T V

Science of Trial Advocacy

The Waiter Pivot

JOHN JERRY GLAS

AMERICAN BAR ASSOCIATION
Solo, Small Firm and
General Practice Division

Cover design by Elmarie Jara/ABA Design

Printed in the United States of America.

27 26 25 24 23 5 4 3 2

A catalog record for this book is available from the Library of Congress.

Dedication

Dedicated to Bob Kerrigan, my mentor, friend, and favorite "Gray Hair."
Thank you for believing in me.

Contents

CHAPTER 3

CHAPTER 4

CHAPTER 8

CHAPTER 14

Forms and tables from this book are available for download at ambar.org/TrialAdvocacy

About the Author

JOHN JERRY GLAS is the Chair of Civil Litigation at Deutsch Kerrigan, LLP in New Orleans, Louisiana, and a Fellow of the American College of Trial Lawyers.

Mr. Glas was born and raised in New Orleans. He earned a bachelor's degree in philosophy from the College of the Holy Cross in Worcester, Massachusetts, and a master's degree in philosophy from the University of Toronto. After returning home to teach theology at his alma mater, Jesuit High School, he earned a juris doctor from the Paul M. Hebert Law Center at Louisiana State University.

Mr. Glas cut his teeth trying cases as a prosecutor for the Orleans Parish District Attorney's Office. After serving as a Senior Assistant District Attorney, Mr. Glas joined Deutsch Kerrigan. Twenty-five years later, he still calls Deutsch Kerrigan home.

Mr. Glas has tried 114 trials. His 76 jury trials comprise 61 criminal jury trials and 15 civil jury trials. During the past decade, he served as national trial counsel for Axon Enterprise, Inc. (formerly TASER International, Inc.), enrolling pro hac vice in 12 states. In 2022, he was selected for the cover of *Super Lawyers Magazine* and the featured article entitled "Direct Connection: How Jerry Glas Develops His Rapport with Juries."

Mr. Glas has enjoyed success on both sides of the aisle. As a state prosecutor, he convicted Douglas Whitton in 1999 of four counts of first-degree murder for the "Mid-City Massacre" in Orleans Parish, Louisiana. As a criminal defense attorney, he secured a "not guilty" verdict in 2010 for former police officer Scott Nugent, who was indicted for manslaughter in Winn Parish, Louisiana. As lead defense attorney for TASER International, Inc., he secured a zero verdict in St. Louis, which *Missouri Lawyers Weekly* ranked as the fourth-largest 2012 defense verdict in Missouri. And as lead plaintiff attorney for Lindale Pipeline, LLC, he obtained a $26 million verdict in Houston, which *Texas Lawyer* ranked the 22nd-largest 2021 plaintiff verdict in Texas.

Mr. Glas is a proud member of the American Bar Association. He previously authored three book chapters for the ABA's *From the Trenches* series.

In his latest offering, Mr. Glas challenges those older and old-fashioned attorneys, whom he lovingly refers to and unfairly stereotypes as "Gray Hairs," to consider the possibility that it is time to revisit trial advocacy. Mr. Glas boldly proposes an alternative approach, which he calls the "waiter pivot," and carefully constructs a new playbook for jury trials.

Acknowledgments

The waiter pivot is not a theory brewed in a sterile classroom. It is a trial strategy produced by the messy process of trial and error in courtrooms. Seventy-six jury trials and *countless* errors by an overconfident and imperfect attorney. I learned from every judge, co-counsel, and opposing counsel. And I owe my career to so many. But I am particularly grateful:

To Jonathan Pierce, for your friendship. Thanks for seeing me through law school, brother.

To my professors at the Paul M. Hebert Law Center at Louisiana State University. Geaux Tigers!

To Prof. Jay Bybee, for coaching the 1995 & 1996 moot court teams. Thanks for picking us.

To Trey Reymond, for going to *The Rock* (1996) instead of studying for the bar exam. Great call.

To the Orleans Parish DA's Office, for giving me the chance to try cases at "Tulane & Broad."

To Magistrate Joseph Giarrusso, Jr., for taking me under his wing. The world misses you.

To my friends and fellow ADAs, for trying the cases that needed trying. Baptism by fire.

To Judges Elloie, Parker, and Cannizzaro, for their patience and advice. Call for the jury!

To Greg Johnson and Brett Wise, for our years of coaching Jesuit High School's mock trial team.

To Charles F. Seemann, III, for making the interview happen. That was my fork in the road.

To the talented lawyers at Deutsch Kerrigan, LLP, for raising me.

To Johnny Cochran, for kicking my butt in his last jury trial. Thanks for the lesson. Still stings.

To Dick Chopin and Peggy Joffe, for our years of teaching Trial Ad at Loyola University New Orleans College of Law. No student learned more than I did.

To Doug Klint, Mike Brave, and Holly Gibeaut, for giving that guy from Louisiana a chance.

To Felice, Edd, and *everyone* in The Trial Network, for helping me find my voice.

To Isaiah Fields, for taking more witnesses than I did. Stop telling everybody.

To Ed Walters, George Hebbler, and James Brown, for years of friendship and encouragement.

To the brilliant lawyers and judges on the LSU Trial Ad Committee, for challenging and inspiring me to be better.

To Kelly Theard, for (eventually) walking back to counsel's table.

To Jonathan Walsh, for crossing the aisle and joining our firm. I meant what I said.

To Denia Aiyegbusi, for quietly handling *everything* while I myopically focus on one case.

To Ray Lewis, for the yellow sticky note after my rebuttal close. Still not funny.

To Claire, Katie, and Molly, for loving me and putting me back together after a loss.

To Lorraine Murray, Ray Lewis, Marisa L'Heureux, and Molly Montanaro, for making this book better.

To Bobbie Molnar, for bringing me Diet Coke. I prefer cans. How hard is that to remember?

Chapter 1

The Waiter Pivot

The Golden Age of Lawyers has ended.

To be honest, it ended a long time ago, but nobody said anything. Nobody wanted to say anything, certainly not the lawyers lecturing at conferences and bragging at cocktail parties. Hey, don't laugh. Many of them are still in denial, pretending the year is 1965 and trying cases the same way lawyers did when *The Sound of Music* was in movie theaters. It's difficult to watch (the lawyers, not the movie), but understandable. After all, it was a glorious time to practice law.

Back then, lawyers had gravitas. They worked in posh downtown law offices. They had magnificent private libraries, not personal passwords. They carried leather briefcases, not cardboard boxes. They wore three-piece suits and hats, even when they slept. And they earned their reputations trying cases in smoky courtrooms, not settling cases in conference rooms.

For generations, these venerable lawyers relied on clients to spread word of their kindness and skill. They did not have marketing departments. They did not spend millions on advertising. They did not define themselves—or demean their profession—with irreverent commercials, slogans, and jingles. Thanks to them, there was a time when jurors pictured lawyers like Atticus Finch (Gregory Peck) and Henry Drummond (Spencer Tracy) roaming the courtrooms of America, seeking truth and demanding justice.

Back then, jurors were also different. Jury duty was a civic responsibility, and jury selection was an honor. Jurors dressed for the occasion. They entered the courtroom solemnly and filed into the pews like they were in church. They sat quietly. They waited patiently. They listened.

It was a simpler time. Jurors knew less about science and medicine. When in pain, jurors did not drive to the public library, research their symptoms, and self-diagnose. Nor did they drive to the nearest college campus, find a bulletin board, and hope somebody "posted" something about their symptoms or their illness. Instead, they made an appointment to see a medical doctor, at that doctor's office and during regular business hours. Jurors wanted an expert opinion because they trusted experts and respected expertise. The mere sight of a lab coat gave them goose bumps.

Jurors were also less experienced. Not less intelligent. Not less capable. Just less familiar with trial practice and procedure. For many, it was their first time in a courtroom. For some, it was their first time hearing words like "hearsay" and "preponderance." They needed the judge to explain the law, and they wanted the attorneys to explain the evidence. Best of all, they had no expectation about the quality of the evidence or the lawyering. Such beautifully blank slates.

Back then, it was easier to drown the jury in a sea of words. Jurors were forced to process hours of testimony without the benefit of visual aids or air conditioning. And, once drowned, jurors had the common decency to stay drowned. Opposing counsel could not rescue them with fancy computer animations, and they could not save themselves by going home and researching online. When in doubt, jurors defaulted to "voting" for the lawyer they trusted the most instead of weighing the evidence admitted during the trial. At least, that is what lawyers told their clients behind closed doors. "Jurors love me," they bragged, smiling that smile.

Right or wrong, jury trials were perceived as popularity contests, and that perception influenced every aspect of trial strategy. Voir dire was for getting jurors to love *you*. Opening statement was for telling jurors what *you* thought of the evidence and for avoiding promises that would get *you* in trouble. Expert witnesses were called to establish *your* expertise and to prove *you* were "right all along." Cross-examination was for demonstrating *your* skill, establishing *your* superiority, springing *your* surprises, and proving *your* case. Closing argument was for telling jurors how *you* wanted them to vote. The goal of every trial was to persuade the jurors to trust *you* and to value *your* opinion. Consequently, how *you* looked presenting the evidence was as important as the evidence presented, and *your* credibility was as important as your expert's. That was a special time for trial lawyers. But that time has passed.

The Golden Age of Lawyers did not end because of a single event or innovation. The whole world inside and outside the courtroom changed. Everyone became a lawyer, even that kid who failed algebra. Expert witnesses became professional witnesses. Trials became mediations. Inexperienced lawyers became judges, and judges became less tolerant of inexperienced lawyers.

Meanwhile, the world discovered computers, cable television, the Internet, social media, Google, Wikipedia, iPhones, Netflix, Skype, and Zoom. Information was no longer hoarded in private and public libraries.

It was everywhere and in everyone's hands. And that is when the great shift happened. Almost overnight, the world decided to eliminate the middleman. Grandchildren stopped calling grandparents with questions about World War II. Dinner guests stopped admitting they had no idea who Pericles was or what *hubris* meant. There was a magical rectangle in their hands that had all the answers and would never judge them.

It was intoxicating. The world already knew that knowledge is power, and that absolute power corrupts absolutely. What the world discovered was that access to knowledge is also power. And that unlimited access to information limits our need for the well-informed. Finally, the world could eliminate people from the process of learning. Why call a human being to make reservations? Why waste time exchanging pleasantries? Why trust someone else to do it right? Why feel compelled to express gratitude at the end of an unnecessary conversation? There's an app for that.

Lawyers were among the last to get the memo. We still saw ourselves as the Great Communicators, and we still clung to the belief that jurors *needed* and *wanted* us in the courtroom. In reality, jurors were increasingly focused on the information and increasingly annoyed by the way lawyers were spinning and spoon-feeding it to them. By the time COVID-19 reared its ugly head in the year 2020 AD, virtual mock trials had already relegated lawyers to one small box in the upper corner of the juror's screen. Lawyers had *literally* been minimized.

Today, jurors are easily frustrated with lawyers and the legal system. They dislike bench conferences (aka "side bars") or anything else that delays the trial. They detest objections because they want to be trusted with all the evidence. They hate courtroom theatrics and repetitive questions. They are convinced that they could ask fewer and better questions. Given the choice, some jurors would send the lawyers home and have the bailiff stack the evidence in a corner of the deliberation room. Just pile it up and get out of their way.

Jurors have become experts in everything and suspicious of everyone. They do not trust lawyers or their hand-picked experts. They will not be manipulated, and they do not want to be "told" anything. If you have a great case, keep your opinion to yourself. They have seen enough courtroom dramas to know that the obvious answer is never correct, and the "slam dunk" trial always ends with a surprise. Tell jurors something is "clear," and they will assume it is not. Tell them the case is a "no brainer," and they will resolve to find what you missed. Tell them to award a specific number, and they will avoid that number like the bubonic plague. They are *not* your puppets. They will reach their own decisions, thank you very much.

Times have changed, and trial lawyers must change with the times. We cannot continue trying cases like our truly talented and beloved mentors and ancestors—who are hereinafter fondly remembered, unfairly stereotyped, and respectfully referred to as "Gray Hairs." We are practicing law in a very different time, and we need to take a very different approach to trial advocacy.

Jurors do not want lawyers. They want waiters. They do not want arguments and objections. They want evidence and deference. They will dislike the first lawyer to engage in obvious "lawyering," and they will appreciate the first waiter to bring them a useful timeline. Instead of denying that reality, let's embrace it. Like good waiters, let's bring them what they want and point out something about the soup they might have missed.

Let's change our approach. Let's dedicate ourselves to learning the art of good service. Instead of being lawyering lawyers, let's become wonderful waiters. It's not about us anymore. "Hello, I'll be one of your waiters for the trial. May I start you off with a helpful graphic?"

Let's resolve to be patient with those Gray Hairs who will scream and holler that the legal profession should never be compared to the service industry. They mean well. Gray Hairs just don't understand how a good waiter can influence every dining decision and how a bad waiter can ruin every restaurant review. By shedding our lawyerly skins and donning the trappings of humble waiters, we can maximize our influence with the jury and better serve our clients. We can be more persuasive and more effective. Hasn't that always been our goal? Isn't that our true calling?

This sea change in our profession is not a death sentence. It is an opportunity for the open-minded. Together, let's write a new playbook that ignores conventional wisdom. Instead of assuming trials are popularity contests, let's assume jurors will base their verdict on the law and the evidence. Yes, I know how crazy that will sound to some. Let's do it anyway.

Jurors know they are the most important people in the courtroom, and they want better service. Let's give it to them. Let's do more than publicly endorse the waiter metaphor. Let's actually change the way we try cases.

Times have changed, and the time has come to revisit trial advocacy. Yes, becoming good waiters is easier said than done, but we must rethink our approach and rewrite our old trial playbook. We have no choice. We must adapt or die. The Golden Age of Lawyers has ended.

The Age of Jurors has begun.

Chapter 2

Voir Dire: Ten Minutes, One Theme, and a Cloud of Dust

During the Golden Age of Lawyers, judges allowed unlimited voir dire, and lawyers took their sweet time questioning potential jurors. It was a beautiful sight. Gray Hairs effortlessly and endlessly visiting with jurors. Fishing for personal bias and prejudice. Finding common ground and experience. Filling the courtroom with the distinct sound of strangers connecting. "No kidding, my son worked there too!" "Really, I played a little ball myself." "Oh, my wife and I love your restaurant!" "Hey, that's good honest work. My dad did it for fifty years . . . God rest his soul."

For decades, Gray Hairs discovered favorite questions—secret windows for peering into a juror's soul and magic keys for unlocking their hidden opinions. Maybe, in the 1960s, it was "What magazine subscriptions do you have?" Or, in the 1970s, it was "What bumper stickers do you have on your car?" Or, in the 1980s, it was "What is attached by magnets to your refrigerator?" Whatever their favorite question was, Gray Hairs loved asking it, and judges allowed it.

Gray Hairs were trusted. Sometimes, they were even allowed to divulge facts and pry into a potential juror's opinion on the evidence to be offered at trial. "Would you hold the opinion of a chiropractor in higher regard than the opinion of an orthopedic surgeon?" "What would you think if a plaintiff saw a lawyer before a doctor?" "Would you give greater weight to a plaintiff's complaints or to a negative x-ray?" "Do you think a plaintiff should be expected to learn a new trade at age sixty?"

To this day, Gray Hairs remember fondly a time when they could ask jurors to commit to a specific verdict. "If I prove she suffered a traumatic brain injury, *could you* return a verdict of $2.5 million dollars?" "If I prove there is no objective evidence of injury, *will you* return a zero verdict?" "If the State proves the defendant was driving the get-away car, *will you* find the defendant guilty as charged of first-degree murder?"

No wonder Gray Hairs at cocktail parties can still be heard bragging that "every trial is over by the end of voir dire." There was a time when that statement was probably true. But that time has passed, and trial lawyers have nobody to blame but themselves.

We ruined a good thing. We asked ridiculous questions. We talked more than we listened. We took delight in shamelessly name-dropping. We shared personal stories and made funny comments. We flirted. We smiled. We dazzled them with our wit and charm. We chose to shine the bright light of voir dire on ourselves.

We reminded everyone that we are nothing more than paid advocates. We became obsessed with saving our precious peremptory challenges and forcing opposing counsel to spend theirs. We asked carefully worded questions until we secured the soundbite we wanted. We harassed unfavorable jurors into making that one admission we desperately needed to challenge them for cause. Meanwhile, we coddled favorable jurors with leading questions and cleverly rehabilitated jurors who should *never* have been allowed to serve on a jury. Trusted with the responsibility of discovering prejudice, we filled the courtroom with the stench of our own bias. Not all trial lawyers did, to be sure. But enough of us did to establish a pattern.

Unlimited voir dire allowed lawyers to become what they are, and we became a threat to the legal system. Not surprisingly, the system fought back. Slowly but surely, judges redefined our right to "intelligently exercise" our peremptory challenges and limited our opportunity to interact with potential jurors.

Today, most federal courts have taken over the questioning of jurors. Many prohibit lawyers from having any interaction with jurors, and few allow more than ten minutes of questioning. Even state courts, those last bastions of voir dire, are starting to fall. Every year, more and more state court judges are conducting voir dire and allowing only "limited follow up" by the lawyers. Every day, judges become more and more convinced they can do a better job of conducting voir dire than the lawyers seated before them. Most days, they are not wrong.

Today, the legal profession stands convicted of abusing the right to voir dire, and our sentence fits our crime. Just look at us. Squirming in our seats while the judge asks questions that have no hope of discovering bias or prejudice. Gritting our teeth while the judge shares personal stories, plays the "do you know so-and-so" game, and befriends potential jurors. Pretending to smile while the judge cleverly rehabilitates jurors who should *never* be allowed to serve. Holding our tongue while the judge thanks our dream juror for admitting a personal preference instead of clarifying what that juror *really* meant and determining whether that juror *really* could be fair and objective. Suffering at the judge's unskilled hands what the judge should be suffering at ours. It is absolute torture, and we absolutely deserve it. We had it good, and we got greedy.

Times have changed. Now, when the court finishes its voir dire of jurors by asking the lawyers if they have "any follow up," we cannot spring out of our seats like we were shot out of a cannon. We cannot ignore the phrase "follow up" and ask whatever we want. We must resist the temptation to rehabilitate jurors whose bias the judge has already exposed. And we should think twice before prying further into a juror's bias after the judge has accepted that juror's assurance they can "fairly and objectively weigh the evidence."

What we need is a new approach to voir dire. We need voir dire strategies that allow us to discover bias and prejudice without pitting ourselves against the judge. We need to ask voir dire questions that send the right message about our client and our confidence in our case. Questions that announce the type of jurors we want, not the type of jurors we fear. Questions that favorably frame the central issue the jury will decide at the end of the trial. Questions that emphasize whatever witness or fact we want to determine the outcome of the trial. Our new playbook for voir dire should involve ten minutes, one theme, and a cloud of dust.

1. Let the Court Voir Dire on Bias and Prejudice

A waiter may ask about food allergies, but a waiter would never ask incredibly personal questions as soon as you sit down at the table. In contrast, lawyers often start the trial by asking incredibly personal questions about bias and prejudice during voir dire. Let's stop doing that.

Questions about bias can bias the questioned. Whenever possible, trial lawyers should move the court to ask those questions designed to discover bias and prejudice. No, the court is not going to ask all the questions on our list. No, the court is not going to follow up regarding potential bias the way we would. But consider the advantages of letting the court do our dirty work.

Jurors recognize when a trial lawyer is unfairly trying to "get rid" of a juror or "save" an obviously biased juror. It does not matter how clever or subtle you think you are being with your questioning. Jurors know what you are doing, and they don't like it. Whether or not you succeed in establishing a single juror's bias and saving *one* of your precious peremptory challenges (or succeed in rehabilitating a juror and forcing opposing counsel to spend *one* of theirs), you will succeed in reminding jurors that you are a paid advocate. The jury will brand you as a "slick lawyer," and it will hurt your credibility. No, jurors do not expect lawyers to be objective, but they care about integrity. One peremptory challenge is not worth risking your gravitas and your voice.

Pressing jurors about bias and prejudice can also send the wrong message about your client and your case. Imagine if a lawyer stood up during voir dire and politely said, "Your Honor, I'm not going to ask any questions of these jurors, and I agree to let opposing counsel pick any twelve jurors they want to serve on this jury."[1] What would that say about the lawyer's confidence? What message would that send about the evidence? Well, the sight of a lawyer desperately questioning a juror can send the *wrong* message. There is always a reason for desperation. If your evidence is so persuasive, why are you so afraid of this one juror?

Today, in addition to hiring jury consultants to prepare a jury questionnaire, trial attorneys should always move the court to ask questions designed to discover bias and prejudice because (a) jurors are more likely to respond honestly to the court; (b) jurors are less likely to resent being asked personal questions when those questions are asked by the court; (c) the court asking the question (in and of itself) sends the message that question is legitimate and such bias or prejudice will not be tolerated; and (d) the court asking these questions frees up an attorney to ask *only* those questions necessary to establish a voir dire theme.

Consider standard voir dire questions seeking to determine whether jurors are biased against corporations, like "Would you be more likely to hold a corporation liable than an individual?" or "Have you read anything about this corporation online?" How many corporation-hating jurors are more likely to share the truth with the court than volunteer their bias to the Big Bad Corporation's attorney, knowing that is exactly what the Big Bad Corporation is trying to "trick" them into doing? How many jurors could be rubbed wrong by the Big Bad Corporation lawyer's tone, facial expressions, or follow-up questions? Isn't there a real possibility that the mere asking of what jurors have "heard" or "read online" about the Big Bad Corporation suggest there must be something bad "out there" about the Big Bad Corporation? Wouldn't it be better for the court to ask

1. Never do this during voir dire. You will be held in contempt of court. The purpose for this outlandish and inappropriate hypothetical was not to endorse such grandstanding. The sole purpose was to reinforce the principle that the better the case, the less an attorney should care about one peremptory challenge. Seriously, if you are that confident in your case, be content to stand up and respectfully say, "No questions, your honor."

the questions? Couldn't the court's asking the questions suggest that the questioning is routine, that the court recognizes the risk of such bias in all cases, and the court will not tolerate such bias in this case?

Consider specific voir dire questions that are sometimes asked during a criminal trial or during a civil trial involving claims of excessive force, like "Have you had a bad experience with a police officer?" or "Do you feel it is never permissible to use pepper spray on a female suspect?" or "Do you feel that a cocaine addict should not be held accountable (or is less responsible) for their actions?" Why would a lawyer for the police officer or the law enforcement agency want to ask those questions? Why would a lawyer risk offending jurors by pressing for details or clarifying what happened during a prior incident with a police officer? Wouldn't counsel for the police officer prefer for the court to pry into the personal opinions regarding the convictions and addictions of their family members?

Consider the advantages of having the court ask voir dire questions based on a medical assumption, like the existence and effect of "hypersexual disorder," which was not included in the first publication of the Diagnostic and Statistical Manual of Mental Disorders, now in its fifth edition. If a lawyer asks questions about the disorder, that lawyer could be perceived as trying to "sell the jury" that the disorder is real, and the client's diagnosis is relevant. In contrast, if the court asks jurors what "peer-reviewed literature" they have read about "the diagnosis of hypersexual disorder," it suggests: (a) the diagnosis is real; (b) there is "peer-reviewed literature" to be read about the diagnosis; and (c) the court itself needs to know whether the jurors have already formed an opinion regarding that diagnosis.

Every trial provides at least one reminder of why we should let the court voir dire on bias and prejudice. During voir dire for the 2016 *White* trial, I sat in my chair and listened while a state court judge asked a perfectly innocent question about whether a juror who had previously filed a medical malpractice action could be fair and impartial. In response, the juror volunteered incredibly personal information and started crying. Her response stunned and silenced the courtroom, prompting the judge to apologize and explain the need for the question. The following is an excerpt from that trial transcript:

> The Court: There was a medical malpractice case where the doctor settled with you, correct?
>
> Prospective Juror: Yes . . .
>
> The Court: I know it is hard to remember. You are not a professional witness. You cannot remember all of those things. The fact that

you had that experience and had a particular case, would that affect your ability to be fair and impartial in judging the facts of this case?

Prospective Juror: I tend to be sympathetic to people. It was no recourse. Because what happened when they did the surgery, she [my daughter] drowned in her own blood. It was, you know, it is something I try not to talk about.

The Court: I'm not—I will tell everybody this. This is not here to stir up feelings and bad memories. It is important for the lawyers and their clients to know.

Prospective Juror: She was 19.

The Court: I'm very sorry, ma'am, that happened. Am I to understand that because of that experience you feel sympathetic to [the plaintiff] and that it would be hard for you not to award her damages even if the evidence does not show her injuries were caused?

As I sat quietly in my chair, I imagined how red my face would have gotten if I had asked the same innocent question and elicited the same emotional response. Would the jury have blamed me for prying into such a painful memory? Would the jury have believed me if (like the judge) I had personally assured them that "I'm not here to stir up feelings and bad memories"? Would the jury have balked at my assurance the question was "important" or thought "that lawyer means important to *his* client"? Would the jury have accepted my apology if (like the judge) I had said "I'm very sorry, ma'am, that happened"? Would I have sounded defensive to even one juror? Would I have been compelled to use a peremptory challenge on that juror? Suddenly, my chair was more comfortable, and I was less irate about the court "stealing" my voir dire.

Stop holding on to your understanding of "the way it has always been done." Forget what Gray Hairs may think of you for "turning over" that part of voir dire to the court. Let the court ask the difficult questions. Let the court apologize for prying into their lives. Let the court explain the need for questions regarding bias and prejudice. File a motion asking the court to start voir dire by asking questions regarding bias and prejudice. List the specific questions you want asked. Free yourself to ask questions that make a good first impression, send the right message, and frame that one central issue for the jury to decide.

2. Don't Fix or Undo Anything the Court Did

No waiter would ever disrespect or disagree with the owner in front of a guest, but lawyers insist on questioning jurors on bias and prejudice even after the judge makes it clear which jurors can be objective and which jurors should never be allowed to serve. Let's stop doing that.

Jurors love judges. Try to remember how you felt the first time you walked into a courtroom. The first time you heard a bailiff declare, "All rise!" The first time you saw a packed courtroom rise as one to stand in respect. The first time a judge, seated on a pedestal platform, smiled at something you said. Recognize what is happening between the judge and the jurors.

By the end of voir dire, the judge will have expressed an interest in each juror, listened intently to every answer, demonstrated patience with many, and shown kindness to some. With every "thank you" spoken, the judge returned their respect and acknowledged their importance. With every smile, the judge made a new friend. Remember that, by the time the judge finishes speaking with the last juror and says, "I'm going to turn you over now to the lawyers," some jurors may feel a twinge of dread or disappointment. Do not ignore that reality.

What Gray Hairs do not realize—and may never accept—is that the jurors belong to the judge by the end of the judge's voir dire. They are spoken for. They have imprinted. And the more professional the judge, the more protective the jurors will be of *their* judge.

Trial lawyers should never disrespect the judge (in the eyes of jurors) by trying to "fix" or "undo" whatever the judge did during voir dire. Never try to rehabilitate a juror whose bias or prejudice the court has already established. If a juror admitted to having a specific bias, and the court personally confirmed that bias (usually by thanking the juror for their candor and quickly moving on to the next juror), do not speak to that juror. Not a word. No matter how unfair you felt the court's questions were. No matter how perfect that juror would be for your client. No matter how badly you want opposing counsel to burn a challenge. Not a word. Seriously. Let it go.

During the 2016 *White* trial, while being questioned by the judge, a medical doctor answered that he would need to know more about the plaintiff's injuries to know whether his medical training would affect his impartiality. In response, the state court judge (a former plaintiff attorney who insisted on conducting voir dire) stubbornly refused to identify the plaintiff's alleged injuries and launched into leading questions arguably designed to secure the soundbite the judge wanted to dismiss for cause that medical doctor. The following exchange occurred:

The Court: The fact that you have familiarity with these types of injuries, would that affect your ability to be fair and impartial in this case?

Prospective Juror: I would have to hear more about the case to be honest.

The Court: **You are not going to hear any more in the voir dire** because the whole point is just the simple the fact that someone was injured and the allegations of those injuries and that there is a dispute on causation. I guess what the lawyers are worried about or maybe not worried about, depending on what you say, the lawyer may like what you say—as always one side may like what you say. One side may not. It is a fact of life.

The lawyer wants you to believe that the injuries were caused while the other side does not want you to believe the injuries were caused. **So you are going to be in this jury trying to treat and diagnose the injury?**

Prospective Juror: I would have to say just the nature of what I hear, yes. I am not sure if I would be as impartial as someone who doesn't have as much medical knowledge.

The Court: It is because of your knowledge that you feel uncomfortable that you might hear something a doctor says that does not comport with your education and training. Is that a fair statement?

Prospective Juror: Yes.

The Court: Thank you.

Yes, this exchange was infuriating. Yes, every bone in my (defense counsel) body wanted to rehabilitate that medical doctor and force plaintiff's counsel to spend a peremptory challenge. After all, medical doctors are not automatically dismissed for cause from cases involving physical injuries. The proper standard for dismissal was not whether the doctor would "be in this jury trying to treat and diagnose the injury" or would "feel uncomfortable" upon hearing testimony that "does not comport" with his medical training. The proper standard was whether the doctor could base his verdict "on the law and on the evidence presented" and "set aside any personal bias or prejudice." But that ship had sailed.

Nothing I subsequently asked and nothing the medical doctor subsequently replied was going to persuade the judge—who was quite proud of soliciting the "yes" he wanted—to change his mind. It was far more likely my questions would anger the court and the jury.

Every lawyer must decide whether the risk of alienating jurors outweighs the reward of (possibly) rehabilitating one juror. Every lawyer must exercise the self-control necessary to let that one juror go *without* a micro-expression of pain or frustration.

Yes, every trial lawyer thinks he or she is the Great Rehabilitator, but there is an increasingly large difference between what great lawyers say and what the average juror hears. Instead of focusing on the potential "reward" from your brilliant line of voir dire questions on bias and prejudice, consider the potential "risk" that jurors will be offended by those questions. When the judge succeeds in getting a medical doctor to admit that she or he cannot forget or ignore their medical training, consider the possibility that jurors will be asking themselves questions like the following:

- Why is that lawyer asking that doctor more questions?
- Didn't that lawyer hear the doctor tell the judge that he "might not be as impartial" as other jurors?
- Does that lawyer think he knows more than the judge?
- Why is that lawyer trying to get a biased juror on the jury?

What is the chance that every juror heard and will remember *verbatim* your brilliant rehabilitation questions? What is the risk that—regardless of what you asked—jurors will incorrectly interpret your questions as *really* an expression of the following:

> Doctor, I know the judge tricked you into admitting you would be "less impartial" in some cases because of your medical training and experience, and I know the judge tricked you into admitting your personal experience with patients would "prejudice" the way you listened to and weighed the testimony, but . . . this judge doesn't know the law and the judge failed to ask you the right questions.
>
> Fortunately, I know more than the judge. Let me clean this mess up because my case is so bad that I desperately need a biased juror like you on this jury. So, isn't it true you meant to say that you would be "less likely" to be fooled by junk science and false medical testimony? Wink, wink, nudge, nudge. Say no more, say no more.

> I mean, putting aside the judge's convoluted questions, is there any way that I can get you to say that you will follow the law and base your verdict on the evidence? Please, I really need you on this jury. I am desperate.

Locking horns with the judge over one juror is rarely a good idea, but there is an exception to the rule. Picture a defense lawyer in a traumatic brain injury case candidly admitting "I would absolutely love to get a neurologist on this jury,"[2] and then desperately trying to rehabilitate the one neurologist on the jury. What would that say about the lawyer and that lawyer's case? Instead of sending the wrong message (i.e., "I want a biased juror because my case is so weak"), rehabilitating the neurologist could send the right message (i.e., "I want a neurologist because the neurological evidence is so strong").

In that specific situation, carefully consider rehabilitating the neurologist even after the court has confirmed bias, but only if that neurologist's bias was based on the neurologist's skill, knowledge, and expertise. And, yes, that exception applied to the (above-quoted) voir dire, where I was tempted to openly try to rehabilitate the medical doctor to send the message: "I want this medical doctor on the jury because the medical evidence favors my client!" For me, the risk that my attempts to rehabilitate the medical doctor would inspire the judge to frown, shake his head, or interrupt me (i.e., "move on, counselor!") outweighed the possibility of sending the message that I *wanted* that doctor on the jury. But it was a tough call.

Resist the temptation to attack a juror whose assurances the court has already accepted. If a juror admitted to having a bias, but the court personally confirmed that the juror could "fairly and objectively weigh the evidence" or "base their verdict solely on the law and the evidence," do not ask that juror another question about their bias. Do not ask the juror to repeat their assurances. Do not ask more complicated or convoluted questions, especially if the court verbally accepted the juror's assurance by replying "fair enough" or "that's all we ask." Why would

2. Never say this during voir dire. You will be held in contempt of court. The purpose for this outlandish and inappropriate hypothetical was not to endorse such grandstanding. The sole purpose was to emphasize the concept that *appearing* to fight for a neurologist could send the right message about your case. Seriously, there are more subtle ways to give jurors the impression your client *wants* a neurologist on the jury. Consider smiling and nodding, asking detailed questions, getting excited by the answers, and sneaking in a well-timed "excellent" when learning that the neurologist routinely handles traumatic brain injury cases.

you ask more questions about a juror whose assurance the court already accepted? Were you not paying attention? Did you not hear the answers? Do you think the juror fooled the judge or the judge is a fool? Why do you so desperately want to get rid of this juror? What is your problem?

Always respect the judge's questioning and opinions regarding the objectivity of specific jurors. Not because you agree with the judge. Not because the judge "owns" the courtroom. But because you know your questioning will not change the judge's ruling on a challenge for cause or the jury's verdict at the end of the trial. And because the risk outweighs the reward.

While a lawyer should never try to "fix" or "undo" what the court established regarding the bias of a juror, the same rule does not apply to what opposing counsel established. When opposing counsel unfairly exaggerates a juror's bias (hoping to successfully challenge for cause that juror), consider rehabilitating that juror. And whenever rehabilitating that juror is a legal or moral imperative, always rehabilitate a juror whose "bias" was solicited by opposing counsel.

3. Forget Speed Dating

A good waiter may politely ask "How are you doing today?" But no waiter is going to frantically ask personal questions as soon as you are seated. So, let's not do that during our voir dire. When the court grants the attorneys only ten minutes of voir dire or only "limited follow up," speed dating will *not* be an option in our new playbook for the Age of Jurors.

By the time the judge is finished questioning the jurors, you should have basic demographic information regarding each potential juror, including their age, gender, race, marital status, education, employment history, litigation history, and prior jury service. You will know whether the jurors are familiar with the attorneys, parties, experts, lay witnesses, or the specific incident out of which the lawsuit arises. Thanks to the jury questionnaire you submitted, you will be holding the answers that your jury consultants wanted. Thanks to the motion you filed requesting specific voir dire questions, you will have heard the jury's answers to the court's questions on bias and prejudice. And you will have some sense of whether the court is inclined to grant any challenges for cause. So how should you spend whatever precious time the court gives you for voir dire?

Do not waste your voir dire frantically questioning jurors. You do not have time to run the old voir dire playbook, and you should not try.

Maybe jurors were transparent in 1955, and lawyers could reliably predict their opinions on the evidence based on their magazine subscriptions and bumper stickers. But those days are over. Modern jurors are more complicated. No single response to a single question will reliably predict that juror's opinion of the evidence and verdict.

It is far more likely that the juror's opinion of a specific claim or witness will be determined by their personal experiences. Maybe your star witness will remind the juror of a dear high school friend. Maybe your expert will sound like the juror's ex-spouse. Accept the reality that you are not going to discover that fact during your ten minutes of voir dire. No line of questioning will reveal whether a specific juror will hate your expert's haircut, clothes, accent, eye contact, bluntness, or favorite sports metaphor.

Resist the temptation to spend your voir dire on a handful of jurors. That is not the solution to your problem. Even if you dedicated your entire voir dire to one potential juror, how well would you really get to know that juror? Consider how many years you have known your parents, siblings, spouse, friends, neighbors, and coworkers. Would opposing counsel *really* know how any of them would vote based on a handful of questions?

I have been married to the same wonderful woman for twenty-five years, and I have no idea how my wife would weigh the evidence, let alone what her verdict would be. She is a beautiful mystery to me, and no lawyer is going to solve that mystery during voir dire. Only the most vain, naïve, delusional, and inexperienced trial lawyer would think otherwise—which is precisely what I thought (and what I was) for a very long time.

Never spend all your time speaking with only those jurors who you are seriously considering cutting. The jury will realize what you are doing, and whoever you do not cut will know there was something about them you did not like. How would you feel if an interviewer admitted that they disliked *something* about you, but considered you the lesser of two evils?

Consider the terrifying possibility that jurors may recognize a common denominator among the handful of jurors you choose to question and draw the wrong conclusion about you. What if all the jurors you question are the same gender? What if all the jurors you question are the same race? What if all the jurors you question are old, unemployed, poor, or divorced? Even if opposing counsel does not make a *Batson* challenge (which they probably will) and does not argue that your disparate questioning is evidence of purposeful discrimination (which they absolutely should), you can lose the jury before you question the first witness. Right or wrong, who you choose to question can define who you are to the jury.

4. Establish a Voir Dire Theme

If trial lawyers should move the court to ask questions about bias and prejudice (which they should), and speed-dating is futile (which it is), how should we spend our precious few minutes of voir dire? What should be our goal when we are finally given a chance to interact with jurors? The answer requires an open mind and a complete shift of focus.

We need to change the way we think about voir dire. We need to shift our focus from the answers to the questions. We do not have time to solicit the answers we want, but we have time to ask questions that send the right message about our client and our case.

Jurors draw conclusions about the lawyers and the parties based on the questions asked during voir dire. What would you think if, at the start of a first date, your date asked you the following three questions: (a) "What is your job?" (b) "What kind of car do you drive?" and (c) "How much did your house cost?" What would you immediately conclude about your date? Well, voir dire is no different.

Gray Hairs often spend voir dire asking questions designed to identify the jurors they do *not* want on their jury. Let's stop doing that. Those questions may occasionally bird-dog a few bad jurors, but those questions will always tell jurors what Gray Hairs fear and suggest there is an evidentiary basis for that fear.

For example, when plaintiff attorneys ask prospective jurors to share their feelings about tort reform, they unintentionally send the message that they fear jurors who hate frivolous lawsuits *and* that jurors who hate frivolous lawsuits will hate their client's lawsuit. Now, is that the best message for a plaintiff attorney to send during voir dire? Of course not. But Gray Hairs who myopically focus on "getting" an answer to their tort reform question will always fail to see how those questions can negatively reflect on them, their clients, and their case.

Instead of asking questions that tell jurors who we do not want and what we fear, trial lawyers should ask questions that tell jurors who we do want and what we love. By doing so, trial lawyers can learn more about the jurors (which is important) and send the right message about them, their clients, and their case.

Let's agree that our new playbook will require trial lawyers to ask questions that establish a voir dire theme. Not a trial theme, but a theme *only for* voir dire. Let's resolve to ask questions that either: (a) send a clear message about the type of jurors we want on the jury; or (b) send a clear message about the central issue for the jury to decide at the end of the trial. Here are a few examples of voir dire themes that can send the right message.

a. "We Want Smart Jurors"

One simple but effective theme for voir dire is "we want smart jurors." By asking questions designed to identify smart jurors, you send the message that "if we get smart jurors, we will win!" You express confidence that smart jurors will understand the evidence, correctly apply the law, and find for your client. You silently promise the law and the facts are on your side. You tacitly suggest that the only type of juror your client fears is a dumb jury.

To send the message that your client wants smart jurors, design a series of voir dire questions that establish the necessary intelligence or experience, like the following:

- Did any of you love science or math in high school?
- Did anyone's college degree require significant reading and analysis?
- Does anyone's job require them to read and analyze a significant amount of material?
- Does anyone's job require them to be particularly logical or methodical?
- Does anyone's job require them to objectively analyze the basis for complaints?
- Does anyone's job require them to objectively analyze conflicting estimates?

These types of questions can prompt jurors to volunteer useful information while sending the message that you and your client want smart jurors. It can suggest (perhaps correctly) that the other side took this matter to trial "counting on" or "hoping for" dumb jurors. And, if any of the "smart" jurors you talked with do *not* get selected, it can have the unintended consequence of suggesting (perhaps incorrectly) that opposing counsel cut the smart jurors. Picture the juror who told you they loved science in high school being elected the foreperson. Is that person more likely to ignore the scientific evidence or discuss the scientific evidence during jury deliberation?

b. "We Want Hard Workers"

Know your audience and know your venue. If the court's questioning reveals that only three or four jurors have college degrees or intellectually demanding jobs, sending the message you want "smart" jurors could seem pretentious and could alienate the jury.

An alternative theme for voir dire is "we want hard workers." By asking questions designed to identify hard-working jurors, you can send the message that your client wants jurors who will take the time to understand the evidence because the evidence favors your client. To send the message that your client wants hard workers, design a series of voir dire questions like the following for a case where medical causation is an important issue:

- Does your job require you to "roll up your sleeves" and read hundreds of pages every week?
- Does your job require you to "roll up your sleeves" and patiently organize large amounts of data?
- Does your job require you to carefully chart data?
- Are you willing to "roll up your sleeves" and wade through thousands of pages of medical records?
- Do you love watching television shows about ERs or hospitals?
- Is there any reason you might not be the right juror to be asked to listen to hours of medical testimony, either because of a problem with hearing, seeing, attention, concentration, or any other issue?

Remember that it is possible to combine certain voir dire themes. By asking both lines of voir dire questions, you can send the message that "we want smart jurors and hard workers."

c. "We Want Fact Checkers"

The outcome of many trials can be determined by how a single witness performs during cross-examination. During voir dire, a trial lawyer is not permitted to divulge impeachment evidence or conflicting evidence. Nor is a trial lawyer permitted to ask jurors to pre-judge evidence or commit to returning a specific verdict. However, if the evidence will not support the plaintiff's testimony, a lawyer can establish a "we want fact checkers" voir dire theme.

The key is to ask questions that use the magic phrase "consider and weigh." Trial attorneys have the right to know whether jurors can "consider and weigh" physical and testimonial evidence during the trial (but not what weight the jurors will assign to that evidence). By focusing on a juror's ability to "consider and weigh" the evidence that contradicts a witness's testimony, you can also send the message that evidence will contradict that witness's testimony and your client will prevail if the jurors care about the facts.

For example, in a personal injury action, a defense attorney may want to establish a "we want fact checkers" theme for voir dire if sufficient evidence will contradict the plaintiff's testimony. To identify fact checkers *and* send the message that the evidence will contradict the plaintiff's testimony, design a series of voir dire questions like the following:

- Will anyone **automatically** assume that the plaintiff is telling the truth or correctly recalling the incident or their symptoms?
- Was anyone here a "fact checker" for a publisher?
- Is everyone willing to roll up their sleeves and check the facts?
- Is everyone comfortable judging the plaintiff's credibility?
- Can you **consider and weigh** whether surveillance video contradicts plaintiff's testimony?
- Can you **consider and weigh** whether eyewitness testimony contradicts plaintiff's testimony?
- Can you **consider and weigh** whether plaintiff made a contradictory statement to police or doctors?

By asking jurors if they can "consider and weigh" certain evidence, you are not asking jurors to pre-judge that evidence, nor are you prying into their opinions on the weight they will give that evidence (which could solicit an objection). Instead, you are determining (a) whether any jurors will *automatically* defer or *automatically* believe the plaintiff's testimony and (b) whether any jurors will refuse to "consider and weigh" certain evidence based on a personal bias or prejudice. Picture a juror volunteering that "CT scans are unreliable" or "neuropsychological testing is voodoo science." Picture another juror confessing that "the plaintiff is the only person who *really* knows whether their memory is worse since the accident."

More importantly, by focusing on the plaintiff's testimony and repeating the word "contradicts," you emphasize that a plaintiff must do more than take the stand and say, "trust me." You send the message that the jury's primary job will be to determine whether the evidence "contradicts" the plaintiff's testimony. You tacitly promise the evidence will contradict the plaintiff, and you express confidence that your client will win if jurors can "consider and weigh" the conflicting evidence. Also, you dramatically improve the chances that, during deliberation, some juror will say, "hey, we can't *automatically* assume what the plaintiff says is true."

d. "The Best Expert Should Win"

The outcome of many trials will be determined by whether the jury believes the testimony of your expert or theirs. When you want the trial to come down to a "battle of experts," design a line of questioning that focuses jurors on the importance of expert testimony and evaluates their ability to compare qualifications, materials, and methodology. By asking questions about their ability to judge experts based on their qualifications, materials, and methodology, you express confidence in your expert's ability to win that "battle of the experts."

During the 2017 *Stroud* trial, which involved a traumatic brain injury claim, we decided that a voir dire theme would be "the best neurologist should win." To identify jurors capable of weighing conflicting neurological testimony *and* send the message that the best expert should win the case, we designed a series of voir dire questions like the following:

- Does anyone work with a **neurologist**?
- Does anyone have a family or friends who are **neurologists**?
- Has anyone ever researched this particular **neurological** issue?
- Does anyone think that the opinion of all **neurologists** should be given equal weight?
- Can everyone consider and weigh whether one **neurologist** is better qualified?
- Can everyone consider and weigh how the **neurologist** reached that opinion or validity of his methodology?
- Can everyone consider and weigh the basis for a **neurologist's** opinion?
- Can everyone consider and weigh whether one **neurologist** failed to read (or failed to request or wasn't provided) all of the medical records?
- Can everyone consider and weigh whether peer-reviewed medical literature supports that **neurologist's** opinion?
- Can everyone wait until they've heard from both **neurologists** before making up their minds?

By repeating a variation of the word "neurologist" in every question, we emphasized that the *Stroud* trial would be a "battle of neurologists." By asking jurors if they could "consider and weigh" qualifications, we expressed confidence that our neurologist was better qualified than their neurologist. By asking jurors if they could "consider and weigh" whether one neurologist failed to read all the medical records, we correctly suggested that *only* our neurologist read all the medical records before issuing an expert report.

Properly executed, a "best expert should win" voir dire can set the stage for an effective opening statement. After hearing ten minutes of questions about neurologists, the jury will absolutely expect you to stand up and tell them why your neurologist is more reliable. More importantly, they will be impatiently waiting for opposing counsel to discuss their neurologist's qualifications, methodology, and opinions.

Do not wait for closing argument to tell jurors that this is a "battle of neurologists" and your neurologist's opinion should win. Start in voir dire. Frame the issue for opening statement. Define the trial. Pick the ground where you want the battle to be fought.

e. "The Treating Physician Should Win"

One potentially effective voir dire theme for plaintiff attorneys is "the treating physician should decide this case." When the outcome of the trial will likely be determined by a "battle of experts," a plaintiff attorney could frame the issue for the jury by focusing on the fact that the plaintiff's expert is a "treating physician." Most jurors will instinctively recognize the importance and advantages of being a treating physician, which means defense counsel will be at a distinct disadvantage. Imagine if a plaintiff attorney used his or her ten minutes of voir dire to frame the "real issue" for the jury by asking the following series of voir dire questions:

- Do any of you work for a doctor who **treats** patients?
- How many of you have a **treating** physician?
- How many of you have seen your **treating** physician for more than a year?
- How many of you trust your **treating** physician?
- Can you consider and weigh how many times a doctor **treated** the plaintiff before the accident?
- Can you consider and weigh how many total minutes the doctor spent **treating** the plaintiff before the accident?
- Can you consider and weigh how many times the doctor has **treated** the plaintiff *since* the accident?
- Can you consider and weigh for how long a doctor has **treated** a plaintiff?
- Can you give the testimony of a **treating** physician the weight it deserves?
- If the court instructs you to give greater weight to a **treating** physician, can you follow that instruction? (This question is only applicable in some jurisdictions.)

By repeating a variation of the word "treating" in every question, a plaintiff lawyer could send the message that the jury's primary job will be to consider and weigh the opinion of the treating physician *and* that the plaintiff will prevail if the jury gives the treating physician's testimony "the weight it deserves."

f. "You Have One Issue to Decide"

The outcome of some trials will be determined by the jury's answer to a single factual or legal question. When your trial team *wants* the entire trial to come down to a single question or issue, ask voir dire questions that focus jurors on the importance of that one issue and evaluate their ability to determine that issue fairly and impartially. By asking questions about only one issue, you can frame the purpose of the entire trial for the jury and express confidence in your ability to prevail on that issue.

Before the 2015 *Ricks* trial, the district court dismissed all of the claims against our client, except the plaintiff's manufacturing defect claim. As trial approached, we were confident that our product met every specification, but we were concerned that plaintiff's counsel would argue that our product *must have* deviated from its design (*res ipsa loquitur*) because the product was not designed to cause cardiac arrest. When the district court allocated only ten minutes for voir dire, we chose to frame the trial by focusing the jury on the issue of whether the product met specifications. Toward that end, I asked voir dire questions like the following:

- Has anyone ever been responsible for making certain that a product *met* **specifications**?
- Has anyone ever worked for the manufacturer of a product that was built to **specifications**?
- Has anyone ever been injured by a product that deviated from **specifications**?
- Has anyone ever filed suit alleging that a product failed to meet **specifications**?
- Is anyone going to assume that, because plaintiff filed a manufacturing defect claim, our product "must have" deviated from **specifications**?
- Can everyone consider and weigh the results of testing designed to determine whether a product deviated from **specifications**?
- Can everyone consider and weigh whether an expert analyzed (or requested) testing of a product before offering an opinion as to whether it met **specifications**?

By repeating the word "specifications" in every question, I suggested that plaintiffs were required to prove that our product somehow deviated from specifications. By asking jurors if they could "consider and weigh" testing that was "designed to determine whether a product deviated from specifications," I suggested that subsequent testing conclusively proved our product did not deviate from manufacturing specifications (which it did not). By asking jurors if they could "consider and weigh" whether an expert considered the results of such testing, I suggested plaintiff's expert had failed to consider the results of the testing (which he had).

In so doing, we framed the "real issue" in the *Ricks* trial as whether our product deviated from specifications. By the time plaintiff's counsel stood up for opening statement, the jury absolutely expected her to identify *how* our product specifically deviated from our own specifications. And, when plaintiff's counsel failed to identify any deviations from specifications (or use the word "specifications") during her opening statement, the jury understood why the case did not settle and why my client chose to take the matter to trial.

g. "We Want People Who Care about This Issue"

Voir dire is an opportunity for a trial lawyer to tell jurors the "real issue" in the case and send the message that your client wants jurors who care about that issue. Executed properly, the "we want people who care about this issue" voir dire theme can (a) persuade jurors your client cares about that issue; (b) suggest your opponent does not care about that issue; and (c) imply that jurors who care about that issue will ultimately find for your client.

Perception can become reality. During the 2021 *Lindale* trial, which involved an incredibly boring dispute over water transfer rights in North Dakota, we decided to use voir dire to send the message that our client (the plaintiff) was taking this matter to trial "because written contracts should be enforced!" Toward that end, we designed a voir dire that (a) started with a series of questions emphasizing the importance of enforcing "written contracts," thereby suggesting the defendant was trying to "wiggle out" of a written contract; and (b) ended with a series of questions that began with the phrase "if the court asked you to determine the intent of the parties," thereby suggesting that the intent of the parties would determine the outcome of the trial. Here are some of the questions we asked.

I. We Want Jurors Who Believe Written Contracts Should Be Enforced

- Do you think that written contracts should be enforced?
- Does anyone think that written contracts should *not* be enforced?
- Has anyone had to painstakingly write a contract?
- Has anyone experienced what it is like to have someone break a written contract with you?
- Has anyone ever had to research how to enforce a written contract?

- Has anyone ever intentionally broken a written contract?
- Does anyone think that people who break written contracts should *not* be held accountable?
- Does anyone think that our community would be better off if we started ignoring written contracts?

ii. The Intent of the Parties Will Determine the Outcome of This Trial

- If the court asked you to determine the intent of the parties, could you consider and weigh the contractual language those parties chose to *include* in the contract?
- If the court asked you to determine the intent of the parties, could you consider and weigh the contractual language those parties chose to *omit* from the contract?
- If the court asked you to determine the intent of the parties, could you consider and weigh how those parties acted immediately *before* they signed the contract?
- If the court asked you to determine the intent of the parties, could you consider and weigh how those parties acted immediately *after* they signed the contract?
- If the court asked you to determine the intent of the parties, could you consider and weigh the testimony of the people who signed the contract?

Taking the bait, opposing counsel in *Lindale* started his voir dire by trying to reassure the jury that the defendant (a worldwide energy company) also believed in enforcing written contracts, but the seed had been sewn. As soon as opposing counsel started asking questions about contractual limitations ("what if a contract doesn't specifically say . . ."), he tacitly confirmed that his client was the party who was trying to "wiggle out of" the written contract. At the end of the trial, the jury found that the worldwide energy company had breached the written contract and awarded more than $26 million to our client.

5. Rehabilitate Quickly, Indifferently, and Consistently

Rehabilitation questions are blatantly obvious attempts to establish whether a juror can be fair and impartial. They stick out like a sore thumb. They cannot be mixed in with whatever line of questions you designed to establish your voir dire theme. Picture a lawyer asking a line of beautifully crafted questions regarding the jury's ability to judge conflicting testimony by two qualified neurologists before abruptly revisiting one juror's feelings about tort reform. That one rehabilitation question will break the spell, and your voir dire theme will be lost.

Never let a handful of rehabilitation questions interrupt your voir dire theme. When a juror is so special that they warrant rehabilitation, either start your voir dire by attempting to rehabilitate that juror (i.e., "Before I get to my questions, I would like follow up with Mr. Johnson about something he said") or finish your voir dire by attempting to rehabilitate that juror (i.e., "Before I sit down, I would like to follow up with Mr. Johnson about something he said"). But never interrupt your carefully crafted series of questions designed to establish your voir dire theme with a non-sequitur question regarding an individual juror's bias.

Never attempt to rehabilitate a juror by proving that they are *not* biased or prejudiced. That is not your job. And even if it was your job (which it is not), it is impossible to disprove the existence of bias and prejudice with a handful of voir dire questions.

Here are some standard rehabilitation questions you can ask regardless of the specific answers given by the juror and the specific bias perceived by opposing counsel.

- Base Your Verdict on the Evidence Presented
    - Will you devote your full attention to the trial?
    - Will you listen to all the testimony?
    - Do you want to hear all the evidence before reaching a verdict?
    - Will you decide the case based solely on the evidence presented?
- Base Your Verdict on the Law
    - Will you listen to the court's instructions on the law?
    - Will you follow the court's instructions on the law?
    - Will you decide the case according to the law?
- Weigh the Evidence Fairly and Impartially
    - Will you weigh the physical and testimonial evidence fairly and impartially?
- Decide the Case Fairly and Impartially
    - Will you decide the case fairly and impartially?

Always attempt to rehabilitate jurors with generic rehabilitation questions. If opposing counsel gets a juror to volunteer that they have a bias against truck drivers, do not ask that juror specific questions about their feeling and experiences with truck drivers. Every bias-specific question you ask about truck drivers will drag the jurors farther away from your voir dire theme. Every substantive response the juror gives about truck drivers will drag that juror—and the other jurors—farther away from your voir dire theme. Stay on target!

Remember that, when a potential juror volunteers (under oath) that he or she has a bias, that voluntary disclosure is the ultimate act of candor with the court. The same lawyer who wants the court to "believe" the juror's admission regarding bias should not ask the court to "ignore" the juror's testimony that they can set aside that bias. The admission and the assertion must be given the same weight. Otherwise, the court rewards the jurors who intentionally hide their bias and punish the jurors who openly discuss it with the attorneys.

Never express any passion or personality while asking rehabilitation questions. Expressions of passion and personality suggest you *want* or *need* to rehabilitate that juror. And that is not why you are asking the questions. Your sole reason for asking rehabilitation questions is to make certain the record is complete. At least, that is how you want to appear.

Find ways to emphasize you have no dog in the hunt. Consider typing your favorite rehabilitation questions on a piece of paper. That way you can calmly walk back to your table, grab the page, and read the questions from the page. No eye contact with the juror. No grinning like a used car salesman. No inflection in your voice. Nothing that might suggest an answer. Nothing that could be interpreted as your coaching the juror. No nodding your head in response to any answer. No lawyering lawyer here, only an Officer of the Court with a routine job to do.

Never ask follow-up questions after the juror responds to your generic rehabilitation questions. Show no interest in the juror's answer to your rehabilitation question. Ask the rehabilitation question, let the juror answer, and ask your next rehabilitation question. No clarification. No confirmation of what the juror meant (i.e., "Is it fair to say that you feel . . ." or "By that, did you mean . . .").

Never reveal *your* bias by asking rehabilitation questions to only favorable jurors or to only jurors of the same race or gender. If two prospective jurors replied that they would be suspicious of a criminal defendant who did not testify at trial, either ask both jurors the same rehabilitation questions or ask neither any rehabilitation questions, even if you would love for the court to dismiss for cause one of the jurors. Look, you either stand for justice or you do not. You either should be asking the rehabilitation questions or you shouldn't. Wonderful waiters bring a menu to every guest who needs a menu. Lawyering lawyers only help the jurors they *want* to serve on the jury.

6. Rehabilitate Jurors Who Just Learned the Law

There may be times when a prospective juror will volunteer an opinion that is based on their misunderstanding or ignorance of the law. For example, a prospective juror may not know that the criminal defendant is legally "presumed innocent" and the jury "can't hold it against a criminal defendant who does not testify." When that happens, do not focus on the juror's initial answers. The question is not how the juror initially responded when asked whether "an indictment meant something to them" or whether they "would hold it against the defendant if he did not testify." The real question is whether, after the law was explained, would that juror *still* give weight to the indictment and *still* hold it against the defendant for not testifying. Simply put, a juror should not be dismissed based on opinions that the juror held *before* being told what the law requires.

It is not always appropriate to rehabilitate a juror whose bias is based on misunderstanding or ignorance of the law. When the judge discovers the juror's bias (i.e., "I would want the defendant to testify if he is not guilty") and chooses not to explain the law to that juror, you should never try to educate *and* rehabilitate the juror in front of the other jurors. That ship has sailed. If the court did not want to explain the law to that juror, the court is not going to allow you to explain the law. And even if the court did permit you to explain the law, your attempt to educate the biased juror may not be well received by the jury. Your attempt to correct the biased juror's misunderstanding or ignorance of the law could be misconstrued as your coaching the biased juror *before* asking your rehabilitation questions. And what would that say about you?

However, it can be appropriate to rehabilitate a juror when opposing counsel exposes the bias and chooses not to explain the law, especially if it was obvious that the juror did not understand the law *and* that opposing counsel was "hiding the ball." First, consider asking the court for the chance to question that juror "in chambers" or "outside the presence of other jurors" to spare that juror from any embarrassment (and to spare the other jurors from seeing how the sausage is made). If you are forced to rehabilitate that juror in open court, start by confirming the testimony ("Earlier, you shared that you would want the defendant to testify if he is not guilty"). Thank the juror for "disclosing" or "sharing" that opinion,

preference, or preconception. Then, ask questions that establish whether the juror is willing and able to set aside that opinion, preference, or preconception (i.e., "If the court instructed the jury that . . . would you . . .").

Here are some standard questions you can ask a juror who misunderstood the law.

- Ability to Set Aside Bias after Instructed/Educated by the Court
  - When you originally expressed your opinion or preference, were you aware of the law?
  - Did you understand the court's explanation of the law?
  - Now that the law has been explained to you, will you follow the law?
  - Now that the law has been explained to you, can you set aside your [opinion, preference, preconception, or bias]?
  - Now that the law has been explained to you, will you base your verdict solely on the law and the evidence presented?
  - Now that the law has been explained to you, will you fairly and impartially weigh the evidence?
- Ability to Set Aside Bias "If the Court Instructed That the Law . . ."
  - When you originally expressed your opinion or preference, what was your understanding of the law?
  - Do you now understand that you were mistaken about the law? (If the court or counsel has told juror what the law requires.)
  - If the court instructed you that the law is/requires . . . , would you follow the law as instructed by the court?
  - If the court instructed you that the law is/requires . . . , could you set aside your [opinion, preference, preconception, or bias]?
  - If the court instructed you that the law is/requires . . . , would you base your verdict solely on the law and the evidence presented?
  - If the court instructed you that the law is/requires . . . , could you fairly and impartially weigh the evidence?

Remember to ask these questions quickly, indifferently, and consistently. Avoid giving the impression that you are only asking these questions because you want a specific juror to serve, unless you want to send that message (i.e., "I would love for a neurologist to be a juror because the medical evidence proves there was no permanent brain damage").

7. Move to Exclude Speeches and Coaching

During the Golden Age of Lawyers, lawyers decided that voir dire was the perfect excuse to tell jurors about themselves. With folksy charm, Gray Hairs would smile and say, "Now, before I start asking personal questions, I figure it is only right that I tell you a little about myself." Gray Hairs would then masterfully introduce and portray themselves as the lovable grandfather, beloved coach, local prosecutor, or former teacher. To this day, some courts still allow attorneys to start voir dire in this fashion. It is incredibly effective and inappropriate.

Voir dire is not about the lawyers. Nobody asks the lawyers any questions. The sole purpose of voir dire is to discover information about the jurors, not reveal information about us. Why does the jury need to know that one of the lawyers was born "a stone's throw from the courthouse"? Why does a Louisiana jury need to know that a lawyer played center for Louisiana State University ("Geaux Tigers!")? Why should any lawyer be allowed to tell the jury he currently coaches the high school football team? No fact about an attorney has any probative value or relevance to any material issue in dispute.

Anticipate and eliminate this obvious attempt to prejudice jurors. When appropriate, file a motion with the court to prevent lawyers from volunteering personal information. Do not wait until trial. Objecting to opposing counsel's introduction is a surefire way to introduce yourself to the jurors as a lawyering lawyer.

Voir dire is not the appropriate time to "coach" jurors on how they should respond to questions they will likely be asked by opposing counsel. In preparation for a voir dire demonstration against a very successful plaintiff attorney, I obtained transcripts of his voir dire examinations. In an obvious attempt to coach jurors on how to respond to defense counsel's questions about sympathy, that plaintiff attorney warned jurors that "the law" required them "not to be persuaded by sympathy, passion, or anything" before openly suggesting that they respond "I'm going to be fair, let the evidence determine that." Incredibly, that plaintiff attorney even asked one juror to *promise* to respond that way when asked. Here is an excerpt from that transcript:

> Plaintiff Attorney: As the Judge told you this is the case of [plaintiff] against five insurance companies . . . The judge is going to tell you that an insurance company is to be treated just as a person. They're called a juridical person. They have the same right. They have the right to sue and to be sued and you treat them the same way. You have to be fair with them. You have to be fair to those

> insurance companies. And we're asking you to be fair to them and to be fair to us. **So if they stand before you and they talk about stuff like sympathy**, you know, the person here may be injured really, really bad whenever the evidence comes before you and they'll ask you, Mr. Jackson can you put sympathy aside? **Judge Dupont is going to order you and tell you the law that you're not to be persuaded by sympathy, passion, or anything**. You just got to let the evidence flow from this stand here, you with me? Let the chips fall as they may. Are you with that?
>
> If the judge, or I, or anyone asks you if would you be fair to both sides, am I feeling you right when you say, Tony, I'm going to be fair, let the evidence determine that. Will you do that?

Prospective Juror No. 115: Yeah.

Always do your homework. Find a transcript of opposing counsel's voir dire. File a motion *in limine* to exclude opposing counsel from discussing the law, warning prospective jurors about questions they may be asked, coaching jurors on what their response *should be* if they want to serve on the jury, and soliciting their promise to give a specific response.

8. Object to Impermissible Questions

There is a difference between knowing *whether* you can object and knowing *when* to object. If opposing counsel asks an objectionable question during voir dire, you will have a fraction of a second to decide. That is why it is important to decide your strategy for objecting during voir dire before voir dire starts.

During voir dire, lawyers should only object to impermissible questions. Be vigilant. Keep a list of impermissible questions and review them before voir dire starts. That list may vary from one venue to another. But your list may include:

- No divulging of facts
- No questions regarding a juror's reaction to potential evidence
- No questions regarding what a juror would "do" or "think" if evidence was presented
- No prying into juror's opinions on the evidence to be offered at trial
- No prying into juror's opinions on the weight to be given certain evidence
- No questions of law that call for pre-judgment of the facts

- No asking jurors to commit themselves to a verdict
- No suggesting the amount of the verdict to be reached
- No asking jurors if they have reservations about awarding a *specific* amount

As part of your due diligence, obtain a prior transcript of opposing counsel's voir dire. If you know that opposing counsel routinely asks certain impermissible questions, file a motion *in limine* with the court seeking to prohibit those impermissible questions (and attach that transcript). That way, you decrease the likelihood that opposing counsel will ask an impermissible question and increase the probability that the court will sustain your objection.

9. Bring Gifts When You Approach the Bench

How you object to an impermissible question can be as important as the objection itself. Remember that potential jurors are watching. When you object and ask to approach, don't just walk to the judge with a frown on your face. Lawyering lawyers approach the bench with only their argument. Wonderful waiters bring *something* to the court.

Whenever possible, approach the bench with something in your hands. Let the jury watch you hand a copy to opposing counsel and the court. Let the jury watch the judge and opposing counsel read the highlighted excerpt of whatever the wonderful waiter brought them. If you filed obtained an order prohibiting that line of voir dire questions, bring it to the bench with the ruling highlighted. If you have a published opinion that specifically prohibits that line of voir dire questions, bring it to the bench with the holding highlighted. If you have neither an order nor a published opinion on point, consider bringing a published opinion or article that generally discusses the purpose of voir dire (i.e., "Your Honor, as the highlighted passage confirms, the purpose of voir dire is to . . .") or specifically prohibits certain broad categories of questions (i.e., "Your Honor, as the highlighted passage confirms, attorneys are prohibited from prying into juror's opinions on the evidence to be offered at trial . . .").

10. Tolerate and Voir Dire on Prejudicial Remarks

Experienced trial lawyers will often try to bait you into objecting to prejudicial remarks during voir dire. Do not take the bait. Do not object. Whereas it is your job (as a wonderful waiter) to object to impermissible questions, it is not your job to whine about name-calling and snide remarks. Want to introduce yourself to the jury as a lawyering lawyer? Jump out of your seat and object to the first prejudicial remark. In so doing, you might as well cry, "Your Honor, opposing counsel is being mean!"

Always tolerate opposing counsel's unnecessary and inappropriate voir dire comments when there is *some* truth to them. If you represent a powerful, global corporation, do not object when opposing counsel correctly calls your client a "big corporation" or a "global corporation" or a "powerful corporation." Only object when a comment is patently false.

Here is another excerpt from the successful plaintiff attorney's voir dire transcript. In this excerpt, the charismatic plaintiff attorney made another speech and successfully baited defense counsel into objecting (in the eyes of the jurors) to the expression "big insurance company."

> Plaintiff Attorney: Now, let me ask you a little bit, I guarantee you if I ask folks out there to raise their hand, folks, y'all don't want to be here today? A lot of them, they're not going to be here. It's something that touches me dearly when I think about those kids over there in Iraq and Afghanistan, you know what they're dying for and fighting for? For us to have twelve people and not the government to stand here and tell us about our case **and not some big insurance company** to come in here and—
>
> Defense Attorney: Your Honor, can we approach?
>
> The Court: Sustained.
>
> Defense Attorney: Thank you.
>
> The Court: Sustained.
>
> Plaintiff Attorney: Twelve jurors make that determination. I gotcha. I'll move on, Your Honor. You folks, you as a jury make that determination. You with me? Will you be fair to both sides? The judge tells you that you gotta be honest and straight up will you do that?

Resist the temptation to take the bait and contemporaneously object to prejudicial comments. Why would a defense lawyer for a big insurance company object to his client being called a "big insurance company"? Is being a big insurance company a bad thing? Did the defense lawyer think that jurors couldn't figure that out for themselves? What message did the judge send by sustaining that objection, other than the message "Hey, let's not call the big insurance company that even though it is true"? To this day, Gray Hairs sit with their chairs pushed back from the table, listening to every word of opposing counsel's voir dire, poised to spring to their feet and object to the first prejudicial comment. Let's stop doing that.

Instead of objecting to a prejudicial but truthful remark, wait for your opportunity to ask questions during voir dire. Then, when it is your turn to voir dire, ask the jurors whether opposing counsel's remark succeeded in biasing or prejudicing that juror against your client. Of course, no juror is going to admit that they are so easily manipulated by opposing counsel. The point of the following questions is to remind the jury that opposing counsel was *trying* to manipulate them because opposing counsel is a lawyering lawyer.

- When opposing counsel referred to my client as a "big insurance company," did he (succeed in his attempt to) bias or prejudice any of you against my client?
- Do any of you know yourself well enough that you can admit that opposing counsel's calling my client a "big insurance company" made you like my client less or like his client more?
- If opposing counsel makes comments like that throughout the trial, will it be more difficult for any of you to remain objective?
- Do any of you feel that you might be more susceptible to manipulation than other jurors because of opposing counsel's personality, charisma, or tactics?

By allowing opposing counsel to make prejudicial remarks during voir dire, you can also create an opportunity for yourself during closing argument. Picture yourself reminding jurors that certain prejudicial remarks (a) started during voir dire; (b) were made in the hope of injecting bias and prejudice (or "passion") into their deliberations; and (c) will only make their job of objectively and impartially weighing the evidence "more difficult." In this manner, opposing counsel's attempt to bias the jury against your client can backfire, succeeding only in biasing the jury against opposing counsel.

Chapter 3

Jury Selection: Picking the Worst Possible Jury

During the Golden Age of Lawyers, Gray Hairs perceived jury selection as the process of picking the best possible jurors (which it is not and has never been). They prided themselves on being able to spot "good jurors" and marketed their instincts during jury selection. Whenever they got a great verdict, they often bragged about "picking" a great jury and patted themselves on the back for "selecting" the juror who served as the foreperson. Not surprisingly, when voir dire ended, Gray Hairs routinely turned to their co-counsel and asked, "Who do you like?," which was the wrong question and a colossal waste of time. Let's stop doing that.

Let's change the way we think about jury selection. Let's stop thinking of jury selection as the process of picking the best possible jury. Let's start thinking of jury selection as the process of picking the worst possible jury. After all, attorneys do not "pick" the jurors who serve on the jury. We "pick" the jurors we challenge for cause, and we "pick" the jurors we excuse by exercising one of our peremptory challenges. When the court gives us six peremptory challenges and tells us to pick a twelve-pack, we don't "pick" the best-possible twelve jurors. On a good day, we "pick" the worst-possible six jurors, and we send that six-pack home by exercising our six peremptory challenges on the worst six jurors.

Let's recognize that jury selection starts with calculating (and constantly re-calculating) the set of mathematically eligible jurors and ends with identifying the worst jurors within that mathematical set. Let's stop asking "Who do you like?" and start asking (a) "Who do you think is the last eligible juror?" and (b) "Who do you hate?" Let's stop myopically focusing on whether the next juror is "acceptable." Let's do the math and carefully consider all the reasons why we should be cutting an "acceptable" juror.

Let's stop bragging that we "picked a great jury." Hopefully, we didn't. Let's start taking pride in the jurors we sent home and stop taking pride in the leftovers who deliberated.

1. Identify Lions and Lambs

Every jury can be divided into Lions and Lambs, and the Lions *eat* the Lambs. The same adversarial system that forbids the use of a prejudicial pronoun during closing argument is more than willing to lock complete strangers in a windowless room, without bailiff or judge, until they reach a verdict. Jury deliberation has become survival of the fittest, and the fittest jurors, not the fittest opinions, survive. It is a gilded cage and a juridical Thunder Dome: "Twelve opinions enter, one verdict leaves!"

Lions can be teachers, preachers, and lawyers (the "Big Three"), but education and employment are *not* the only factors. Jurors become Lions for different reasons. Sometimes, jurors become Lions because of their age, intelligence, diplomacy, sensitivity, charm, gravitas, prior jury service, or personal experiences. Sometimes jurors become Lions because of the friendships they develop with other jurors. Sometimes jurors become Lions because they take better notes or demonstrate better recall of the facts during deliberation. Sometimes, an entire generation can develop a reputation for producing Lions by speaking "early and often" during deliberation, by refusing to compromise, and by demonstrating an ability to persuade or exhaust other jurors (yes, I am looking at you, millennials).

Unfortunately, it is not always possible to spot Lions during voir dire. Sequestration gives jurors the opportunity to become what they are, and Lions may rear their heads for the first time during deliberation. Remember how Juror #8 (played by Henry Fonda) slowly and brilliantly persuaded eleven jurors to change their verdict in the classic 1957 movie *Twelve Angry Men*? Well, if I had been the prosecutor (during that fictitious trial), I may have correctly guessed that Juror #4 (played by E.G. Marshall) was a Lion because he was so smart and Juror #10 (played by Ed Begley) was a Lion because he was so loud, but I would never have guessed that Henry Fonda's soft-spoken character was a Lion, let alone a Lion capable of devouring the other eleven jurors.

Sometimes, Lions are elected the foreperson. In 1997, when I was a prosecutor, the Honorable Charles L. Elloie in Criminal District Court for the Parish of Orleans had the uncanny ability to predict which juror would be selected to serve as foreperson. It was a sixth sense he developed after presiding over hundreds of criminal jury trials. After jurors left the courtroom to deliberate, Judge Elloie would sometimes ask us to identify who would be selected as the foreperson. It was a challenging exercise, and it is the reason why I started writing "Lion" and "Lamb" next to prospective jurors. For a time, I even associated "Lion" with potential foreperson.

Lions do not always serve as the foreperson. In *Twelve Angry Men*, the foreman (played by Martin Balsam) turns out to be a Lamb, more of

a follower than a leader. In the real world, many Lions will intentionally or instinctively avoid being elected the foreperson. What Judge Elloie developed was the ability to identify natural leaders on the jury. That is the same skill trial attorneys must develop over years of observing focus groups, watching mock trial deliberation, and trying cases to verdict.

Let's dedicate ourselves to hunting Lions during voir dire. Let's write down whether we think a potential juror is a "Lion" or a "Lamb." And let's not stop there. Let's determine and note whether prospective jurors are Friendly Lions, Ugly Lions, Mystery Lions, Friendly Lambs, or Ugly Lambs. No, there is no mathematical formula we can apply or magical questions we can ask to consistently spot Lions. When Lion hunting, there is no substitute for experience. Enlist jury consultants, Gray Hairs, and litigation savvy clients. Explain your mission and ask for their help.

2. Determine the Last Eligible Juror

Nothing is more important than spotting Lions during voir dire, but identifying Lions and Lambs is only the first step. Every attorney needs a system for using that information during jury selection, and every system should be based on the same premise: only worry about the Lions who have a mathematical chance of serving on the jury. The mathematically ineligible Lions are going home, and the mathematically eligible Lambs are getting eaten.

Before jury selection, always identify the set of mathematically eligible jurors, which is a very simple calculation. Before jury selection starts, trial lawyers always know the total number of jurors being selected (TJ) and the total number of peremptory challenges (PC) or "cuts" that the parties can exercise. By adding the total number of jurors being selected and the total number of peremptory challenges (TJ + PC), a lawyer can identify the Last Eligible Juror (LEJ). The Last Eligible Juror is the last juror who will be placed on the jury if *all* parties exhaust their peremptory challenges (TJ + PC = LEJ).

For example, if the jury will consist of six total jurors (TJ = 6), and the court allows three peremptory challenges to the plaintiff and three peremptory challenges to the defense (PC = 6), both lawyers should recognize at the start of jury selection that the Last Eligible Juror is Juror #12 (Landry) and the set of mathematically eligible jurors includes Juror #1 (Anders) through Juror #12 (Landry), as illustrated in Table 3.1. In this example, each lawyer could draw a line at Juror #12 (Landry) and cut the worst three jurors within that set.

Table 3.1 Calculate the Last Eligible Juror

Juror	Name	Plaintiff Cut	Defense Cut	Dismissed For Cause	Juror Selected	Notes
1	Anders					
2	Brown					
3	Connolly					
4	Drennan					
5	Emilio					
6	Foster					
7	Gillen					
8	Heller					
9	Irving					
10	Jensen					
11	Krupp					
12	Landry					Last Eligible Juror
13	Morris					
14	Nunez					
15	Ortego					

There is a meaningful difference between thinking of jury selection as "picking the best possible jury" (i.e., the jurors who stay and deliberate) and thinking of jury selection as "picking the worst possible jury" (i.e., jurors who are sent home). That difference manifests when attorneys must *refrain* from exercising all of their peremptory challenges to "pick the worst possible jury."

For example, if the Last Eligible Juror is Juror #12 (Landry) and the worst three jurors for the defense are Jurors #10 (Jensen), #11 (Krupp), and #12 (Landry), defense counsel should *refrain* from exercising a single peremptory challenge because, if plaintiff uses all three of plaintiff's peremptory challenges, Juror #9 (Irving) would become the last juror selected. In this scenario, defense counsel should "save" all three cuts for the last three mathematically eligible jurors, even though defense counsel will never get to exercise those peremptory challenges because jury selection will end with Juror #9, as illustrated in Table 3.2.

3. Move the Court to Rule on Challenges for Cause First

During jury selection, every court allows an unlimited number of challenges for cause, and every dismissal for cause of a mathematically eligible juror changes the set of mathematically eligible jurors. As a result, no attorney can intelligently exercise their peremptory challenges until they know which jurors will be dismissed for cause.

Always move the court to rule on challenges for cause at the start of jury selection and *before* the court asks the attorneys to "accept" or "cut" the first juror. For example, as shown in Table 3.3, if the attorneys are picking a jury of six, and the court allows each side three peremptory challenges, the Last Eligible Juror at the start of jury selection is Juror #12 (Landry). That changes each time the court dismisses for cause a mathematically eligible juror. When the court dismisses for cause Juror #2 (Brown), the Last Eligible Juror becomes Juror #13 (Morris). When the court dismisses for cause Juror #5 (Emilio), the Last Eligible Juror becomes Juror #14 (Nunez). And when the court dismisses for cause Juror #14 (Nunez), the Last Eligible Juror becomes Juror #15 (Ortego).

Conversely, it should be noted that the dismissal for cause of a juror who is not mathematically eligible does not change the set of mathematically eligible jurors. In Table 3.3, when the court dismissed for cause Juror #16 (Phillips), that dismissal changed nothing because Juror #16 (Phillips) was not a mathematically eligible juror. Juror #15 (Ortego)

Table 3.2 Save Peremptory Challenges for the Worst Eligible Jurors

Juror	Name	Plaintiff Cut	Defense Cut	Dismissed For Cause	Juror Selected	Notes
1	Anders				Juror #1	
2	Brown	P#1				
3	Connolly				Juror #2	
4	Drennan	P#2				
5	Emilio				Juror #3	
6	Foster				Juror #4	
7	Gillen				Juror #5	
8	Heller	P#3				
9	Irving				Juror #6	
10	Jensen		[save]			*Ugly Lion*
11	Krupp		[save]			*Ugly Lion*
12	Landry		[save]			*Ugly Lion* Last Eligible Juror
13	Morris					
14	Nunez					
15	Ortego					

Table 3.3 Changes to the Last Eligible Juror

Juror	Name	Plaintiff Cut	Defense Cut	Dismissed For Cause	Juror Selected	Notes
1	Anders					
2	Brown			Dismissed		
3	Connolly					
4	Drennan					
5	Emilio			Dismissed		
6	Foster					
7	Gillen					
8	Heller					
9	Irving					
10	Jensen					
11	Krupp					
12	Landry					~~Last Eligible Juror~~
13	Morric					~~Last Eligible Juror~~
14	Nunez			Dismissed		~~Last Eligible Juror~~
15	Ortego					**Last Eligible Juror**
16	Phillips			Dismissed		
17	Quinlan					

was the Last Eligible Juror before Juror #16 (Phillips) was dismissed for cause, and Juror #15 (Ortego) was the Last Eligible Juror after Juror #16 (Phillips) was dismissed for cause.

4. Determine Probability of Potential Dismissals for Cause

When a court refuses to rule on challenges for cause before starting jury selection, a trial attorney can still "play the odds" by identifying the likelihood (in terms of a percentage) the court will grant each potential challenge for cause (for both sides). With that information, trial attorneys can identify the Last Likely Juror (LLJ) and the Last Possible Juror (LPJ).

Whenever a court refuses to rule on challenges for cause at the start of jury selection, an attorney should (a) identify each potential challenge for cause; (b) determine the probability (percentage) that the court will dismiss for cause those jurors; (c) calculate the Last Likely Juror based on those percentages; and (d) calculate the Last Possible Juror by assuming that the court will grant every potential challenge for cause.

For example, if a jury will consist of six jurors and the court allows each side three peremptory challenges, the Last Eligible Juror at the start of jury selection will be Juror #12 (Landry). If the court refuses to rule on challenges for cause "up front" (i.e., at the start of jury selection), and the plaintiff attorney believes there is a 25 percent chance the court will dismiss for cause Juror #11 (Krupp) and a 100 percent chance the court will dismiss for cause Juror #13 (Morris), the Last Likely Juror remains Juror # 12 (Landry), but the Last Possible Juror (LPJ) becomes Juror #14 (Nunez), as illustrated in Table 3.4.

While it is never ideal to "accept" or "cut" jurors without knowing who will be dismissed for cause, this system allows attorneys to choose whether they want to be conservative and "save a cut" for the Last Possible Juror. In Table 3.4, if Juror #14 (Nunez) was an absolute nightmare, an attorney could "gamble" that the court would ultimately deny opposing counsel's challenge for cause of Juror #11 (Krupp) and choose *not* to save a cut for Juror #14 (Nunez). Alternatively, an attorney could "play it safe" and "save a cut" for Juror #14 (Nunez) in case the court granted opposing counsel's dismissal for cause of Juror #11 (Krupp). Regardless of the outcome, that discussion with co-counsel (and/or the client) and decision by the lead trial attorney only happens if the trial team is using this system for jury selection and has done the math.

Table 3.4 Identify the Last Likely Juror and Last Possible Juror

Juror	Name	Plaintiff Cut	Defense Cut	Dismissed For Cause	Juror Selected	Notes
1	Anders					
2	Brown					
3	Connolly					
4	Drennan					
5	Emilio					
6	Foster					
7	Gillen					
8	Heller					
9	Irving					
10	Jensen					
11	Krupp			25%		
12	Landry					**Last Likely Juror**
13	Morris			100%		
14	Nunez					**Last Possible Juror**
15	Ortego					
16	Phillips					
17	Quinlan					

5. Cut Ugly Lions and Ignore Ugly Lambs

There will be times when an attorney is not given enough peremptory challenges to cut all the Ugly Lions and all the Ugly Lambs. Every attorney needs a system for jury selection that quickly and definitively handles that unfortunate situation.

Let's agree to use our precious peremptory challenges *first and foremost* to send Ugly Lions home. Let's resolve that we will have the intestinal fortitude needed to allow eleven Ugly Lambs to serve on the jury before we accept one Ugly Lion. And make no mistake. Intestinal fortitude is exactly what is required. It is not easy for a defense attorney to say "acceptable" when the Ugly Lamb has filed two personal injury lawsuits in four years. Nor is it easy for a plaintiff attorney to say "acceptable" when the Ugly Lamb "went to grammar school" with the defendant. But every lawyer needs to trust their system, and no system should fear an Ugly Lamb the same as an Ugly Lion.

For example, if the Last Eligible Juror is Juror #12, and the defense attorney recognizes that Juror #8 (Heller), Juror #9 (Irving), and Juror #10 (Jensen) are Ugly Lions, that defense attorney should not hesitate to say "acceptable" to the six Ugly Lambs that precede those three Ugly Lions. When an attorney has only been given enough peremptory challenges to cut Ugly Lions, it does not matter how ugly a Lamb is because that Lamb is serving on the jury. Again, we are not picking the "best possible" jury of six. We are picking the "worst possible" jury of three, and that jury (which we are sending home) consists of Juror #8 (Heller), Juror #9 (Irving), and Juror #10 (Jensen), as illustrated in Table 3.5.

Again, this system is not for the faint of heart. In Table 3.5, at the end of jury selection, the client is going to ask you (as his defense attorney) why you didn't exercise a single peremptory challenge to "get to" Juror #7 (Gillen). "I could have stood there and taken the first six jurors in a row," the client will complain before demanding to know why you didn't like Juror #7 (Friendly Lion) better than Juror #6 (Ugly Lamb). "Of course, I liked Juror #7 better than Juror #6," you will respond. "But I didn't pick Juror #6 (Foster) over Juror #7 (Gillen); I picked Juror #6 (Foster) over Jurors #8 (Heller), #9 (Irving), and #10 (Jensen)." If the confused client needs more, you may have to explain by adding, "In reality, I didn't pick *any* of the jurors who are serving on your jury. I picked the three worst jurors (Heller, Irving, and Jensen), and I made certain those three jurors went home. By the way, that is a common misperception about jury selection. We really pick the jurors we send home. Only the leftovers deliberate."

Table 3.5 Cut Lions and Ignore Lambs

Juror	Name	Plaintiff Cut	Defense Cut	Dismissed For Cause	Juror Selected	Notes
1	Anders				Juror #1	*Ugly Lamb*
2	Brown				Juror #2	*Ugly Lamb*
3	Connolly				Juror #3	*Ugly Lamb*
4	Drennan				Juror #4	*Ugly Lamb*
5	Emilio				Juror #5	*Ugly Lamb*
6	Foster				Juror #6	*Ugly Lamb*
7	Gillen					*Friendly Lion*
8	Heller		[save]			*Ugly Lion*
9	Irving		[save]			*Ugly Lion*
10	Jensen		[save]			*Ugly Lion*
11	Krupp					
12	Landry					
13	Morris					
14	Nunez					
15	Ortego					

6. Beware Mystery Lions

There will be times when a trial attorney recognizes that a juror is a Lion but has no idea whether that juror will be an Ugly Lion or a Friendly Lion. On those rare occasions, a trial attorney should remember how dangerous Lions can be and brand that juror a "Mystery Lion."

Jury selection is not a time for optimism. Never look at Lions through rose-colored glasses. Being wrong about a Lamb may cost your client that one juror's vote. Being wrong about a Lion can cost your client the trial. When in doubt, classify a Lion as a "Mystery Lion." Whenever possible, cut Mystery Lions. Thus, your philosophy or protocol for exercising peremptory challenges must be to cut Ugly Lions first, Mystery Lions second, and Ugly Lambs third.

There may be times when an attorney should consider using a peremptory challenge on an Ugly Lamb instead of a Mystery Lion. For example, if the first six jurors are all Ugly Lambs and the next four jurors are all Mystery Lions, it may be preferable to cut the Ugliest Lamb and accept the least mysterious of the Mystery Lions. In that unfortunate situation, an attorney may have a better chance during the trial of persuading the Mystery Lion than persuading six Ugly Lambs. Desperate times require desperate measures.

7. Beware Potentially Divisive Friendly Lions

Nobody wants to agree with the jerk in the room. When picking a jury, do not be content with identifying Friendly Lions. Always ask yourself whether that Friendly Lion's personality or beliefs could have unintended consequences. Instead of gobbling up Lambs, some Lions will actually cause the Lambs to band together. That is why savvy criminal defense attorneys may refrain from cutting the embattled Republican senator if they believe that the senator's personality or extremely conservative beliefs will ultimately alienate and unify the other jurors. Instead, they may accept the senator and pray that the senator is the *first* to speak in favor of finding the defendant guilty as charged.

Picking a biased or irrational Friendly Lion can backfire. For the 2015 *Crayton* trial, we stipulated that our truck driver was "100 percent solely responsible" for causing the motor vehicle accident. During opening statement, I told jurors that our driver was "100 percent solely responsible" for the accident, and we only needed them to determine what constituted fair compensation for any injuries caused by the accident.

During closing argument, I again reminded jurors that our driver was negligent, and that his negligence caused the accident. Nevertheless, one conservative juror reportedly insisted that the plaintiff caused the accident and should receive nothing. After deliberating for some time, the other jurors asked the judge to remove the conservative juror. Instead of gobbling up Lambs, that Lion managed to unite the other jurors in their common disdain, either for him or his opinions. The verdict was still favorable for the defense, but picking that conservative juror had unintended consequences.

Picking a potentially divisive Lion can also have unintended consequences. During voir dire for the 1997 *Nelson* trial, I saw that my best friend's date to a high school dance (Helen) was a potential juror. I immediately called the jury's attention to the fact that Helen and Trey had double-dated with me and my girlfriend. I even made the obligatory joke at my best friend's expense (i.e., "Helen, I'm going to ask you a very important question, and I'll remind you that you are under oath . . . Did you have fun with Trey?"). The jurors all laughed, and I figured that would be the last I saw of Helen, but I was wrong. During jury selection, opposing counsel accepted Helen as a juror. When I asked opposing counsel "why in the world" she didn't cut Helen, opposing counsel said, "Because she is going to hold you to a higher standard."

Whether or not Helen held me to a higher standard (and she may have) during the 1997 *Nelson* trial, Helen succeeded in hanging-up the jury. Five jurors voted to convict Mr. Nelson of a lesser included offense, and Helen voted to convict Mr. Nelson "guilty as charged." The court was forced to declare a mistrial, and I had to retry the case.

At the conclusion of the subsequent 1998 *Nelson* trial, the jury unanimously convicted Mr. Nelson of the lesser included offense. That retrial confirmed that Helen was not a "Divisive" Lion. She was not the reason why six jurors voted to convict Mr. Nelson of the lesser included offense in 1998 (when she was not on the jury), nor was she the reason why five jurors refused to vote "guilty as charged" in 1997 (when she was on the jury). But Helen's vote is a reminder that picking a potentially controversial Lion can have unintended consequences, including mistrials being declared because of hung jurors.

8. Cut Friendly Lambs to Reach Friendly Lions

There may be times, after opposing counsel has exhausted their peremptory challenges, when an attorney must choose between accepting and cutting that Friendly Lamb to reach a Friendly Lion. Do not hesitate to cut Friendly Lambs to accept the Friendly Lions. For example, if the plaintiffs use their three cuts on the first three jurors (Anders, Brown, and Connolly), a defense attorney could be blessed with a string of six Friendly Lambs followed by a Friendly Lion. In that situation, the defense attorney should absolutely cut a Friendly Lamb like Juror #9 (Irving) to make a Friendly Lion like Juror #10 (Jensen) the final juror selected, as shown in Table 3.6.

During the 2012 *Fahy* trial, we finished voir dire late in the day and the court recessed for the night, telling us that jury selection would start in the morning. That night, at dinner, my client asked, "Who do you think plaintiff's counsel will use his three cuts on?" Without hesitation, I assured my client that there was "no way" opposing counsel was going to use all of his cuts because (if we both exhausted our cuts) the Last Eligible Juror would be a medical doctor, who was a *ferociously* Friendly Lion for my client.

The next morning, the court dismissed for cause only one mathematically eligible juror, which meant that the medical doctor (our Friendly Lion) would become the penultimate juror if both parties exhausted their cuts. I sighed. If plaintiff's counsel exercised only one peremptory challenge, he could make certain that the medical doctor (our Friendly Lion) did not serve. But then, inexplicably, plaintiff's counsel failed to do the math and used all three of his peremptory challenges.

As calmly as I could, I asked the court for a few minutes, walked over to the gallery, and explained the decision to my clients. The medical doctor was a Lion. If we used two of our cuts to reach her, and put her on the jury, we could be trying the case to a "jury of one." To their credit, my clients decided that they wanted the case decided by a medical doctor who would understand the medical and scientific evidence—whether it won or lost them the trial. I returned to my seat, double checked my math, and the medical doctor was sworn in as a juror.

The *Fahy* trial resulted in a 9-3 jury verdict, with the majority returning a defense verdict (no award) in favor of my clients. Weeks later, the plaintiff filed a motion for a new trial that included allegations about that medical doctor. That motion was correctly denied by the court, but it is worth noting that opposing counsel produced an affidavit from one of the three dissenting jurors, who swore under oath that the medical doctor "was adamant during the deliberations about how she was voting and she may have influenced other jurors." When I read that affidavit, I laughed out loud. Well, of course the medical doctor influenced other jurors! She was a Lion, and Lions *eat* Lambs. That's what Lions do. That's what Lions *always* do during jury deliberation. Opposing counsel had nobody to blame but himself.

Table 3.6 Cut Friendly Lambs to Reach Friendly Lions

Juror	Name	Plaintiff Cut	Defense Cut	Dismissed For Cause	Juror Selected	Notes
1	Anders	P#1				
2	Brown	P#2				
3	Connolly	P#3				*Mystery Lion*
4	Drennan				Juror #1	*Friendly Lamb*
5	Emilio				Juror #2	*Friendly Lamb*
6	Foster				Juror #3	*Friendly Lamb*
7	Gillen				Juror #4	*Friendly Lamb*
8	Heller				Juror #5	*Friendly Lamb*
9	Irving		D#1			*Friendly Lamb*
10	Jensen				Juror #6	*Friendly Lion*
11	Krupp					*Ugly Lion*
12	Landry					*Mystery Lion* **Last Eligible Juror**
13	Morris					
14	Nunez					
15	Ortego					

9. Exhaust Cuts to Preserve the Right to Appeal Rulings on Cause

Some states prohibit a criminal defendant from appealing the erroneous *denial* of a challenge for cause unless that defendant exhausted his or her peremptory challenges. Other states have held that prejudice is presumed when a challenge for cause is erroneously denied, and a criminal defendant's peremptory challenges have all been exhausted.

Always learn, before trial, whether exhausting your peremptory challenges is necessary to preserve your client's right to appeal the court's (erroneous) denial of your challenge for cause. That way, if the court denies your challenge for cause, you can consider the appellate advantages of exhausting your peremptory challenges before the final juror is selected.

For example, as shown in Table 3.7, if a court erroneously denies a criminal defendant's challenge for cause of Juror #8 (Heller), and that jurisdiction requires a criminal defendant to exhaust its peremptory challenges, the defense attorney should cut Juror #8 (Heller) and consider cutting Friendly Lambs like Juror #9 (Irving) and Juror #10 (Jensen) to preserve the defendant's right to appeal the court's denial of the challenge for cause, even though an Ugly Lamb like Juror #11 (Krupp) will likely become the final juror selected.

10. Save Cuts to Eliminate Their Right to Appeal Rulings on Cause

Some states also prohibit a party from appealing the erroneous *granting* of a challenge for cause unless the party who benefitted from that erroneous ruling exhausted their peremptory challenges. For example, Louisiana Code of Criminal Procedure Article 800(B) provides: "The erroneous allowance to the state of a challenge for cause does not afford the defendant a ground for complaint, unless the effect of such ruling is the exercise by the state of more peremptory challenges than it is entitled to by law."

Always learn, before trial, whether saving a peremptory challenge will prohibit your opponent from appealing the court's (possibly erroneous) granting of your challenge for cause. That way, if the court grants your challenge for cause, you can consider the appellate advantages of saving one peremptory challenge.

Table 3.7 Consider Exhausting Cuts to Preserve Appellate Issues

Juror	Name	State Cut	Defense Cut	Dismissed For Cause	Juror Selected	Notes
1	Anders	S#1				
2	Brown				Juror #1	
3	Connolly	S#2				
4	Drennan				Juror #2	
5	Emilio				Juror #3	
6	Foster				Juror #4	
7	Gillen				Juror #5	
8	Heller		D#1	Challenge Denied!		We should appeal the denial of our challenge for cause!
9	Irving		D#2			*Friendly Lamb*
10	Jensen		D#3			*Friendly Lamb*
11	Krupp				Juror #6	*Ugly Lamb*
12	Landry					**Last Eligible Juror**
13	Morris					
14	Nunez					
15	Ortego					

For example, as shown in Table 3.8, if the prosecutor believes the court may have erroneously granted the State's challenge for cause of Juror #3 (Connolly), that prosecutor should consider the appellate advantages of accepting an Ugly Lamb like Juror #9 (Irving) as the sixth and final juror rather than exhaust the State's peremptory challenges by using the State's third cut on Juror #9 (Irving).

11. Avoid Ending Jury Selection before a String of Ugly Lions

Courts often pick alternate jurors, who will only participate in jury deliberation if the court is forced to remove or release a "seated" juror from service prior to verdict. There is no way of knowing whether the First Alternate will get to serve on the jury. And there is no way of calculating the probability that the First Alternate will get to serve because there are too many confounding variables (including sickness). At best, it is reasonable to conclude that the longer the trial, the more likely the First Alternate will get to serve.

Most courts treat the selection of jurors as a separate and distinct process from the selection of alternates. Those judges give the parties a certain number of cuts during the selection of the jury (i.e., "we're picking twelve jurors and each side has three cuts") and a certain number of cuts during the selection of alternates (i.e., now we're picking two alternates, and each side gets one cut"). Typically, a lawyer who "saves" a peremptory challenge during jury selection does not get to exercise that challenge during alternate selection. Spend it or lose it.

Always ask the court during the pre-trial conference (a) whether the court intends to pick alternates; (b) how many alternates the court intends to select; (c) what the court's process for selecting alternates will be; and (d) how many peremptory challenges each side will be given during the process of selecting alternates.

Always look at the potential alternates prior to exhausting your peremptory challenges. No, it does not matter if the last juror selected will be followed by a string of Ugly Lambs. The possibility of having Ugly Lambs for alternates should *never* affect jury selection. But you should always worry about the possibility of having a pride of Ugly Lions serving as alternates.

Avoid having Ugly Lions selected as alternates. Whenever possible, consider "saving cuts" or "spending cuts" to avoid ending jury selection at the start of a string of Ugly Lions. No, you are never going to "spend a

Table 3.8 Consider Saving Cuts to Eliminate Appellate Issues

Juror	Name	State Cut	Defense Cut	Dismissed For Cause	Juror Selected	Notes
1	Anders	S#1				
2	Brown	S#2				
3	Connolly			X		Yikes. Court may have erred in granting our challenge.
4	Drennan				Juror #1	
5	Emilio				Juror #2	
6	Foster				Juror #3	
7	Gillen				Juror #4	
8	Heller				Juror #5	
9	Irving				Juror #6	*Ugly Lamb*
10	Jensen					
11	Krupp					
12	Landry					
13	Morris					
14	Nunez					
15	Ortego					

cut" on a Friendly Lion. Nor will you ever abstain from cutting an Ugly Lion for fear of having an Ugly Lion selected as an alternate. But stay vigilant and recognize when cutting or accepting a Lamb (any kind of Lamb) could be the difference between having an Ugly Lion selected as an alternate.

For example, there may a situation where, after plaintiffs exhaust their peremptory challenges, a (vigilant) defense attorney realizes that exercising a second and third peremptory challenge will result in the defense's facing a string of four Ugly Lions during the selection of alternate jurors. In that situation, the defense attorney may want to "save" two cuts to make certain the first alternate juror is not an Ugly Lion, as illustrated in Table 3.9.

12. Be Prepared for Back Strikes

Back strikes are the bane of my existence during jury selection. Some courts allow back strikes during jury selection. Some courts allow back strikes, but only until the final juror has been accepted by both parties. And some courts allow back strikes *even after* the final juror has been accepted by both parties.

Always ask the court during the final pre-trial conference whether they allow back strikes during jury selection, and make certain you know whether that right to exercise back strikes abruptly ends when all parties have said "accept" for the final juror. For example, when you are picking a jury of six (a "six pack"), and the court allows back strikes *until* the final juror is accepted by both parties, be ready to exercise at least one of your back strikes as soon as the fifth juror is accepted by opposing counsel.

The best back strike strategy is to accept every juror until you are forced to exercise a back strike. Why wouldn't you? Let opposing counsel exercise their peremptory challenges contemporaneously. Maybe opposing counsel will cut one of the jurors you were considering cutting. For example, as shown in Table 3.10, if the court allows back strikes until the sixth and final juror is accepted by both parties, and defense counsel considers Juror #1 (Anders) and Juror #2 (Brown) to be Mystery Lions, defense counsel should say "accepted" for both jurors, save two cuts for those jurors, and make certain to back strike both jurors *before* the sixth juror is accepted. After all, there is a chance (however small) that plaintiff counsel will contemporaneously cut Juror #1 (Anders) or Juror #2 (Brown), saving you two peremptory challenges!

Table 3.9 Avoid Having a String of Ugly Lions as Potential Alternates

Juror	Name	State Cut	Defense Cut	Dismissed For Cause	Juror Selected	Notes
1	Anders				Juror #1	
2	Brown				Juror #2	
3	Connolly	P#1				
4	Drennan				Juror #3	
5	Emilio	P#2				
6	Foster				Juror #4	
7	Gillen	P#3				
8	Heller		D#1			*Ugly Lion*
9	Irving				Juror #5	*Ugly Lamb*
10	Jensen				Juror #6	*Ugly Lamb*
11	Krupp	P#1-A				
12	Landry				**Alternate**	
13	Morric					*Ugly Lion*
14	Nunez					*Ugly Lion*
15	Ortego					*Ugly Lion*
16	Phillips					*Ugly Lion*

Table 3.10 Accept Every Juror Until Forced to Exercise a Back Strike

Juror	Name	State Cut	Defense Cut	Dismissed for Cause	Juror Selected	Notes
1	Anders	P#1				*Mystery Lion*
2	Brown		Backstrike #1			*Mystery Lion*
3	Connolly				Juror #1	
4	Drennan				Juror #2	
5	Emilio				Juror #3	
6	Foster				Juror #4	
7	Gillen				Juror #5	
8	Heller	P#2				
9	Irving		D#1			*Ugly Lion*
10	Jensen				Juror #6	

Beware judges who allow back strikes *and* who alternate asking the question (i.e., the court will ask plaintiff whether Juror #1 is acceptable, then ask defense whether Juror #1 is acceptable, then ask defense whether Juror #2 is acceptable, then ask plaintiff whether Juror #2 is acceptable). When attending a pre-trial conference before those judges, both trial attorneys need to know whether the deadline for exercising a peremptory challenge is (a) any time *before* the ultimate juror is "accepted" by both attorneys; (b) any time *before* the first attorney says "accepted" for the ultimate juror; or (c) any time *before* the second attorney says "accepted" for the ultimate juror. The only way to know is to ask the court.

Chapter 4

Mock Trials: Stop Trying to Win

During the Golden Age of Lawyers, trial attorneys discovered the many advantages of participating in mock trials to "road test" their arguments, evidence, demonstrative exhibits, and witnesses. As technology improved, the format of those mock trials evolved. Today, in addition to traditional "in-person" mock trials, jury consultants offer a variety of virtual jury research platforms, which allow attorneys and jurors to participate remotely. But all mock trials involve the presentation of evidence and the harvesting of opinions. And all mock trials involve one absolutely critical decision: Before the start of every mock trial, attorneys must decide whether the goal of that mock trial will be winning or learning. That is the fork in the road.

If the goal is to "win" the mock trial, the dream scenario is to have every panel of jurors unanimously vote in favor of your client as soon as the foreperson calls for a vote. Then, as you and your client watch with pride, the jurors will sit around and agree. Agree with each other. Agree with your experts. Agree with your analysis and argument. Agree with your position. Of course, you won't learn anything, except that a handful of people found your truncated presentation more persuasive than the truncated presentation by an attorney who will not be making those arguments at trial. But the compliments will rain down, drowning you and your client in confidence. Enjoy the positive feedback and your great victory!

If the goal is to learn what jurors think of the evidence and argument, your dream scenario is to have 35 percent of the jurors agree with you, 35 percent of the jurors agree with opposing counsel, and 30 percent of the jurors be genuinely "neutral" when individually polled *before* the start of deliberation. Then, as you and your client watch, all hell will (hopefully) break loose as jurors express their strongly held opinions and strenuously disagree. Disagree with each other. Disagree about the evidence. Disagree about the witnesses. Disagree about what is "right" and "wrong." Misinterpret arguments. Misquote attorneys. Share personal stories and make impassioned pleas. From the safe side of the one-sided glass, you and your client will suddenly find yourselves tuned into the wilderness channel, watching as the Lions challenge each other and gobble up the Lambs. Grab a pen and a legal pad. Take copious notes. Enjoy the carnage!

Yes, there will be times when a client needs to know *whether* your side can win at trial or *what* the jury's verdict could be on *your* best day. On those rare occasions, when only the verdict matters, the mock trial should mirror as closely as possible the real trial. Assign lead trial counsel to represent your client and tell lead counsel not to hold back. Tell them to make every argument they intend to make at trial. Discuss every important piece of evidence. Share every demonstrative exhibit. Offer every metaphor and analogy. Take the same approach and use the same tone they intend to use during the real trial, even if that means criticizing opposing counsel's argument, witnesses, and personal hygiene. Forget balancing the presentations. Forget balancing the presenters. Cry "Havoc!" and let slip the dogs of war.

On every other occasion, the goal of the mock trial should be to get the jurors talking about the evidence and the argument. Forget their verdict. After all, these jurors will not be serving on your actual jury. What matters is their deliberation. Design your mock trial to harvest their personal stories, observations, comparisons, questions, confusion, and concerns. When pressed, what arguments will a hostile Lion make? When uncertain, what questions will the Lambs have about the accident or your client? When frustrated, what bias or prejudice will raise its ugly head during deliberation? And what completely irrelevant issue will jurors raise and criticize counsel for not addressing, if only to solicit agreement in the room or interrupt momentum during deliberation? Properly mined, these golden nuggets can change your client's fortune at trial.

The bottom line is that all mock trials are *not* created equal. The return on your investment will always depend on the choices you make months before the mock trial or focus group starts. Here are some suggestions for how to reduce the chances that your mock trial results in a single-vote victory and how to increase the chances your mock trial will inspire sustained and passionate discourse. Good luck!

1. Balance the Presentations

The goal is to get the jurors talking about the evidence and argument, not about the disparity in the two presentations. Balance the presentations. Do not allow one presentation to include 180 PowerPoint slides when the other presentation involves only 10 slides. Do not allow one presentation to last 60 minutes when the other presentation last only 30 minutes. Do not allow only one presentation to include expensive trial graphics, custom illustrations, 3D animations, and witness video clips. Imbalance is the enemy. Imbalance skews results.

Whenever possible, submit the slides for both presentations to your jury consultant and ask the jury consultant to incorporate those slides into the same PowerPoint deck template. If the jury consultant does not have the bandwidth to redesign the slides prior to the mediation, assign the same person to prepare both presentations, even if that person will not be playing either attorney during the mock trial. The more similar the presentations, the more the jury will focus on and discuss the evidence presented.

During the course of civil litigation or criminal prosecution, attorneys will always spend a disproportionate amount of time developing favorable evidence, arguments, and demonstrative exhibits for their client. And that is only natural. By the time the mock trial rolls around, a defense attorney should have an opinion on the right way for the defense to present its case. But that same defense attorney may have no idea how to prepare opposing counsel's presentation, refine opposing counsel's arguments, and create opposing counsel's demonstrative exhibits.

That is why mock trial preparation should always start by assigning and preparing *opposing* counsel's presentation. If you wait until the week before a mock trial to "throw some slides together" for opposing counsel, the jury will notice the disparity in the presentations, and that disparity will skew the results. Always plan ahead. Be aware of an attorney's natural tendency to spend more time on charts, graphs, timelines, slides, and arguments that they may actually get to use if the case goes to trial. Whenever possible, stagger the deadlines for completing the two presentations and require trial counsel to circulate *opposing* counsel's presentation before circulating their own presentation.

2. Balance the Presenters

The goal is to get the jurors talking about the evidence, not the presenters. Do not let your mock trial become a beauty pageant or an oratory competition. Nothing can skew the results of a mock trial like assigning the trial-tested, brilliant Gray Hair to represent the client during the mock trial and asking the less-experienced associate to play opposing counsel.

In 2022, an insurer hired our trial team to parachute into a case one week before the insured, a national trucking company, was holding a mock trial. The client asked us to attend the mock trial, hoping that it would help us "get up to speed." It was a complete disaster. The talented Gray Hair who had been hired by the trucking company to serve as lead trial counsel for the defense had a polished and prepared presentation that allowed him to demonstrate his complete command of the law and evidence. In contrast, the same Gray Hair was perfectly content to have his associate read a typed script for the plaintiff's presentation. The case involved complex cardiac issues, and the poor associate struggled to pronounce many of the words. Not surprisingly, the Gray Hair won, and we learned absolutely nothing during deliberation.

In retrospect, it would have been better for the Gray Hair to have stayed home that day and to have asked an equally inexperienced associate to read a typed script for the defense presentation. Maybe then, the jurors would have ignored both presenters, rolled up their sleeves, and figured out what happened for themselves.

3. Clearly Define the Goal for Both Presenters

Trial attorneys can be extremely competitive ("Type A") personalities. They love to win. In fact, they hate losing more than they love winning. Asking a Gray Hair to help you "balance" the presentations can be tantamount to asking Muhammad Ali to throw a boxing match. But that is exactly what has to happen. Every attorney participating in the mock trial has to be committed to balancing the presentations, instead of "winning" the mock trial.

The real problem here is that fewer jury trials mean fewer opportunities for trial attorneys to impress their clients. The mock trial presentation may be the only opening statement or closing argument that clients ever see an attorney give. That is why trial attorneys often approach the mock trial as an audition. This is their time to shine, and that makes them dangerous. Their desire to "crush" opposing counsel during the mock trial can destroy that perfect jury ratio (35/35/30) headed into jury deliberation. Truth be told, the vanity of trial attorneys can be the biggest confounding variable in a mock trial.

The only way to eliminate that particular confounding variable is to get everybody on the same page. As soon as the mock trial is scheduled, hold a phone call to discuss "mock trial strategy, preparation, and division of labor." Identify the fork in the road. Discuss the pros and cons of both approaches to mock trial. Solicit the client's opinion. Find out whether the theme song for your mock trial will be Queen's "Another

One Bites the Dust" or Bonnie Raitt's "Let's Give Them Something to Talk About."

If the client's goal is to see lead trial counsel in action and to determine whether jurors will find lead trial counsel's approach persuasive, so be it. The customer is always right. Of course, you should still find a worthy adversary, but you can tell counsel to take the gloves off. Give the client the no-holds-barred, barbed-wire steel cage match that the client wants to see. Leave your pen and legal pad at home. Bring popcorn.

But if the client's goal is to inspire jurors to argue about the evidence and argument (as opposed to deferring to lead trial counsel), openly discuss your concerns that the presenters may be tempted to try to "win" the mock trial. Make it clear that the goal of the mock trial will be to generate the maximum amount of (quality) discussions during deliberation. Explain how and why a "dominating" performance by lead trial counsel could be counterproductive. Every trial attorney needs to hear the client say that they *want* counsel to "hold back" or to "dial it down." Only then will counsel relax. Only then will everyone listen to the jury consultant's advice about what will improve your chances of inspiring discussion and debate.

In college, I was so desperate to impress the rowing coach that I spent the entire first practice trying to pull *harder* than the other seven men in the boat, instead of trying to pull *with* the other seven men in the boat. Eventually, our wise coach pulled his skiff up alongside our shell, looked at me, and said, "Son, I know you can row hard. What I want to see is whether you can row right. Can you do that for me?" That was exactly the acknowledgment and the guidance that I so desperately needed. It allowed me to relax and focus on my technique. Similarly, lead trial counsel may need to hear the client say, "I know you are a good trial lawyer. I know you will do an excellent job at trial. What I want to see is whether you can mock try this case right. And that means balanced presentations from balanced presenters. Can you do that for me?"

4. Design Wild Swings into Both Presentations

Different jury consultants use different protocols, equipment, and questionnaires. Many mock trials involve a 60-minute presentation ("clopening") by the plaintiff, followed by a 75-minute presentation ("clopening") by the defense, followed by a 15-minute rebuttal by the plaintiff. During each presentation, jury consultants use an audience response system to track whether jurors find the arguments and evidence to be helpful.

Between presentations, jury consultants also use that audience response system to poll the mock jurors, recording their personal opinions and preferences *before* they deliberate with other jurors.

For this mock trial format, when the goal is to generate discussion, the ideal scenario is (a) for the plaintiff's presentation of the evidence to be so persuasive that at least 75 percent of the jurors "agree" or "strongly agree" with the plaintiff when polled after the plaintiff's "clopening"; (b) for the defendant's presentation of the evidence to be so persuasive that 50 to 75 percent of the jurors "agree" or "strongly agree" with the defendant when polled after the defendant's "clopening"; and (c) for the plaintiff's brief rebuttal to be *only* effective enough for the final poll to reveal 35 percent "agree" or "strongly agree" with the plaintiff, 30 percent are neutral/undecided, and 35 percent "agree" or "strongly agree" with the defense.

Toward that end, mock trial presentations should be carefully designed and staged to create swings in jury polling as shown in Figure 4.1.

Disastrous mock trials are those without any swings in polling. Persuasion requires movement. Without movement in polling results, there is no reliable method for jury consultants to determine whether the evidence or argument persuaded any jurors.

No defendant wants to spend $100,000 on a mock trial only to witness (a) a plaintiff presentation that convinces only 15 percent of the jurors to "strongly agree" or "agree" with the plaintiff; (b) a defense presentation that persuades none of the undecideds; and (c) a plaintiff rebuttal that

Figure 4.1 Ideal mock trial polling.

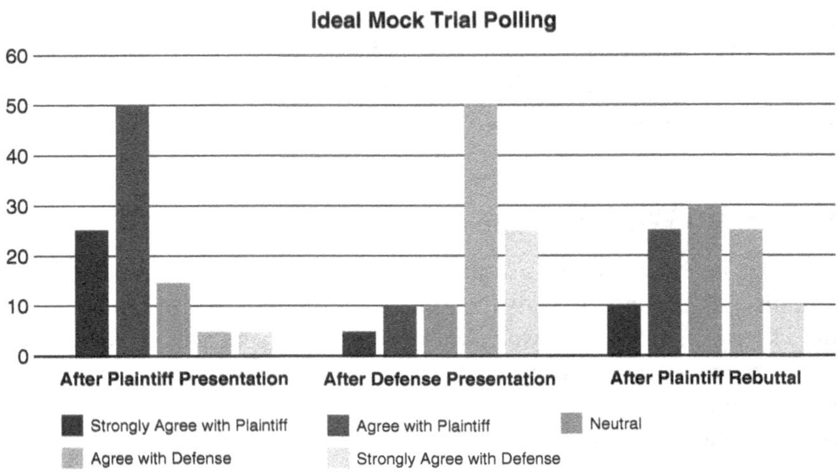

Figure 4.2 Nightmare mock trial for the defense.

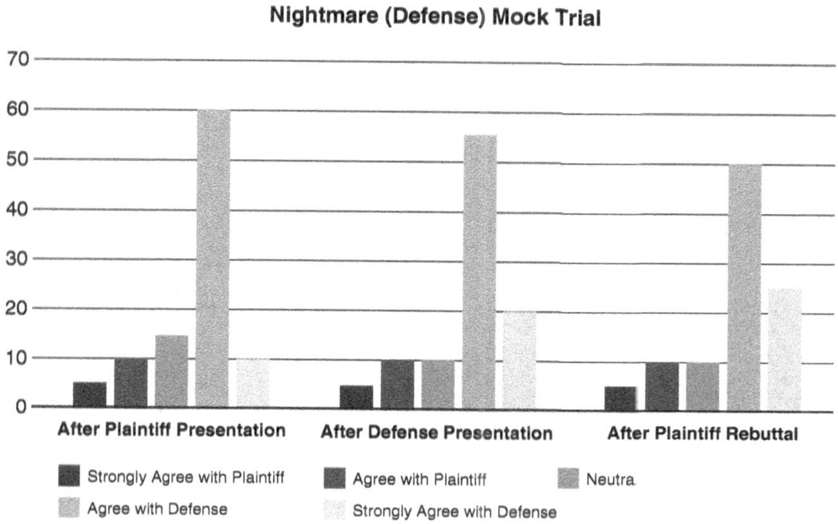

swings no jurors back to the plaintiff. For a defendant, the worst-case scenario is not losing the mock trial. The worst-case scenario is winning the mock trial because the jurors make up their mind *before* hearing the defendant's arguments and evidence. When the mock trial looks like Figure 4.2, the jury consultants may only learn about the mock jury's natural bias or (more likely) the jury's complete dissatisfaction with the plaintiff's presentation.

Designing swings during a mock trial requires careful planning. The attorneys must agree on who will disclose the important evidence and when that evidence will be disclosed. Consider the examples in Table 4.1 of how the attorneys can generate swings by timing the introduction of evidence, the disclosure of facts, and the making of specific arguments.

To achieve dramatic swings, both presenters must resist the temptation to steal thunder. Make no mistake. Stealing thunder has no place in a mock trial. The goal of the plaintiff's 60-minute mock trial presentation is not to present the evidence on both sides of every argument. That would render the defendant's 75-minute presentation either unnecessary or uninteresting. Similarly, the goal of the defendant's 75-minute presentation is not to address every argument the plaintiff could possibly make during rebuttal. That would moot the need for the plaintiff's rebuttal.

Stealing thunder during a mock trial presentation also "robs" jury consultants of the opportunity to learn more about the thunder. Yes,

Table 4.1 Example of Staging Mock Trial Swings

Plaintiff Presentation	Defense Presentation	Plaintiff Rebuttal
Plaintiff's neck pain started the same day.	Plaintiff reported "no injury" to the police officer.	The officer only asked if Plaintiff was "okay."
	Plaintiff did not seek medical attention for two days.	Plaintiff took daughter to school event that Sat. Went to ER at 1:00 a.m. on Monday morning.
Plaintiff was diagnosed at ER with a neck injury.	Plaintiff's ER diagnosis was a cervical strain.	That diagnosis was before Plaintiff got a cervical MRI.
Conservative treatment did not eliminate her pain.	Plaintiff went to one week of PT (prescribed six weeks).	Plaintiff had to leave work for PT and it was not helping.
MRI revealed herniated disc at C6-7.	Defense neurosurgeon says film only shows C6-7 bulge.	Every treating physician and the radiologist say "herniation."
	Before accident, Plaintiff went to chiropractor for neck pain for five years.	Before accident, Plaintiff was only treated for flare-ups and had not been to chiro for six months.
Plaintiff's ESI at C6-7 provided no relief.	Because no relief, ESI did not identify pain generator.	Because no relief, Plaintiff's pain was likely discogenic.
Plaintiff underwent C6-7 fusion.	Defense neurosurgeon said no need for surgery.	Testimony of treating physician entitled to greater weight.
	Plaintiff had a subsequent, more serious accident that was 100 percent her fault. Surgery occurred after that accident.	Plaintiff's neurosurgeon recommended the C6-7 fusion one month before the subsequent accident.
Plaintiff will likely need adjacent level C5-6 fusion within ten years.	Studies do not support speculation regarding adjacent level fusion.	Probability for adjacent level fusion increased when initial fusion at C6-7.
Plaintiff has not worked since the C6-7 fusion.	No doctor has restricted her from returning to work. Fusion was successful. Neck is stronger now.	Surgery only addressed instability at C6-7. It did not resolve her neck pain. If Plaintiff could return to work, she would. She loved that job.
	Defense private investigator obtained video of Plaintiff enjoying roller coaster ride last month.	Plaintiff has good days and bad days. Her daughter begged her to go on the ride. Her neck was sore for a week.

audience response systems allow jurors to rate the "helpfulness" or "persuasiveness" of the attorney's pre-emptive *response* to opposing counsel's argument (i.e., rate the "stealing"), but they do not permit the jury to properly rate opposing counsel's argument (i.e., rate the "thunder"). Moreover, there is a tremendous difference between the jurors making voluntary helpful/persuasive ratings during the presentations and jurors participating in mandatory polling regarding specific questions after those presentations.

Fair warning: Gray Hairs will always push back when asked not to steal thunder and when told to remove those pre-emptive arguments from their presentation. "There is no way that I am going to lose credibility by telling the mock jurors that physical therapy did not help the plaintiff only to have opposing counsel reveal that the plaintiff only went to three physical therapy sessions," the Gray Hair will say. "That would never happen during a real trial." Of course, Gray Hairs are correct on both accounts.

Gray Hairs are correct about opposing counsel's trial strategy. During opening statement, plaintiff's counsel will likely steal the defendant's thunder by disclosing that plaintiff only went to three physical therapy sessions and explaining *why* plaintiff stopped. But again, when the goal of the mock trial is to learn (not win), imitation can be counterproductive. Allowing the Gray Hair to steal defense counsel's thunder would (a) generate a single "helpful/persuasive" click on the audience response system for each issue during the Gray Hair's clopening, instead of multiple clicks for each issue over the course of all three presentations; (b) deprive the defendant of a meaningful clopening on each issue; (c) moot the need for a plaintiff rebuttal on each issue; and (d) deprive jury consultants of the polling swings that generate clicks and define persuasion.

Gray Hairs are also correct about losing credibility. Gray Hairs *will* lose credibility with mock jurors when opposing counsel discloses that plaintiff only went to three physical therapy sessions. Swings do come at a price, and the presenters have to be willing to pay that price. When the additional evidence is disclosed by opposing counsel (i.e., "What counsel did not tell you is . . ."), jurors will be surprised and disappointed. But that surprise and disappointment is exactly what is needed for a meaningful swing.

That surprise and disappointment can also have the unintended consequence of reminding jurors that *both* attorneys are paid advocates. And that reminder can be very helpful. When the goal of the mock trial is to learn, nobody wants jurors to "trust" or "defer" to *either* of the presenters. Jurors must think for themselves. They must consider and weigh evidence for themselves. Otherwise, their deliberations will only parrot the attorneys.

Consistency is the key to generating swings without skewing results. When designing swings, make certain that (a) both presentations focus on *only* the favorable evidence and argument; (b) both presenters refrain from disclosing and responding to unfavorable evidence and arguments during their presentations; (c) neither presenter *ever* misrepresents a fact (which is unforgiveable); and (d) both presentations include swing-inducing disclosures of new facts and swing-inducing introduction of new evidence. Jurors must be reminded that both presenters are "only advocates." Either incorporate swings for both presenters or eliminate all swings from the mock trial. In this regard, it is all or nothing.

5. Skew the Results for Celebrity

There are exceptions to the rule that mock trials should involve balanced presentations and balanced presenters. Jurors do not deliberate in a vacuum. Sometimes, a locally popular, particularly charming, or famous opposing counsel or opposing party will directly affect the way jurors consider and weigh the evidence. Sometimes, a particularly abrasive, detestable, or infamous client will directly affect the way jurors consider and weigh the evidence. When the goal of the mock trial is to learn, attorneys need to learn what jurors are going to say and think *after* the celebrity witness testifies or *after* the celebrity attorney implores them to rule for their client. That means either disclosing the identity of the celebrity to the mock jurors or finding a way to simulate the same degree of excitement, bias, and prejudice during deliberations.

When you identify a (game-changing) confounding variable, do not hide that confounding variable from your mock jurors. Instead, consider ways of intentionally skewing the results to test the true strength of your evidence and argument.

For example, when it is likely that the real jurors will *want* to agree with opposing counsel or will *want* to find for the opposing party (or will *hate* your client), consider telling the mock jurors before the mock trial starts that the mock trial was funded by opposing counsel. Tell them that opposing counsel is paying their fees and treating them to lunch. Only then will you learn whether your approach to closing argument will persuade the jurors to set aside their bias and prejudice. Only then will your client learn what type of juror is capable of returning a verdict they *know* will upset the attorneys who hired them (i.e., willing to bite the hand that is feeding them). Only then will your client learn which items of evidence and which arguments are likely to "make the cut" and be discussed during deliberation.

Before one mock trial, we did not have videotaped depositions of either parent, but we knew their testimony in the wrongful death case was going to be very powerful. We were able to find online an incredibly moving video interview of the parents talking about the loss of their child. While the video would never be admissible at the real trial, we chose to *start* the mock trial by playing that video because we anticipated the plaintiffs calling the parents to the stand at the start of the trial, and similarly skewing the jury in their favor. The video included a beautiful montage of their child, which was set to haunting music. We chose to play that video *with* the haunting music because we wanted to bias and prejudice the jurors *against us* during the plaintiff's case. We wanted to see whether we could take a 100 percent "strongly agree" with the plaintiff polling result after the plaintiff's presentation and swing that vote with our scientific and medical evidence. Our goal was to learn whether our evidence could overcome the anticipated bias.

6. Streamline the Mock Trial with Stipulations

Jurors today know that the vast majority of cases settle before trial. Consequently, jurors often walk into the courtroom wondering why your case did *not* settle and asking themselves one question: Who is being unreasonable? By stipulating to as many facts and issues as humanly possible, you can answer that question for the jury. Picture the judge instructing the jury that "defendant has stipulated that they were 100 percent solely responsible for this accident, and you are only being asked to determine what constitutes fair compensation for any injuries you find were caused by the accident." Right or wrong, jurors who hear that stipulation will wonder what injury the plaintiff is claiming that "probably wasn't caused by the accident."

In one case, we stipulated that our client was 100 percent solely responsible for causing the accident *and* that the accident caused all of plaintiff's orthopedic injuries. We reserved only our right to challenge whether the accident *also* caused plaintiff's alleged traumatic brain injury. In so doing, we gained credibility with the jury, took the poison out of the trial, and focused the jury on only those factual issues we wanted them to determine.

Mock trials are the perfect time to test the effect of stipulations. Ideally, you should hold two separate mock trials, making the stipulation in only one mock trial. In the alternative, if you have only time for one mock trial, consider layering the evidence during that mock trial so that

(a) at least one panel of mock jurors is told the stipulation and is not presented with the evidence likely excluded from trial because of that stipulation and (b) at least one panel of mock jurors is not told the stipulation, is presented with all of the evidence, and is asked to determine the issue resolved by the stipulation. In this manner, the jury consultants can help you evaluate the likely effect that the stipulation would have on jury deliberations.

7. Hold a Focus Group before the Mock Trial

Attorneys do not have to choose between doing a focus group and doing a mock trial. When your client can afford the additional expense, consider the advantages of doing a focus group *before* holding the mock trial. Jury consultants love conducting focus groups because they can control the presentation of the evidence and they know how to solicit the comments, concerns, and conversations your client needs. The focus group format can allow the jury consultant to do all of the following:

- Ask more detailed questions regarding each juror's prior bias and prejudice toward a client, witness, product, or specific issue.
- Solicit opinions on specific issues, evidence, and arguments, instead of hoping jurors will discuss those issues, evidence, and arguments during mock trial deliberations.
- Solicit opinions on specific demonstrative exhibits (i.e., "Is this helpful?"; "What does this exhibit tell you?"; "What questions do you have about this chart?").
- Solicit opinions from all of the jurors, instead of allowing one juror to dominate the conversation or intimidate and influence other jurors (because Lions also *eat* Lambs during mock trials).
- Control the direction of jury deliberation (i.e., "Let's talk more about liability"; "What do you think about the causation issue?"; "Is anyone concerned about . . .?").
- Test and compare different themes and metaphors ("Does that make sense?"; "Do you like that metaphor better?"), instead of picking one theme for an entire mock trial and finding out *after* the mock trial whether that metaphor was effective.
- Add a fact or introduce an exhibit *in response* to something that a juror says.

With the benefit of this focus group information, attorneys can decide what evidence to emphasize, what questions to answer, what demonstrative exhibits to use, and what bias to address during the subsequent mock trial. By starting with a focus group, you can learn more about streamlining and presenting your case than you might learn from watching several mock trial deliberations. If you only have time to do two mock trials, your client may be better served by doing one focus group and one mock trial.

Ideally, you should hold the focus group weeks before the mock trial to give the attorneys time to change their presentations, get answers to the questions asked by jurors, and obtain any documents requested by the jurors. In the past, to reduce the cost of out-of-town jury research, we have often scheduled a focus group on Day 1 and a mock trial on Day 2 (after a very long night spent revising our presentation). We have even done a focus group in the morning and a mock trial in the afternoon (after a very stressful lunch spent revising our presentation). Now, we have the option of conducting a virtual focus group *weeks* before the "in person" mock trial.

8. Exclude Prejudicial and Controversial Evidence

When the goal of the mock trial is to generate disagreement and discussion among the jurors, resist the temptation to introduce evidence, disclose facts, or make arguments that the court may exclude from trial. Never tell mock jurors about a prior conviction or show mock jurors a devastating social media post when you are not *absolutely* certain that the court will admit that evidence at trial. Yes, that evidence is "sexy." Yes, that evidence can affect the outcome of the trial. But you already *know* the prejudicial effect that evidence will have on jurors *if* that evidence is ultimately admitted. So, while it may be entertaining, there is no need to hear jurors discussing that evidence during a mock trial.

Nothing is worse than watching mock jurors walk into the deliberation room and proceed to talk *only* about the sexy evidence that may be excluded from the trial. What have you learned? If your goal was to determine *whether* you can win at trial, you have just paid a lot of money to determine that you can win *if* the prejudicial evidence is admitted. If your goal was to learn from jurors by generating disagreement and discussion, you have just paid a lot of money to hear a single (predictable) conversation that may never take place. And hearing that single conversation just cost you the chance to hear disagreement and discussion about the other evidence.

During a 2023 mock trial, we faced a decision. We knew the wheelchair-bound plaintiff had incorrectly denied being charged with a felony crime during his deposition. In fact, when the wheelchair-bound plaintiff answered "no," he was wearing an ankle monitor concealed under his pants leg and awaiting trial for the felony crime of sexual battery. Because plaintiff was claiming that the motor vehicle accident was the sole cause of stress in his marriage and that the motor vehicle accident eliminated his interest in sexual intimacy, there was a chance the court would allow the defense to disclose more than the fact that he was charged "with a felony crime." Together, the defense team quickly decided that there was no point in disclosing the truth to the mock jury because we knew how that information would likely affect the way jurors perceived the plaintiff.

Mock trials are often held long before the deadline for filing motions *in limine* to exclude controversial expert opinions and evidence. Yes, there are reasons to wait until the deadline to file a *Daubert* motion seeking to exclude a controversial expert opinion, including the risk that your motion will inspire opposing counsel to retain a new expert. But the same is not always true for controversial evidence. Whenever possible, do not wait for the deadline to file a motion seeking to exclude opposing counsel's controversial evidence or a (pre-emptive) motion *in limine* seeking a ruling from the court on the admissibility of *your* controversial evidence. The earlier the ruling, the more likely you can schedule the mock trial to take place *after* the court rules on those motions.

9. Layer the Evidence from Least to Most Persuasive

During focus groups, the jury consultant often controls the order in which he or she discloses facts and presents evidence. When the jury consultant has the ability to solicit opinions after each new piece of evidence, it is imperative to organize the presentation of the evidence from (what you think is) your least persuasive evidence to (what you think is) your most persuasive evidence. Never start by having the jury consultant present your most persuasive evidence because that evidence will dominate the juror's deliberations, skew their opinions, and help them process subsequent evidence. All you will learn is that the focus group was most impressed by your most persuasive evidence (which you already knew). What you will not learn is what opinions, observations, comparisons, questions, confusion, and concerns the focus group has about your less persuasive evidence. In short, by burying the lede for the mock jurors, you can learn how to better present the "lesser" evidence and improve the chances that the "lesser" evidence is *also* discussed during the real jury's deliberation.

For example, we had a product liability case where we could support the design of our product with four different types of evidence, which we ranked from least to most persuasive as follows: (1) strictly mathematical calculations; (2) complicated product modeling; (3) helpful expert testimony; and (4) amazing video demonstrations. For a focus group directed by the jury consultant, it would have been a mistake to start by showing the amazing video demonstration because those demonstrations would have skewed the focus group's opinion and would have mooted the need for defense attorneys and experts to explain the other evidence.

Instead, by starting with the least persuasive evidence (strictly mathematical calculations), we could learn what the jurors thought about that evidence and how we could present it better. Similarly, by continuing to feed jurors our less persuasive evidence (product modeling and expert testimony), we could learn more about that evidence. Then and only then was it appropriate to show the jurors our most persuasive evidence (video demonstrations) and enjoy the jury's discussion about that evidence. By carefully layering the evidence for the focus group, you can increase the likelihood that your client will learn more about each layer, instead of only learning about the most persuasive layer.

10. Layer the Evidence by Removing or Adding Jury Panels

It is more difficult to layer evidence for a mock trial than for a focus group, but there are times when your client needs to know the effect of a single confounding variable. When that happens, the best option is (a) to divide the mock jurors into separate panels and (b) to organize the mock trial so that at least one panel is presented with the confounding evidence/argument and at least one panel is *not* presented with that evidence/argument. Only then will the jury consultants be able to reliably determine the effect of the confounding evidence/argument.

Always consider whether to layer (game-changing) factual evidence. For the previously mentioned case involving the wheelchair-bound plaintiff who denied having a pending felony charge, our defense team recognized (a) the possibility that the disclosure of that evidence could skew the results and (b) the possibility that the court could exclude the prejudicial evidence altogether. To hedge our bet, we decided to layer the evidence.

In an abundance of caution, we divided the mock jurors into three panels. All three panels heard the plaintiff's presentation. All three panels heard the defense's presentation. All three panels heard the plaintiff's rebuttal. Then, we sent two of the panels to their (separate) rooms to start deliberating and asked the third panel to the presentation room. To that third panel, and *only* to that third panel, we then permitted (a) defense counsel to share the prejudicial information regarding the plaintiff's arrest for a felony and his denial (under oath) of being charged with a felony and (b) plaintiff's counsel to respond. That way, the jury consultant was able to learn how the felony charge and the plaintiff's perjury affected the *only* mock trial panel to hear that evidence.

Also consider whether to layer (game-changing) evidence and issues to increase the discussion about specific evidence and issues. Once, we had a trucking case that involved a threshold issue of law (motor carrier versus broker). The defense team recognized that the horrible injuries would likely skew the way the jurors considered the threshold issue of law. In fact, we were genuinely concerned that the mock jurors would *skip* the threshold issue of law and immediately discuss how much to pay each plaintiff. To hedge our bet, and to guarantee at least three panels engaged in lively discussions regarding liability, we decided to divide the jurors into six panels and to organize the mock trial so that three panels *never* learned about the injuries. The format we used to layer the evidence, in which three panels heard damages evidence and three panels did not, is shown in Table 4.2.

Table 4.2 Mock Trial Format

	In Room	**Party**	**Presentation**
1.	Panels 1–3	Plaintiff	Accident & Injuries
2.	*Polling, followed by a break.*		
3.	Panels 1–3	Defendant	Accident & Injuries
4.	*Polling, followed by a break.*		
5.	Panels 1–3	Plaintiff Rebuttal	Accident & Injuries
6.	*Polling, followed by a break.*		
7.	Panels 1–6	Plaintiff	Motor Carrier Issue
8.	*Polling, followed by a break.*		
9.	Panels 1–6	Defendant	Motor Carrier Issue
10.	*Polling, followed by a break.*		
11.	Panels 1–6	Plaintiff Rebuttal	Motor Carrier Issue
12.	*Polling, followed by separated panel deliberations.*		

By layering the evidence in this fashion, we were able to learn (a) how the three panels who *knew* the family's injuries determined the threshold legal issue (motor carrier versus broker) and (b) how the three panels who had *no idea* whether the accident resulted in any physical injuries determined the same threshold legal issue. More importantly, we guaranteed ourselves that three panels would *only* discuss the liability issues (because they had not been presented with any evidence of damages).

11. Obtain and Play Videos of Witnesses

Some trial lawyers are lazy, and some trial lawyers like the sound of their own voice. Perhaps you have noticed. Not surprisingly, when given the choice between *playing* a video clip from an expert's deposition and simply *telling* the jury what that expert will say, many lawyers will choose to talk instead of standing silently. Not surprisingly, when given the choice between identifying specific start/stop times for a video clip (1:03:21–1:03:45; 1:07:23–1:08:02) and simply slapping a photo on a PowerPoint slide, many lawyers will conveniently decide that "jurors get bored watching videos."

Always show the jury a clip of the witness. Jurors are suspicious of lawyers. When a lawyer tells jurors that Dr. Wonderful "will testify that this type of injury is impossible," jurors will wonder whether the lawyer is exaggerating. Jurors need to see and hear Dr. Wonderful, and you need to know whether the jurors liked Dr. Wonderful. We are constantly surprised by the way jurors react to certain witnesses. We have had jurors dislike the tone or manner of witnesses who we thought were going to be our "star" witnesses, and we have had jurors adore witnesses who we personally disliked. Again, the purpose of a mock trial and a focus group is *not* to confirm what *you* already think about your witnesses. The purpose is to learn what the *jurors* think about your witnesses. Press "play" and find out.

Since COVID and the emergence of remote depositions, videotaping depositions has quickly become the norm for many attorneys. But there may be times when a witness has not yet been deposed or their deposition was not videotaped. Do not be content to have the attorney slap a picture of the witness on a PowerPoint slide and describe their testimony. Find creative ways to provide the jury with video of the witness. When it is your witness, create a video clip. When it is not your witness, legally search online and social media for any video of the witness. Consider hiring an actor to fairly portray the witness in a video clip.

Figure 4.3 Human diagram with pain ratings.

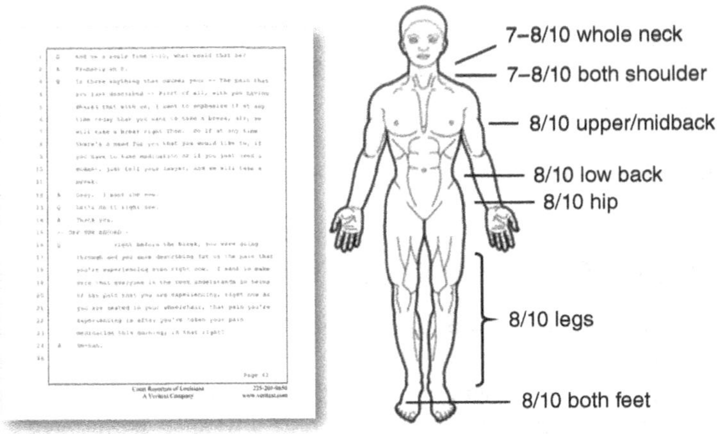

As a last resort, find creative ways to make their deposition testimony "come to life." Do not be content to *only* read from the deposition transcript. For example, we had a case where the most insightful moment of a plaintiff's deposition testimony was when he rated his pain as at least a 7 out of 10 for (literally) every area of his body, *despite* his being on pain medication *and* his having his spinal cord stimulator turned up "to the maximum setting." Rather than just read those pages of the transcript to the mock jurors, we paired the deposition pages with a diagram of the human body to track how he rated each area. Figure 4.3 shows the final slide.

This is how we tried to make the plaintiff's testimony "come to life." Starting with the plaintiff's neck, we worked our way down the body, adding the deposition transcript page and plaintiff's rating to the human figure. Even though the jury never got to see or hear the plaintiff repeatedly respond, "8 out of 10," these slides helped us capture the extent of plaintiff's subjective complaints. That "human body diagram thing" was repeatedly mentioned by the mock jurors, generating discussion and debate.

12. Identify Large Verdict Ranges or Suggest Ridiculous Awards

There are jury consultants who will insist that *both* presenters identify a specific damages award "as an anchor" and break down that award for the mock jury (i.e., past medicals, future medicals, lost earnings, general damages). Consider ignoring that advice.

Jurors hate being told a specific number. In an attempt to either be fair or *appear* fair to other jurors, they will avoid that number like the plague. That is why you should avoid assigning any significance to a mock jury's rejection of the specific amount that plaintiff's counsel demanded in plaintiff's last demand letter. Nor should you assign any significance to the mock jury's rejection of the specific amount that the defense attorney requested unless the jury rejected defense counsel's request that the jury award nothing.

If the goal of the mock trial is to learn, consider either (a) having the presenter provide the jury with a verdict range as an "anchor" or (b) having the presenter provide the jury with a ridiculously high (for plaintiff) or ridiculously low (for defense) number as an "anchor." Both approaches can have the same desired effect of making jurors think *for themselves* and argue *amongst themselves.*

Do not focus myopically on the final number that a handful of specific mock jurors reached. That number is almost always about compromise and the specific Lion(s) in the specific room on that specific day of mock trial. Always focus on the discussion and debate regarding each item of damages. With what number did each juror start? Why did they start at that number? What did they say to defend that number? What argument caused them to abandon that number? Why did they hold the line at a certain number, rejecting higher or lower amounts? That is the gold that you should be mining from a mock trial.

13. Emphasize the Vote's Importance

Different jury consultants have different strategies for convincing jurors to take a mock trial exercise seriously. Some jury consultants will tell jurors that the parties have agreed to "accept their verdict" or to "allow their verdict to resolve the case." Whatever their approach is, and whatever combination of words they use to impress the importance of their verdict, it may not be enough. Both attorneys should always find a way to persuade jurors that the mock trial is more than just an exercise.

Before a 2023 mock trial, I heard a juror tell the check-in person that they were "here for the focus group." Between check-in and deliberation, we needed to find a way to convince that individual (or trick that individual) into believing that the mock trial is "for all the marbles." Find out what your jury consultants plan on telling the jurors and find out how you can help.

Whether I am playing the part of plaintiff's counsel or defense counsel, I end every mock trial presentation with the same plea. I tell jurors,

> I know that this is not a courtroom. I know that we are in a hotel, and that this may not feel like a *real* trial to you. There is no judge wearing a black robe. There is no bailiff. And you are seated in stackable chairs, not a jury box. But make no mistake. Today *matters* to my client. By agreement, I can't say anything more, but I will say this: The outcome of this trial *matters* to my client. Your verdict today *matters*. Your vote today *matters*.

That suggestion and show of restraint can be exactly the type of reminder that mock jurors need, especially those who doubted the jury consultant's declaration that the verdict will resolve the dispute.

14. Take Note of Prejudicial Comments

Some lawyers myopically focus on the verdict reached during the mock trial or focus group, and that is a mistake. Pay attention to every comment that distracts or prejudices the jury against your client. Label a page "Ideas for Voir Dire and Closing Argument" and write down every prejudicial comment during jury deliberations and focus group discussions. That way, after the mock trial or focus group, you can decide whether (a) to file a motion *in limine* to prohibit opposing counsel from making those remarks; (b) to address that bias during *voir dire*; and/or (c) to call that bias to the jury's attention during closing argument.

It may not be a popular trial strategy, but we have found it effective to use our closing argument to *warn* the Lions on the jury what they might hear other jurors say and *give* the Lions the soundbite they need to confront and kill that bias. During closing argument, we will find a way to suggest how jurors respond to specific arguments or emotional appeals during deliberation. For example, to combat prejudicial remarks heard during a mock trial, we might tell jurors during closing argument:

- If a juror says, "That's the price of doing business," that juror has stopped weighing the evidence.
- If a juror says, "That's why they have insurance," that juror has stopped weighing the evidence.
- If a juror says, "Why wouldn't they warn about everything?" that juror has decided to ignore the judge's jury instructions on inadequate warnings.

- If a juror says, "If it happened on their property, I don't care if it's their fault," that juror is ignoring the jury instruction that there is no strict liability.
- If a juror says, "This is a drop in the bucket for them," that juror has stopped weighing the evidence and stopped treating my client fairly and impartially.
- If a juror wants to talk about what another insurance company did to them once, that juror has stopped weighing the evidence and has stopped being fair and impartial.

There is always a risk/reward to addressing bias and prejudice during closing argument, and that risk/reward should be discussed with a client, but the first step is *always* to figure out during mock trials what type of prejudice will rear its ugly head during jury deliberations. Toward that end, attorneys should encourage jury consultants not to "kill" prejudicial comments or "stop" tangential discussions during focus group and mock trial discussions. There's gold in them hills!

Chapter 5

Pretrial and Trial Tips: Adding to Your Tool Belt

During the Golden Age of Lawyers, trial attorneys tried more jury trials and practiced more often in their own backyard. Over time, they got to know the judges, the bailiffs, and the court staff in *every* section of court. Through trial-and-error, they learned exactly where to stand, what to say, and what to do in each courtroom for each judge. It was the ultimate home-field advantage, and Gray Hairs secretly pitied visitors from other states. Only local counsel knew which way the wind blew in the Fourth Quarter.

Today, there are more sections of court and fewer jury trials to go around. Prosecutors, public defenders, and a small band of local litigators still know everyone's birthday in the courtroom and enjoy a degree of home-field advantage. But to their credit, civil and criminal courts have *procedurally* leveled the playing field with rules of procedure, rules of evidence, court websites (addressing frequently asked questions), online instructional videos, status conferences, scheduling orders, and pretrial conferences.

Regardless of the courtroom, every trial attorney needs to know how to handle their first pretrial conference with a judge and how to approach every trial. Here are some tips of the trade.

1. Stop Filing Omnibus Motions in Limine

Aggressive motion practice has long been a staple of trial strategy. For years, we have been regaled with stories about "relentless" partners who "drowned" opposing counsel with paperwork and "broke their backs" with pretrial motions. We have been encouraged to engage in "aggressive" motion practice, including the filing of omnibus motions seeking to exclude all manner of prejudicial arguments and evidence. The logic was sound. If the motions were granted, we succeeded in excluding inadmissible evidence and deterring inappropriate argument. If the motions were denied, we protected the record and forced plaintiff's counsel to spend their time on briefing instead of trial preparation. What nobody told us is that aggressive motion practice and filing omnibus motions can backfire.

We learned that lesson when we parachuted into the 2021 *Lindale* case as trial counsel for the plaintiff. It was only two months before trial. We knew we were outnumbered, and we fully expected defense counsel to slam us with pretrial motions. They did not disappoint. During the next two months, opposing counsel filed: (a) a motion for summary judgment on liability; (b) more than 30 motions *in limine*, including a motion seeking to exclude lost profits, which they later reasserted as a motion for directed verdict; (b) an exhibit list with 1,111 trial exhibits (with a 75-page table of contents); and (e) objections to testimony on almost every page of our only videotaped trial perpetuation deposition. Saving the best for last, defense counsel filed five motions between 10:23 p.m. and 10:47 p.m. the night before the pretrial conference.

The tide turned during that pretrial conference. The court did not seem to appreciate opposing counsel's gamesmanship. The court did not seem to enjoy making twenty-seven separate rulings on their motions *in limine*, including motions to prohibit us from mentioning that the defense was a "Norwegian company" and that our client was a "family-owned company." Nor did the court seem to enjoy hearing argument and ruling on opposing counsel's objections to 17 of the 36 pages we designated of Mr. Brown's videotaped deposition testimony.

Over the course of that marathon pretrial conference, it became clear that the defense was moving to exclude comments we would never make and evidence we would never introduce. It was a completely unnecessary, time-consuming, and often insulting exercise. With their premature objections and motions, defense counsel was tacitly accusing us of being unprofessional and not knowing the law of evidence.

We welcomed the opportunity to demonstrate our reasonableness and willingness to compromise. As lead defense counsel sent different associates to the podium to argue the motions they had been assigned, we smiled and took turns saying, "no objection" or "of course not" or "we would never." We did not unconditionally surrender, but we picked our battles. And when we finally stood and said, "Now, we do have a problem with this motion," we had the court's full attention. For us to object, defense counsel must have crossed a line.

By the end of that pretrial conference, it was also clear that we were willing to let the defense try their case, but the defense was desperate to prevent us from trying ours. Which told the court something about the defense team and about their case. Now, it could have been coincidental, and we could have seen what we wanted to see (lawyers often do), but the court and the court staff seemed to greet us differently the next day. Suddenly, we were those nice lawyers from New Orleans, who flew into town to try the case and let the chips fall where they may.

Maybe our approach was unusual. Maybe we were not what they were expecting. Far from "mad dog" litigators, we were polite and . . . exceptionally ordinary. Just there to do a job. Perform a service. A case needed trying, and we were happy to try the case. Like waiters who spot a table that needs bussing. No big deal. No need to complain or yell. No need for help. This is what we do. We try cases. We call this "Thursday."

2. Have a Pretrial Conference Checklist

Because of their trial experience and familiarity with the court, Gray Hairs often approached a pretrial conference like a social visit. "Good to see you, Your Honor. Hard to believe it's been a month since that last trial with that lawyer from . . . now, I forget where that company lawyer was from, but nice enough . . . gracious in defeat, I'll say that. Bought me a drink afterwards." And why not? They earned it. Gray Hairs knew exactly how the court did everything from conducting voir dire to charging the jury.

Today, pretrial conferences should be more than meet-and-greets. In a civil case, the odds are that neither counsel has tried a jury trial before this particular judge in this particular courtroom. Table 5.1 shows a cheat sheet to help your trial team get the answers they need; it is available for download at ambar.org/TrialAdvocacy.

3. Create a "Hot Docs" Binder

There is nothing wrong with listing every possible exhibit in your preliminary exhibit list, especially when you are still working the problem and don't know what exhibits you will need during your direct and cross-examinations. After all, you can't win a trial on the day you file your exhibit list, but you can lose a trial. So, in an abundance of caution, go ahead and list every document mentioned by every witness during the litigation.

But do not make the mistake of drowning your jurors in exhibits. Soon, every courtroom will be paperless, and every attorney will be able to electronically file thousands of exhibits with a click of the button. Whereas Gray Hairs would *never* have wheeled hundreds of boxes containing thousands of exhibits into the courtroom, lawyers may soon be tempted to take the same approach to filing exhibits that they take to listing exhibits (i.e., "the more, the merrier!").

Table 5.1 Pretrial Conference Checklist

Jury Questionnaire	**Yes**	**No**
Does the court permit jury questionnaires?		
Does the court have a preferred format for questionnaires? If so, what format?		
Do the parties have to agree on the questionnaire? Will the court resolve disputes?		
To whom should the parties submit the (joint) questionnaires? By when?		
When/how will the court share the results of the questionnaire?		
Voir Dire		
Does the court conduct voir dire?		
May parties submit questions for the court to ask during voir dire? By when?		
How many jurors does the court voir dire at the same time? How are they seated?		
Does the court allow the attorneys to question jurors?		
Does the court impose a time limit for each attorney's questioning of jurors?		
On request, will the court individually voir dire a juror to avoid tainting the pool?		
Jury List		
Does the court publish the list of jurors before voir dire? If so, when?		
What information is included in the list of jurors?		
Jury Selection		
What is the court's system for jury selection?		
Will the court rule on challenges for cause before jury selection? ("to allow attorneys to determine the mathematically eligible jurors")		
Does the court permit back strikes? If so, what is the court's policy?		
How many alternate jurors will the court be picking?		
Evidence		
In what format does the court want exhibits submitted? By what date?		
What technology does the courtroom have? May we schedule time to practice with it?		
How does the court want attorneys to mark, share, introduce, and publish electronic documents?		
Before opening statement, will the court admit evidence without objection?		

May the attorneys publish pre-admitted evidence during opening statement?		
By what date should the parties exchange demonstrative exhibits?		
May we provide jurors with a binder of pre-admitted documents ("hot docs")?		
Opening Statement		
How long does the court give each side/attorney for opening statement?		
By what date should the parties exchange opening statement slides?		
Objections		
How does the court like to handle objections? • Say "objection" and ask to approach • State tag ("objection, hearsay") and wait for further instructions • All objections will be handled in presence of jury unless attorneys ask to approach		
Bench Conferences		
Where does the court hold bench conferences (chambers, opposite bench side)?		
Will bench conferences be on the record?		
Scheduling Defense Witnesses		
By what date/time will the plaintiff/prosecution be required to rest?		
If no agreement on date/time, will the court grant a Motion for Equal Time?		

Resist that temptation. Trial lawyers should always revisit their exhibit list before deciding what exhibits to introduce into evidence at trial and to publish to the jury. Clients and co-counsel may initially be confused when we schedule a video conference to discuss our exhibit book, but by the end of that conference, they understand. The exhibit book is where the rubber meets the road. Assembling your exhibit book will always require the entire defense team to agree on what is important and what is not. It is often the most difficult conversation, and it often requires additional research, follow-up calls with witnesses, and (sometimes) a mock trial.

Actions speak louder than words, and a trial attorney's exhibit book should be consistent with that attorney's trial theme. If the defense trial team believes that only the results of the MRI scan matter, consider limiting your trial exhibits to the MRI images, a colorful medical graphic highlighting the MRI findings, the radiologist's original report regarding the MRI scan, subsequent medical records in which treating physicians discuss the MRI scan, and (maybe) a handful of peer-reviewed articles and studies establishing the reliability of MRI scans. Two examples should demonstrate the importance of consistency between your message and your exhibits.

During the 2017 *Stroud* case, the plaintiff, who was claiming a traumatic brain injury, had seven years of medical evaluation, testing, and treatment. Seven years of complaints. Seven years of physical examinations and psychological evaluation. Seven years of anecdotal stories about losing her temper or forgetting her keys. The courtroom was not paperless, and we had a decision to make. Yes, we could have copied, three-hole punched, and put into binders *every* document generated over that seven-year period. But that would not have been consistent with our trial theme, which was that only the first seven months after the accident mattered.

Before the 2017 *Stroud* trial, we held an "exhibit book" telephone conference. We walked the client through every medical record and diagnostic image during the first seven months. During that first seven months, we could prove that (a) every neurological exam was normal; (b) every cranial nerve exam was normal; (c) every diagnostic test and image was normal (i.e., CT, MRI, EEG); and (d) no doctor had diagnosed plaintiff with a concussion. In fact, the word "concussion" did not appear in a medical record for the first seven months. Together, we decided that our exhibit book would only be seven months long.

Accordingly, we created a "hot docs" binder that included—in chronological order—every important medical record during that seven-month period following the accident. Anything that happened after those seven months had nothing to do with us and did not belong in our binder. We then gave each juror a binder of those records, and that binder sat in their laps throughout the trial. During deliberations, the jury did not have to sort through eight binders to find what records our experts discussed. All they had to do was request our binder and they could re-read, re-create, and re-live the entire defense case.

Similarly, before the 2021 *Lindale* trial, thousands of pages of documents had been produced by our client (Lindale) and the defendant (Equinor) during discovery. Based on our experience in the 2017 *Stroud* case, we refused to take the bait. Instead of drowning the jurors in a sea of documents that they would never sort through during deliberation, we carefully chose 96 exhibits to include in Lindale's exhibit book. That exhibit book stayed on the jury's lap for the entire trial, and (almost) every exhibit in that binder was discussed by a witness during direct or cross-examination (i.e., "Turn to tab 57, please").

In contrast, opposing counsel in *Lindale* took the opposite approach. On Day 1 of the trial, they carted into the courtroom a wall of boxes containing 1,111 separate defense exhibits. For the next two weeks, the jury stared at the neatly stacked unopened boxes of defense exhibits. And, during deliberations, they did not call for a single one of those defense boxes.

But beware. Not every judge will allow trial attorneys to distribute a binder of "hot docs" to the jury, especially in a paperless courtroom. Before the 2016 *White* trial, we respectfully requested that the court allow us to distribute a binder of the documents we intended to actually use during direct and cross-examination. Despite the fact that the courtroom was *not* paperless, the court denied that request. Inexplicably, the court insisted that it would be "prejudicial" to the plaintiff for the defense to provide a binder of "hot docs" when the plaintiff (a) had no notice of our intention to narrow our exhibit list; (b) no opportunity to review those exhibits; and (c) no opportunity to assemble their own binder of "hot docs."

It is difficult to understand how opposing counsel could be prejudiced or ambushed by important exhibits listed on the defendant's exhibit list. Nevertheless, to avoid similar rulings, consider doing one or all of the following: (1) file an amended exhibit list that only includes the "hot docs"; or (2) file an amended exhibit list that starts with the "hot docs" (i.e., Exhibits #1–75 are "hot docs"; Exhibits #75–400 can be everything else), so that you can ask to publish Exhibits #1–75 to the jury before the first examination; and (3) provide opposing counsel with a courtesy copy of the exhibit book in advance of trial.

There is a fairly obvious downside to narrowing your exhibit book and providing opposing counsel with your "hot docs" binder prior to trial. In so doing, you will always lose the element of surprise, and you will always help opposing counsel with their trial preparation. Without fail, opposing counsel will (a) go through every exhibit in your binder with a fine-toothed comb; (b) identify any *unfavorable* documents you omitted from your binder (i.e., "And you know why counsel left out this physical therapy note . . . because it didn't fit their story. Well, never let the truth get in the way of a good argument!"); and (c) opposing counsel will provide every one of their experts with a copy of your binder and review every document with them during trial preparation.

Of course, the days of distributing physical binders containing "hot docs" to each juror are numbered. Judges presiding over trials in paperless courtrooms will eventually (a) prefer for the same document to be electronically shared on every monitor, rather than take the unnecessary risk that a page is missing (or accidentally included) in one of the juror's binders; and (b) make certain that jurors are looking at the same page on the same exhibit, rather than take the unnecessary risk that jurors will flip to the next page or the last page in your binder. But do not miss the forest for the trees. The point is to make sure that your exhibits are consistent with your theme, regardless of the manner in which you publish those exhibits to the jury.

The silver lining is that paperless courtrooms will allow attorneys to immediately publish Exhibit 37 on the jury box monitors, instead of having to ask the witness (and the jury) to "turn to page 37." Personally, I look forward to that day, when I no longer have to wait for the distinct sound of flipping pages to end before asking my next question.

When that day comes, and paperless courtrooms everywhere celebrate the death of trial binders, it will be even more important for trial attorneys to start their exhibit books with their "hot docs" so that the jury doesn't have to wade through thousands of electronically stored documents to find the 75 relevant documents. By starting your exhibit book with your 75 "hot docs," jurors in those paperless courtrooms will know what to request (i.e., "Bailiff, we would like to see Defense Exhibits #1–75) or what to access on their deliberation room monitors (i.e., "Let's start by pulling up the defendant's first 75 exhibits.).

When that day comes, trial attorneys should still bring one binder of their "hot docs." And, during closing argument (if the court permits), trial counsel should encourage the jury to call for the "hard copies" of Exhibits #1–75 at the start of their jury deliberation.

4. Prepare an Exhibit-Witness Introduction Spreadsheet

Many trials will involve only a handful of witnesses and exhibits. For all other trials, prepare a spreadsheet that will help you keep track of the exhibits that need to be introduced by each witness. Nothing is worse than tendering a lay witness and realizing that you forgot to introduce a document that you wanted to use during a subsequent direct examination, cross-examination, or closing argument. The best way to prevent that moment of extreme regret is to make time before trial, find an empty conference room, take your exhibit list, and write down which witness should introduce each exhibit at trial. That exercise has often changed the order in which we ultimately called witnesses and required us to schedule "one more" meeting with certain lay witnesses to discuss specific trial exhibits.

After you have identified the right witness to introduce each exhibit, consider generating a simple spreadsheet. Yes, for jury trials involving very few exhibits (i.e., a possession of cocaine trial), attorneys do not need a spreadsheet. But when you have voluminous exhibits or many witnesses, that spreadsheet will allow you to (a) search for specific exhibits and (b) sort by each witness. So, when the employer takes the stand, you can sort by the employer's name, and instantly you have a list of every exhibit that needs to be introduced with that witness.

The exhibit-witness introduction spreadsheet can also be an excellent way to keep track of when each exhibit was admitted into evidence. Nothing is worse than realizing, on appeal, that you failed to introduce an exhibit or failed to proffer an exhibit (that the court refused to admit). By including an "Admitted" column and a "Proffered" column, your trial team can keep track of the court's admission of exhibits. The night before closing argument, when your trial team is exhausted and can't remember whether the court admitted Exhibit #137, the exhibit-witness introduction spreadsheet can become your new best friend. Table 5.2 shows a sample format.

Instead of limiting your spreadsheet to exhibits, you could create a fact/exhibit-witness spreadsheet that would additionally identify every critical fact, admission, statement, and opinion. That would allow your team, before calling Jane Smith to the stand, to sort by "witness" and instantly see a list of every exhibit counsel has to introduce *and* the specific testimony counsel has to solicit for Jane Smith. Of course, the bigger the case, the more difficult it would be to compile a complete list of every fact that needs to be solicited during trial. But for smaller cases involving younger attorneys, the exercise could be helpful.

Table 5.2 Exhibit-Witness Introduction Spreadsheet

#	Plaintiff Exhibits	Witness	Admitted	Proffered
15	Company policy on drug testing	Owner	Pretrial	
16	Company policy on drug use	Owner	Pretrial	
17	Prior positive drug test for driver	Supervisor	Pretrial	
18	Prior reprimand for driver	Supervisor	Pretrial	
19	Driver's social media post on Feb. 2	Friend	Day 2	
20	Driver's phone records on Feb. 2	Driver	Day 5	
21	Driver's handwritten statement on Feb. 3 (after accident)	Officer	Day 1	
22	Police officer's citation	Officer		Day 1

5. Use Rule 1006 Summaries

There are times when making a single point would seemingly require an attorney to introduce hundreds or thousands of documents. To prove that the plaintiff consistently complained of neck pain and had limited range of motion, plaintiff's counsel could introduce ten years of physical therapy records. To prove that the plaintiff's medications did not change in dosage or increase in frequency after the accident, defense counsel could introduce twenty years of pharmacy records. But no attorney wants to alienate or lose the jury by engaging in the pedestrian exercise of reviewing thousands of pages of documents for the sake of discussing a handful of relevant facts on each page.

Instead, trial attorneys traditionally retain experts to review and testify regarding the records. We pay medical doctors to review voluminous medical records. We pay economists to review voluminous tax and employment records. We pay forensic experts to extract, review, and summarize cell phone data. In this regard, as a profession, we have grown dependent on expert witnesses to do our heavy lifting. But expert witnesses are not a perfect solution. During deliberations, jurors cannot ask the court to "replay" the expert's testimony or ask the bailiff to bring them the expert's demonstrative exhibits.

The alternative is to prepare and introduce a Rule 1006 summary. Federal Rule of Evidence 1006 provides as follows:

> The proponent may use a summary, chart, or calculation to prove the content of voluminous writings, recordings, or photographs that cannot be conveniently examined in court. The proponent must make the originals or duplicates available for examination or copying, or both, by other parties at a reasonable time and place. And the court may order the proponent to produce them in court.

When we parachuted into the 2021 *Lindale* trial, we had voluminous documents, but no expert witnesses. Because prior counsel had allowed the expert report deadline to pass, we had to find a way to establish how many barrels of water the defendant purchased from other water providers for the 94 frack jobs performed from June 28, 2015 to November 6, 2019. For us, the solution was to provide opposing counsel with a Rule 1006 summary and the opportunity to check our numbers and our math (for the conversion from gallons to barrels). Table 5.3 shows one of the pages from that Rule 1006 summary.

Remember that a Rule 1006 summary does not have to be presented in a summary table. There is a difference between a table and a chart.

Table 5.3 Statoil/Equinor wells fracked that did not use Lindale as the water provider.

	Well Name	Start Date	Completion Date	Operator Name	Total Base Water Volume (gals)	Barrel Conversion	Source
77.	Allison 23-14 #2TFH	4/1/2019	4/19/2019	Equinor Energy LP	7,033,902	167,474	FracFocus
78.	Allison 23-14 #3H	4/1/2019	4/21/2019	Equinor Energy LP	9,601,578	228,609	FracFocus
79.	Allison 23-14 #4TFH	4/22/2019	5/9/2019	Equinor Energy LP	7,059,612	168,086	FracFocus
80.	Allison 23-14 #5H	4/23/2019	5/9/2019	Equinor Energy LP	9,772,141	232,670	FracFocus
81.	Allison 23-14 #6TFH	4/29/2019	5/9/2019	Equinor Energy LP	7,230,730	172,160	FracFocus
82.	Elmer Hovland 23-14 XE #1H	5/11/2019	5/27/2019	Equinor Energy LP	10,241,296	243,840	FracFocus
83.	Allison 23-14 #7H	5/11/2019	5/28/2019	Equinor Energy LP	10,483,284	249,602	FracFocus
84.	Allison 23-14 #8TFH	5/11/2019	5/28/2019	Equinor Energy LP	7,396,673	176,111	FracFocus
85.	Jarold 25-36 #7H	7/2/2019	7/9/2019	Equinor Energy LP	9,777,088	232,788	FracFocus
86.	Jarold 25-36 #8TFH	7/12/2019	7/10/2019	Equinor Energy LP	9,603,203	228,648	FracFocus
87.	Jarold 25-36 #2TFH	7/2/2019	7/14/2019	Equinor Energy LP	4,241,286	100,983	FracFocus
88.	Jarold 25-36 #5H	7/17/2019	8/1/2019	Equinor Energy LP	9,691,544	230,751	FracFocus
89.	Jarold 25-36 #6TFH	7/17/2019	8/1/2019	Equinor Energy LP	9,816,798	233,733	FracFocus
90.	Jarold 25-36 XW #1TFH	7/17/2019	8/1/2019	Equinor Energy LP	9,750,655	232,158	FracFocus
91.	Sam 30-31 #3H	10/18/2019	10/26/2019	Equinor Energy LP	8,520,172	202,861	FracFocus
92.	Sam 30-31 #6TFH	10/18/2019	10/26/2019	Equinor Energy LP	6,433,970	153,190	FracFocus
93.	Sam 30-31 #7TFH	10/27/2019	11/6/2019	Equinor Energy LP	6,334,499	150,821	FracFocus
94.	Sam 30-31 XE #1H	10/27/2019	11/6/2019	Equinor Energy LP	9,483,517	225,798	FracFocus
				Total GALs	*787,533,886*	*18,750,950*	

Figure 5.1 Timeline showing 2015 fracked wells.

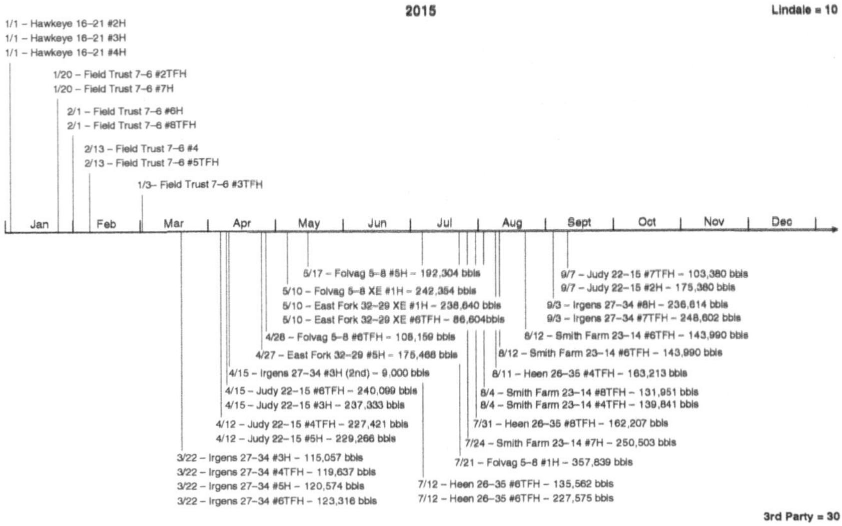

Tables represent facts and figures in a row and column format. Charts represent data more graphically, including timeline charts, bar charts, line charts, pie charts, organizational charts, tree charts, flow charts, and pedigree charts (family trees). Rule 1006 is not limited to summary tables. The statue specifically permits the use of "a summary, chart, or calculation" to prove the content of voluminous documents.

During the 2021 *Lindale* trial, we wanted jurors to *see* how abruptly the defendant stopped purchasing frack water from our client and started purchasing water from other vendors. The table format for the Rule 1006 summary had all of the relevant information, but it did not paint the picture for the jury. That is why we prepared the Rule 1006 timeline in Figure 5.1, showing the frack jobs defendant did (above the line) give to our client and did not (below the line) give to our client.

While preparing for another trial, we recognized how important it would be to visually show the jury that our accident did not cause an increase in the plaintiff's medication. Rather than include the (almost impossible to figure out) pharmacy records from October 28, 2012 until July 27, 2017, we prepared the Rule 1006 summary shown in Table 5.4. Whether or not opposing counsel spent the time going through every pharmacy record we produced to confirm our dates and data (and I seriously doubt that they did), opposing counsel did not object to it, which proved our point "at a glance."

Table 5.4 Table showing prescription meds.

2015	09	30	Clonazepam	1mg	30	Walgreens
2015	11	02	Clonazepam	1mg	30	Walgreens
2015	12	02	Clonazepam	1mg	30	Walgreens
2015	12	29	Clonazepam	1mg	30	Walgreens
2016	01	28	Clonazepam	1mg	30	Walgreens
2016	03	01	Clonazepam	1mg	30	Walgreens
2016	03	01	Clonazepam	1mg	30	Walgreens
2016	03	30	Clonazepam	1mg	30	Walgreens
2016	04	27	Clonazepam	1mg	30	Walgreens
2016	05	28	Clonazepam	1mg	30	Walgreens
2016	07	04	Clonazepam	1mg	30	Walgreens
2016	07	05	Clonazepam	1mg	30	Walgreens
2016	08	08	Clonazepam	1mg	30	Walgreens
2016	10	09	Clonazepam	1mg	30	Walgreens
2016	10	09	Clonazepam	1mg	30	Walgreens
2016	12	08	Clonazepam	1mg	30	Walgreens
2016	12	08	Clonazepam	1mg	30	Walgreens
2017	02	03	Clonazepam	1mg	30	Walgreens
2017	04	05	Clonazepam	1mg	30	Walgreens
2017	06	02	Clonazepam	1mg	30	Walgreens
						After Accident (06/16/2017)
2017	06	30	Clonazepam	1mg	30	Walgreens
2017	07	27	Clonazepam	1mg	30	Walgreens

That is the unintended consequence of producing a Rule 1006 summary. Producing a Rule 1006 summary in any format (table, chart, graph) always shifts the burden to opposing counsel to review the voluminous documents and either stipulate or identify inaccuracies. Perhaps for that reason, opposing counsel can be more willing to stipulate to a Rule 1006 summary than stipulate to the accuracy of an expert-prepared chart that appears in an expert report.

6. Bring Appellate Counsel and Know How to Use Them

Good waiters limit the number of times they interact with their customers and try their best to make each interaction positive and pleasant. Similarly, whenever possible, trial attorneys should limit their interaction with the judge, especially those interactions requiring oral argument and a ruling by the court. Judges are human, and jurors see everything. It only takes one negative exchange or one perceived slight during a bench conference to change the way the judge treats an attorney for the rest of the trial. And a micro-expression of disapproval by a beloved judge can change the way jurors perceive counsel and consider their arguments. By including appellate counsel as part of the team, trial attorneys can choose when to approach the bench, when to participate in an argument, and when to stay on the sidelines.

Trial attorneys should always be focused on the *next* witness. Every trial involves surprises, and many of those surprises require legal research and writing. Instead of spending the night preparing for the next direct examination or cross-examination, trial attorneys can find themselves reading opposing counsel's memorandum, researching the case law cited by opposing counsel, preparing a memorandum in opposition, or outlining an oral argument. Which is sometimes *exactly* what opposing counsel wanted and planned. By the end of the seventh day of testimony, trial counsel can be running on fumes.

Appellate counsel can be the answer. Pick your sports metaphor. Let appellate counsel be your blind-side tackle, protecting you from every time-killing issue. Let appellate counsel steer your case like a coxswain, gently moving the evidentiary tiller or encouraging you to row harder with a witness or issue. Whatever sports metaphor you land on, find appellate counsel you can trust and add them to your trial team.

Nothing is better than watching opposing counsel and your appellate co-counsel walk into the judge's chambers for a marathon jury charge conference, while you keep your seat and keep preparing for the next day. But that is only the tip of the iceberg. Appellate counsel can handle all of the following during the trial:

- Research, prepare trial briefs, and argue unexpected motions *in limine*
- Research, prepare trial briefs, and argue unexpected evidentiary objections
- Argue critical objections at the bench
- Make proffers of physical evidence (outside the jury's presence)
- Call witnesses and solicit proffered testimony (outside the jury's presence)
- Review daily transcripts and protect the record
- Research, prepare trial briefs, and argue Rule 50 motions
- Identify potential closing argument issues
- Make timely motions for new trial and requests for curative instructions
- Research, prepare, and argue jury instructions
- Research, prepare, and argue proposed jury verdicts

During the 2015 *Ricks* wrongful death trial, TASER International, Inc. ("TASER"), provided me and my co-counsel (Isaiah) with an appellate attorney (Pam). Every day, Pam would listen to the trial testimony, suggest appropriate objections, and anticipate the next legal issue. Every night, in addition to handling any pop-up motions, Pam would read the daily transcripts and work on our draft Rule 50 motion. On the fourth day of trial, after I cross-examined the plaintiff's cardiac electrophysiologist, plaintiff's counsel rested. Pam calmly asked to approach the bench and handed the court a polished Rule 50 motion, complete with citations to trial testimony. The court took a recess, read the motion, heard oral argument, and granted TASER's directed verdict, dismissing the plaintiff's claims with prejudice. Instead of preparing to call TASER's first witness, we went back to the hotel and packed.

During the 2021 *Lindale* trial, Lindale Pipeline, Inc. ("Lindale") similarly provided Ray Lewis and me with appellate counsel (Natasha), who was outnumbered at least three to one by Equinor's appellate counsel. Because of COVID restrictions, the jury was seated in the gallery, witnesses testified from the empty jury box, and the number of counsel inside the courtroom was limited. Thankfully, the court provided anterooms for each party and livestreamed the trial. Natasha watched the trial from Lindale's anteroom and handled all of the legal research and writing. As soon as the court recessed, Natasha would enter the courtroom and help with any motions or issues raised by opposing counsel, while I stepped away from our table and sat down at the end of a long row of chairs along the bar. The message was clear: Ray and Natasha have got this. I am only here to handle the next witness. Sigh, good times.

Chapter 6

Opening Statement: Try a TIARA

During the Golden Age of Lawyers, attorneys sometimes treated opening statements like closing arguments, boldly declaring that they were right and opposing counsel was wrong. They refused to acknowledge disputed issues of fact. They refused to discuss unfavorable testimony and evidence. They refused to acknowledge or address any weakness in their case. With absolute conviction, they told jurors what they "should" focus on, *and* what they "should" conclude, *and* how they "should" vote during deliberation.

Today, jurors know that most civil cases result in settlement and most criminal prosecutions result in plea agreements. They want to know which side is to blame for this case not being resolved, and they suspect that one of the lawyers is to blame. If your opening statement doesn't answer that question for jurors in a hurry, they will assume it is you.

Let's stop approaching opening statement like a closing argument. Let's refrain from answering every juror's question with a resounding: "This case did not settle because I told my client that I am right, they are wrong, and there is no chance we lose this trial!"

Let's approach opening statement as an opportunity to demonstrate our willingness to discuss the good, the bad, and ugly. When a guest asks if the soup is "too spicy," only a bad waiter would ignore the question and insist that the guest should be asking whether the soup "comes with croutons." A good waiter calmly acknowledges the soup "does have a little chili pepper in it" and discloses "you may taste the pepper at first," but explains how the "combination of fresh tomato and garden-picked basil perfectly balances the chili pepper."

In so doing, a good waiter prepares the guest for that first taste of pepper so that the guest won't panic, push the soup aside, and curse the waiter for being dishonest. Further, by shifting the question from "Will I taste *any* spice?" to "How well does the tomato and basil *balance* the spice?," the waiter engages the customer's curiosity and increases the likelihood that the guest will want to order the soup and decide for themselves. Like a good waiter, trial attorneys should use opening statement to earn the jury's trust and frame the conversation, instead of ignoring or avoiding the controversy altogether.

Let's stop giving opening *arguments* and start giving opening *statements*. Avoid saying anything that would draw an "argumentative" objection or (even worse) prompt the judge to order us to stop "arguing" during our opening statement. That is what happens to lawyering lawyers, not wonderful waiters.

Never make it personal. Do not criticize opposing counsel for their mistakes, omissions, or choices. Instead, present the evidence in a way that helps jurors decide, for themselves, that opposing counsel either lied or was mistaken during their opening statement.

Choose the right tone for your opening statement. Discuss the evidence in the same way that a good waiter might describe the specials. Never bore jurors by reading your opening statement or delivering it in a monotone or disinterested voice. But never scare jurors with your passion or overwhelm jurors with your personality. Be pleasant, polite, and personable. In a word, be professional. After all, you are here to serve them.

Let's write a new playbook for opening statements during the Age of Jurors. Let's hide nothing. Let's admit everything we do not dispute. Let's candidly reveal every disputed issue of fact. If the *entire* trial should come down to one decision, let's identify that decision and discuss it with the jurors openly and honestly.

Let's define the "perfect" opening statement as a statement that frames the ultimate issue, lays out *both* cases, removes all surprises from the trial, and reduces the trial itself to nothing more than the pedestrian process of calling the witnesses (who will say what we told the jurors they would say) and introducing the exhibits (which we told the jurors they would see). Of course, no trial will ever "perfectly" mirror an opening statement. But let's make that our goal.

Let's adopt a simple opening statement format that can be applied to every civil and criminal trial. While the substance of an opening statement will always depend on the factual and legal issues involved in that specific case, every attorney needs a system or process that helps them decide how to organize and approach their opening statement.

Let's use the acronym "TIARA" for our system because it is easy to remember and because Gray Hairs will absolutely hate it. You know who you are. Sitting there, repulsed by the mere idea of associating opening statements with something a child might wear to a tea party. Well, if you

Table 6.1 Opening Statement

T	Teaser	Start with a 30-second (memorized) teaser.
I	Introductions	Introduce yourself, your co-counsel and your clients.
A	Allegations	Identify the key factual allegations (not the law).
R	Review	Review the evidence regarding those factual allegations.
A	Alamo	End with a 30-second (memorized) statement.

are too vain or too proud to use a TIARA, even as an acronym, you are not ready to be a wonderful waiter. So, pull yourself together. Table 6.1 shows our new format for opening statements.

Like anything else, there is a right way and a wrong way to design a TIARA. When applied properly, the TIARA system can save you time, help you avoid objections, impress the jury, and positively affect the outcome of the trial. Here are some practice tips, examples, exercises, and explanations regarding each part of a TIARA opening statement.

1. Start with a Teaser

Every opening statement should start with a teaser that grabs the jury's attention and drives home a single idea, argument, image, or emotion. The shorter the better, but teasers should not last more than 30 seconds. Do not let your teaser become a trailer. Ever seen a movie trailer that included so many movie clips that you felt like you had seen the whole movie? Don't do that. Don't try to hastily summarize all the evidence before you (less hastily) review all the evidence. Instead, increase the impact of your teaser by narrowly tailoring it.

Avoid turning your 30-second teaser into a 30-second closing argument. Yes, opposing counsel is less likely to object during the first 30 seconds of your opening statement, which means you may have a little more latitude during your teaser. But the risk of being "too argumentative" always outweighs the reward. Picture the judge sustaining an "argumentative" objection during the first 30 seconds of your opening statement. That would be tantamount to the judge telling you to stop being a "lawyering lawyer." Is that how you want to start your opening statement? No, that juice is not worth the squeeze.

Adopt a practical approach to selecting a teaser. Thinking of the "perfect" teaser can be the most challenging part of writing an opening statement. By the time trial arrives, most attorneys know the evidence well enough to discuss every witness and every exhibit, but a good teaser can be elusive. Brilliant lawyers have wasted countless hours perseverating on the "perfect way" to start their opening statement. Let's stop doing that.

Always start by considering the advantages of using the "fork-in-the-road" teaser. The jury is already wondering why the parties did not settle or the defendant did not plead guilty. The best way to start the trial can be to stand up and tell the jury what is undisputed and what is disputed. Show them the fork in the road. Make it crystal clear why they are needed.

> "Both sides agree that the defendant was 100% solely responsible for this accident. We agree that the plaintiff herniated a disc in her neck. We agree that she hit her head on the steering wheel, and we agree that she briefly lost consciousness. We are here today, and we need your help, because we do not agree with the plaintiff's claim that she has permanent brain damage and her claim that she can never work again."

a. Top Ten Teaser Ideas

There are times when a "fork-in-the-road" teaser is not a viable option, especially when your client concedes nothing and disputes everything. Whenever you cannot think of the "perfect" teaser, and you can't use a "fork-in-the-road" teaser, review the following teaser ideas in search of inspiration.

i. One Sentence Teaser

Make a plain and direct statement regarding a key factual or legal issue. Surprise the jury by *not* sounding like a lawyer. Cut through all the evidence and argument. No, you should not repeat Vinny Gambini's infamous opening statement in *My Cousin Vinnie*. Seriously, don't do it. You will be held in contempt of court. But you can cut to the chase.

ii. One Theme Teaser

Establish your theme for the entire trial. Sometimes, your voir dire theme will be directly related to your trial theme. For example, if every question you asked during voir dire included the word "specification" or the phrase "deviation from specifications," your trial theme could be "no deviation, no defect." Sometimes, your trial theme may be indirectly related to your voir dire theme. For example, if your voir dire theme was "best neurologist wins," your trial theme could be "mild concussions get better, not worse." Sometimes, your trial theme can be completely unrelated to your voir dire theme. For example, if your voir dire theme was "we want smart jurors," your trial theme could be "follow the money."

iii. One Quote Teaser

Start with an applicable quote. Yes, some jurors will find it hokey. But if the specific quote will give your argument gravitas or resonate with Lions, consider starting with that quote. Do not limit yourself to familiar quotes. Do not quote controversial individuals (especially controversial politicians and actors). And do not force a quote because you think you will sound smarter (for quoting Aristotle) or seem kinder (for quoting Mother Theresa). Always judge a quote on its own merits.

iv. One Moment Teaser

Describe one key moment, especially if the case involves a complicated timeline. Focusing the jury on one moment can tell them what really matters and can sometimes help them organize all the other moments (as *before* or *after* that one moment). Consider whether there was a "turning point" in the defendant's conduct that led to the defect or the plaintiff's injury. Consider whether there was a "turning point" in the plaintiff's recovery that limits or caps your liability. Consider whether a single medical test or physical examination or statement changed everything. If there is such a turning point, consider describing that moment for the jury.

v. One Element Teaser

Focus the jury's attention on one legal element. Every criminal trial requires the prosecution to prove certain legal elements. Every civil trial requires the plaintiff to prove certain legal elements. In many cases, only one legal element will be disputed. Focusing on that disputed legal element emphasizes the importance of that element and focuses the jury's attention on the ultimate issue they must decide. That is the issue you want the jury thinking about while they listen to each witness.

vi. One Exhibit Teaser

Focus the jury's attention on a single exhibit. Maybe there is one document or one video that impeaches a key witness. Maybe it is a diagnostic image like an MRI or the result of a physical examination. Whatever it is, do not make the jury wait until your direct examination days later to hear about it for the first time. Put it front and center in your opening statement.

vii. One Witness Teaser

Focus the jury's attention on the testimony of a single witness. By focusing on that one witness, you emphasize the importance of that witness and build anticipation for when that witness takes the stand. Be absolutely certain of what that witness will say on the stand because the "one witness" teaser can backfire if that witness changes their testimony. Do not disappoint the jury by exaggerating their testimony or brag about "how strong" or "how persuasive" their testimony will be. Let the jury decide for themselves.

viii. One Perspective Teaser

Describe a critical event or exhibit from the perspective of a single witness if it clarifies what happened or resolves a disputed fact, especially if that witness is a third party with no interest in the outcome of the case.

ix. One Metaphor/Simile Teaser

Compare the key issue, claim, or defense involved in the trial to something in nature or modern life. Consider animals, people, machines, professions, events, occasions, and situations that might perfectly frame the claim or the crime being tried.

x. One Movie/Book/Play Teaser

Focus the jury on a (preferably popular) plot, scene, premise, or exchange between characters. Never spoil the ending to the movie. Jurors will never forgive you if you spoil the ending to a movie that the juror has not seen.

When you are still unhappy with your teaser, force yourself to (a) write ten teasers based on the above-listed top ten teaser ideas and (b) select the best of your ten written teasers, no matter how bad that teaser may be. Give yourself one minute to write each teaser and a total of five minutes to select your favorite (or allow lead counsel to select their favorite). Then, when you have selected your favorite—no matter how bad it is—stop worrying about your teaser and start working on the rest of your opening statement. Trust the exercise. It works.

Remember that teasers often change while you are organizing or writing your "Review" (the "R" in TIARA) of the evidence. While thinking of what to say about specific witnesses or exhibits, the perfect teaser may punch you in the face. Again, trust the process and remember that a good review of the evidence is far more important than a good teaser.

b. Criminal Trial Teaser Examples

There is a benefit to seeing how the top ten teaser ideas can be applied to the same criminal fact pattern. Picture an assistant district attorney prosecuting "John Smith" for the premeditated murder of "Paul Brown" on February 2. The prosecutor wants to start with a teaser and can prove: (1) David heard John say he was going to kill Paul because Paul was sleeping with John's ex-girlfriend (Susan); (2) two witnesses saw John enter Paul's house immediately before the murder; (3) Paul was shot once in the back and then once at point-blank range; and (4) John's fingerprint was found on the murder weapon. Here is how that prosecutor could apply those facts to each of our top ten teaser ideas.

i. One Sentence Teaser

"John Smith shot and killed Paul Brown because Paul was dating his ex-girlfriend, Susan. Ladies and gentlemen of the jury, my name is . . ."

ii. One Quote (Dr. Magrath) Teaser

"Dr. George Magrath once said that robbery, jealousy, and vengeance are the three motives responsible for nearly all murders. Well, on February 2, John Smith killed Paul Brown, and his motive was one of the Big Three. It was jealousy. Ladies and gentlemen of the jury, my name is . . ."

iii. One Theme (Choices Have Consequences) Teaser

"Choices have consequences. This trial is about the defendant's series of choices. Mr. Smith chose to act on his jealousy. He chose to go to Paul Brown's apartment. He chose to aim his gun at Paul. He chose to pull the trigger the first time. He chose to pull the trigger a second time. And those choices must have consequences. Ladies and gentlemen of the jury, my name is . . ."

iv. One Moment (After the First Shot) Teaser

"Paul Brown was lying face down. Shot in the back. Bleeding to death. And that is the moment when John Smith [point to defendant] walked five feet closer to his victim. The defendant aimed the hot muzzle at Paul's face and pulled the trigger one more time. Ladies and gentlemen of the jury, my name is . . ."

v. One Element (Premeditation) Teaser

"He had a lot to remember. On February 2, John Smith had to remember what time Susan left for work. He had to remember to conceal the gun. He had to remember the story that would persuade Paul to invite him inside. And, after shooting Paul twice, John Smith had to remember to wipe clean the gun and leave it at the scene. But the defendant remembered everything. And when a plan really comes together, like it did for the defendant, we say the murder was premeditated. Ladies and gentlemen of the jury, my name is . . ."

vi. One Witness (David) Teaser

"It was a Thursday, and it was David. David, who had been John Smith's friend since grammar school. The guy who he drank beer with and shot pool with. The guy he told everything. The one guy who knew how he felt about Susan. The one guy who would understand. It was late, and it was David. So, the defendant told David: 'I am going to kill Paul.' And one month later, John Smith did exactly that. Ladies and gentlemen of the jury, my name is . . ."

vii. One Exhibit (John's Fingerprint) Teaser

"In 1882, the first criminal fingerprint identification was used to convict a woman who left her bloody print on a door post. Since then, millions of fingerprints have been compared, and no two fingerprints have ever been identical, not even for identical twins. Today, the FBI has more than 54 million fingerprint records. One of those fingerprints is the defendant's fingerprint. And it is identical to the fingerprint found on the murder weapon. Ladies and gentlemen of the jury, my name is . . ."

viii. One Perspective (Paul's Final View) Teaser

"Paul Brown hated the green tile of the hallway. He hated it so much that he purchased new tile. Then, two days before the green tile was going to be replaced, the doorbell rang. It was Susan's ex-boyfriend, John Smith. Paul let him in the house and offered him a drink. As Paul led him down the hallway, he heard a gunshot and felt the bullet slam into his back. Paul fell face-first, and the last thing Paul saw before he died was the green tile of that hallway. Ladies and gentlemen of the jury, my name is . . ."

ix. One Metaphor/Simile (Thorn in the Side) Teaser

"Paul Brown was a thorn in John Smith's side. Paul was living in John's apartment building and dating John's ex-girlfriend. The defendant saw Paul every day. The defendant thought of Paul in his apartment . . . with his girlfriend . . . every day. He felt that thorn in his side every day. Until February 2, when the defendant decided to get rid of that thorn in his side. And John Smith did that by shooting and killing Paul. Ladies and gentlemen of the jury, my name is . . ."

x. One Movie/Book/Play Teaser

"There are so many iconic scenes in the movie *Titanic*, but the most cold-blooded moment may be when Cal orders his butler to frame Jack by slipping the necklace into Jack's coat. It is the reason why Jack is handcuffed while the boat is sinking. That scene is an ugly reminder that ex-boyfriends can be cold, calculated, and ruthless. And this trial will remind you of the same fact. Ladies and gentlemen of the jury, my name is . . ."

c. Civil Trial Teaser Examples

Teasers for civil trials can be more elusive than criminal trials. The law governing personal injury actions may be straightforward, but the law governing other types of actions (i.e., product liability, breach of contract, intellectual property, etc.), and the evidence itself can be difficult to summarize and explain.

There is still a benefit to applying our top ten teaser ideas to the civil trial fact pattern. Picture a plaintiff attorney filing a product liability action on behalf of "Barbara Johnson" against the manufacturer of a ladder, claiming the ladder was defective because it used cheap and inferior metal. Here is how a plaintiff attorney could apply those facts to our top ten teaser ideas.

i. One Sentence Statement Teaser

"This company chose to use cheap metal, and the cheap metal broke. Ladies and gentlemen of the jury, my name is . . ."

ii. One Quote (Franklin) Teaser

"Benjamin Franklin once said that 'The bitterness of poor quality remains long after the sweetness of low price is forgotten.' This company chose to use cheap metal in the design of their ladder. They chose to enjoy the sweetness of low price, knowing that their customers would someday taste the bitterness of poor quality. That day came, and that customer was Barbara Johnson. Ladies and gentlemen of the jury, my name is . . ."

iii. One Theme (Profit over Safety) Teaser

"Every company faces the same decision every day: profit or safety. Spend money buying the best materials or save money buying cheaper materials. Some companies choose safety over profit. This company chose profit over safety. And Barbara Jordan paid the price. It's a terrible price, a price she will continue paying every day for the rest of her life. Ladies and gentlemen of the jury, my name is . . ."

iv. One Moment (Choice of Metals) Teaser

"It was Friday afternoon. The new CEO walked into the room and looked at the two ladder prototypes. Same design. Two different metals. Go with the one that costs less, the CEO told the engineers before walking out of the room. The meeting lasted five minutes. Barbara Jordan's injuries will last a lifetime. Ladies and gentlemen of the jury, my name is . . ."

v. One Element (Defect) Teaser

"There is nothing particularly interesting about the design of this ladder, except for the choice of metal. The metal this company selected was cheaper and weaker. That is why the ladder rung broke and Barbara fell. The metal was unreasonably dangerous. The metal was the defect. This company's decision to use cheaper and weaker metal is why we are here. Ladies and gentlemen of the jury, my name is . . ."

vi. One Witness (Dr. Reymond) Teaser

"Dr. Reymond has a PhD in mechanical engineering. He holds 147 patents. He has examined and tested hundreds of products. On March 14, he opened the crate that was delivered to his lab, pulled out this company's ladder, and shook his head. He would still perform all the testing we requested, but he already knew what that testing would reveal: they used the wrong metal. Ladies and gentlemen of the jury, my name is . . ."

vii. One Exhibit (Bill of Materials) Teaser

"This is called a 'bill of materials.' This is the document that specifies the raw materials needed to manufacture this ladder. This is the piece of paper on which the company specified they wanted to use a cheaper and weaker metal. This is the piece of paper on which they deviated from the design specifications. This is the piece of paper that cost Barbara Jordan everything. Ladies and gentlemen of the jury, my name is . . ."

viii. One Perspective (Terrance's) Teaser

"Terrance worked for this company for thirty years. Thirty years of designing products. Thirty years of manufacturing products. Thirty years of taking pride in every product the company sold. So, when the new CEO chose the cheaper, weaker metal, Terrance walked back to his office, called his wife, and told her he was retiring. Four years later, the cheaper metal cost Barbara Jordan everything. Ladies and gentlemen of the jury, my name is . . ."

ix. One Metaphor/Simile (Red Flag) Teaser

"One month before they started testing this ladder, the defendant decided to change their testing protocol. That decision was the red flag. It was a warning that something was wrong with this ladder. One year later, the ladder failed, and Barbara Jordan was paralyzed. Ladies and gentlemen of the jury, my name is . . ."

x. One Movie/Book/Play (Tucker: The Man and His Dream) Teaser

"Anyone who sees the movie about Preston Tucker and his quest to build a better automobile comes away impressed by the man's passion and his pride in the Tucker Torpedo. This is not that type of movie. This is not that type of company. This is the story about a ladder manufacturer who decided to use cheaper metal and the woman who was hurt by their selfish decision. Ladies and gentlemen of the jury, my name is . . ."

2. Introduce Yourself, Your Team, and Your Case

During the Golden Age of Lawyers, it became customary for some Gray Hairs to start their opening statement by introducing themselves to the jury, even if the judge had already introduced the lawyers before voir dire. It was a nice custom. It was formal and respectful, reminiscent of the way good waiters always introduce themselves at the start of their service. Let's keep that custom, but let's not start opening statements talking about ourselves. Let's wait about thirty seconds.

End your teaser by reintroducing yourself and your case. It serves as the perfect segue, marking the end of your teaser and the start of your review of the evidence. After the teaser, stop talking. Pause for a moment. Let the teaser sink in. Drop the drama. Change your tone and your pace. In your most professional and steady voice, start with "ladies and gentlemen" or "members of the jury." Table 6.2 shows two examples of how the teaser and the introduction fit together.

Never disregard the importance of introducing yourself and your co-counsel. When waiters introduce themselves, it signals the start of the dining experience, suggests the waiter is required to make that introduction, and assures us that our waiter is well-trained and professional. Similarly, when you introduce your trial team, it signals that your opening statement

Table 6.2 Examples of Teaser and Introduction

Criminal Trial Example		
T	Teaser	*"Paul Brown was lying face down. Shot in the back. Bleeding to death. And that is the moment when John Smith [point to defendant] walked five feet closer to his victim. He aimed the hot muzzle at Paul's face and pulled the trigger one more time."*
I	Introductions	*"Ladies and gentlemen of the jury, my name is ____ and I represent the State of Louisiana. This is the case of the State of Louisiana versus John Smith."*
Civil Trial Example		
T	Teaser	*"There is nothing particularly interesting about the design of this ladder, except for the choice of metal. The metal this company selected was cheaper and weaker. That is why the ladder rung broke, and Barbara fell. The cheaper metal renders this ladder unreasonably dangerous. The metal is the defect. The choice of metal is why we are here."*
I	Introductions	*"Ladies and gentlemen of the jury, my name is ______ and [along with co-counsel,______,] I represent the plaintiff, Barbara Johnson. This is the case of Barbara Johnson versus ABC Manufacturer."*

is structured, suggests the court expected you to make that introduction, and tells the jurors that you are well-trained and professional. In short, it reassures jurors that they are in good hands. Let opposing counsel ignore the importance of an introduction, and unintentionally leave the jury wondering why *the other waiter* forgot to introduce their trial team.

3. Discuss the Allegations, Not the Law

During the Golden Age of Lawyers, some courts allowed Gray Hairs to discuss the law during their opening statements. With the court's blessing, Gray Hairs explained the legal elements of the claim and the applicable legal standards before reviewing the evidence. But those days are over. Today, most judges insist that they—and they alone—explain the law to the jury.

Never step on the court's toes by discussing the law or defining legal terms during opening statement. Never analyze what the "statue requires." Never declare what "legal elements must be proved." Yes, if the court allows you to repeat the definition of second-degree murder during opening statement, you should absolutely provide the jury with that definition. But avoid saying anything that would solicit an objection or prompt the court to say, "I'll instruct the jury on the law, counselor. Move on."

Instead of lecturing the jury on the law and telling them how to apply it (like a lawyering lawyer), discuss the factual allegations with the jury in a way that identifies and addresses the ultimate legal issues. Like a good waiter explaining the Reveillon menu, provide jurors with a "roadmap" of their choices:

> "Today's Reveillon menu is amazing. Four courses. The first course will be your choice of Rémoulade of Poached Barataria Pass White Shrimp or Beef Carpaccio. The second course is your choice of Creole Onion Soup en Croûte or Turtle Soup. The third course is your choice of Seared Black Drum with Saffron Jus or Roasted Rabbit Loin. And, for dessert, your choice of Chocolate Absinthe Trifle or Crêpes Suzette."

Never rely on the jurors to "figure out" their decisions during the trial or be content to cover those decisions during closing argument. Tell them up front.

> "Today's trial is amazing. Three courses. First course is your choice of whether the owner knew or should have known there was water on the floor. Second course is your choice of whether or not the owner had a reasonable opportunity to clean up the water. Third course is your choice of whether the water caused the plaintiff to lose his balance and fall."

If the whole trial comes down to a single factual determination (and many trials do), openly discuss that determination with the jury without discussing the law. For example, in a premises liability case involving a rotten railing, do not tell the jury during opening statement that "plaintiff bears the burden of proving, by a preponderance of the evidence, the legal element of notice (of defect)." Resist the temptation to tell the jury that "notice can be satisfied by proving actual knowledge or constructive knowledge." Refrain from defining "actual knowledge" or "constructive knowledge." Instead, let the jury know, "Everyone agrees that the railing was rotten. What we need you to decide is whether the owner knew or should have known that the railing was rotten. That is the decision you will be asked to make at the end of this trial."

Table 6.3 shows two concrete examples of how a prosecutor and a plaintiff could focus the jury on the allegations, instead of soliciting an objection by discussing the legal elements during our hypothetical criminal and civil cases.

Table 6.3 Discussing Allegations, Not the Law

Criminal Trial Example		
T	Teaser	*"Paul Brown was lying face down. Shot in the back. Bleeding to death. And that is the moment when John Smith [point to defendant] walked five feet closer to his victim. He aimed the hot muzzle at Paul's face, and pulled the trigger one more time."*
I	Introductions	*"Ladies and gentlemen of the jury, my name is ____ and I represent the State of Louisiana. This is the case of the State of Louisiana versus John Smith."*
A	Allegations	*"John Smith is charged with the crime of second-degree murder. At the end of this trial, you will be asked to determine whether the defendant (1) shot Paul Brown on February 2 and (2) intended to kill or do great bodily injury to Paul Brown."*
Civil Trial Example		
T	Teaser	*"There is nothing particularly interesting about the design of this ladder, except for the choice of metal. The metal this company selected was cheaper and weaker. That is why the ladder rung broke and Barbara fell. The cheaper metal renders this ladder unreasonably dangerous. The metal is the defect. The choice of metal is why we are here."*
I	Introductions	*"Ladies and gentlemen of the jury, my name is ______ and I represent the plaintiff, Barbara Johnson. This is the case of Barbara Johnson versus ABC Manufacturer."*
A	Allegations	*"This is a product liability action, in which my client claims that the defendant manufactured an unreasonably dangerous ladder. At the end of this trial, you will be asked to decide whether the use of this type of metal (1) deviated from the manufacturer's own specifications and (2) made the ladder unreasonably dangerous for its normal use."*

4. Review the Evidence

During the Golden Age of Lawyers, some Gray Hairs became convinced that "less is more" when it comes to opening statement. Today, some lawyers still stubbornly refuse to roll up their sleeves and walk the jury through all the evidence. Instead, they are perfectly content to make conclusory statements (i.e., "The evidence will show the defendant was negligent") without reviewing the physical and testimonial evidence supporting *and* contradicting those statements (i.e., "Yes, the defendant will testify . . . but we will call . . . and we will show . . .").

It is not clear why some lawyers stubbornly refuse to try their whole case during opening statement. Maybe they don't know the facts as well as the associates who worked up the case. Maybe the evidence is too voluminous or the timeline is too complicated. Maybe they are not comfortable using courtroom technology. Maybe they feel that a full review would be too boring or tedious. Maybe they are afraid that the evidence may "come out differently during the trial," and opposing counsel will remind jurors of their "promises" during opening statement. Whatever the reason, some lawyers shorten and simplify their opening statement. Let's stop doing that.

Let's resolve to identify all the physical and testimonial evidence that will be placed on *both* sides of the scale for every material issue in dispute. Let's show the jury our timelines, charts, and graphs. Let's prepare the jury to hear unfavorable evidence and influence the weight they will assign to that evidence.

a. Select the Right Structure

Trial attorneys should not try to memorize their entire opening statement, nor should they randomly review the physical and testimonial evidence during their opening statement. By the time the trial starts, you know what to tell the jury about each witness and exhibit. The real challenge is organizing or structuring an opening statement.

The right structure for an opening statement will always depend on the particular facts and issues involved in the case, but there are several methods of organization that can generally be applied to civil and criminal jury trials.

i. By Witness Review

Review the witnesses that will be called during the trial. For each witness, make certain to:

1. Identify the witness and explain who the lay witness is ("Mr. Gregory is the owner of the store at the intersection where the accident happened and the only eyewitness") or discuss the expert's qualifications ("Dr. Maggi is board certified in forensic pathology and performed the autopsy").
2. Summarize the lay testimony ("Mr. Gregory will testify that he was standing outside his store and saw . . .") or the expert testimony you will solicit ("Dr. Maggi microscopically examined the heart and found . . .").
3. Note any facts that support that lay witness's observation ("Mr. Gregory has 20/20 vision, had an unobstructed view of

the intersection, was standing only ten yards from the point of impact, and reported what he witnessed to the police within ten minutes of the accident") or support that expert witness's opinions ("Dr. Maggi authored the official autopsy report, signed the death certificate, and subsequently published a peer-reviewed case study about this specific case").

4. Discuss any key exhibits you will introduce with that witness ("Mr. Gregory used his phone to video the accident scene and you will see . . .") and any key exhibits you will review with that witness ("We will show Dr. Maggi the cardiac ultrasound taken five years before this accident, and he will point out for you . . .").
5. Compare the witness's testimony to the testimony of other witnesses ("Mr. Gregory's eyewitness testimony will directly support/contradict the testimony of . . .").
6. Optional and dangerous: Emphasize the significance of the testimony ("If Mr. Gregory is correct, this accident was solely caused . . .") or the logical consequences of the testimony ("If Dr. Maggi's autopsy findings are accurate, plaintiff was susceptible to . . .").

ii. Chronological Review

Review the events in chronological order ("You will learn that on November 17, 2019, only months before the accident, plaintiff went to the ER"). For each event, make certain to:

1. Summarize what each lay witness will say about the event ("You will hear the plaintiff admit that he went to the ER").
2. Discuss any key exhibits you will introduce regarding the event ("You will see the ER triage record, on which the nurse checked . . .").
3. Summarize any expert testimony regarding the event ("Dr. Frassica will show you the MRI taken that day, and she will circle for you the subdural hematoma. She will testify that the bleeding . . .").
4. Compare the evidence regarding the event to the testimony of other witnesses ("The plaintiff will insist that he was not diagnosed with a concussion on November 17, 2019, only months before the accident, but you will see the discharge summary, which states . . .").
5. Optional and dangerous: Emphasize the significance of the event or the logical consequences of the event ("This event explains the abnormal findings on plaintiff's recent MRI of the brain").

iii. Legal Element Review

Review the specific legal elements required for a criminal conviction or for civil liability. For each legal element:

1. Identify the legal element ("We will present physical and testimonial evidence that the defendant knew the stairs were defective").
2. Summarize what each lay witness will say about that legal element ("We will call Mrs. Rogers, the previous tenant, who will testify that she complained on three separate occasions that her guests had tripped on the same steps because the riser height was inconsistent").
3. Discuss any key exhibits you will introduce regarding the event ("You will see photos showing tape measures on the stairs. You will see that the riser height is not inconsistent. We will show you a lawsuit filed three years before this accident claiming that the same steps were defective.").
4. Summarize any expert testimony regarding the legal element ("We will call Mr. Loeber, who will testify that he issued an expert report in the prior case citing the same stairs violated the building code because the risers varied more than 3/8 of an inch between the tallest and the shortest riser").
5. Compare the evidence regarding the legal element to the testimony of other witnesses ("The defendant will deny knowing that the steps needed to be fixed, but you will have the opportunity to see the photos taken months before this accident and to read the prior lawsuit involving the same steps").

iv. Liability and Damages Review

In civil cases, explain that the physical and testimonial evidence in every civil case can be divided into evidence of liability or evidence of damages. Review the physical and testimonial evidence by first reviewing the evidence of liability and then the evidence of damages.

b. Consider Case-Specific Structures

Certain cases will provide additional methods of organizing the evidence and structuring your opening statement. For example, when a civil case involves the allegation of a traumatic brain injury, we often start our review of the evidence by drawing a line on a flip chart and writing "Injury" above the line and "Impairment" below the line, as shown in Figure 6.1.

Figure 6.1 Drawing to start review of evidence

Injury

Impairment

We tell the jury that all the physical and testimonial evidence may be divided into evidence of "Injury" and evidence of "Impairment." First, we review the evidence of a brain injury, which typically includes neurologist testimony, neuroradiologist testimony, brain imaging (like MRI or CT scans), Glasgow Coma Scale Scores, classic symptoms (like loss of consciousness and vomiting), and ER findings (like abnormal neurological or cranial nerve exams). Then, we review the evidence of cognitive or behavioral impairment including neuropsychological testing and anecdotal reports by family and friends. For the rest of the trial, we will return to that page of the flip chart or reference "Injury" or "Impairment" whenever we want jurors to know which aspect we are addressing.

c. Use Bridges to Emphasize the Burden of Proof

When a case involves multiple disputed legal elements, consider introducing a visual reminder that the prosecutor and plaintiff bear the burden of proving every element of their case. Think of a visual that will constantly remind jurors (a) of each element opposing counsel must prove and (b) that opposing counsel bears the burden of proving each element.

My favorite visual is a series of bridges the plaintiff and prosecutor must build (with evidence) to "get where they want to go," like the one shown in Figure 6.2. If the plaintiff and prosecutor fail to meet their burden of producing sufficient physical and testimonial evidence regarding even one bridge, the jury must return a defense verdict. Remember to identify the bridges by the factual allegation and the legal element. Also remember that the order of the bridges is important.

For example, in a premises liability case, the defense may want to organize its review of the evidence by identifying three bridges (legal elements) the plaintiff has to build to prove the restaurant owner was liable: (1) prove the stairs were unreasonably dangerous (defect); (2) prove the owner knew (actual knowledge) or should have known (constructive knowledge) of the defect; and (3) prove that the defect caused plaintiff to fall (causation). By identifying the three bridges in this specific order,

Figure 6.2 Three bridges the plaintiff and prosecutor must build.

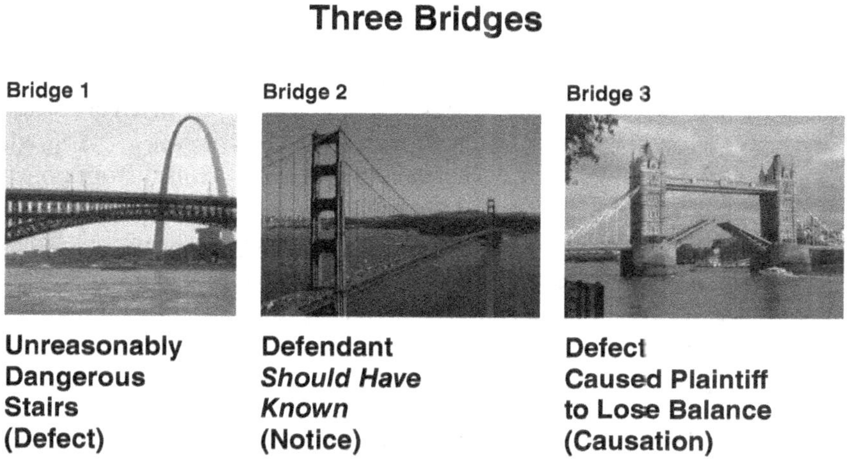

defense counsel can emphasize that, even if the stairs were defective, plaintiff still bears the burden of proving the other two elements to "get where they want to go."

The bridge visual also provides for flexibility in terms of trial strategy. If plaintiff's counsel spends their entire opening statement talking about the first bridge (i.e. "we will prove that the stairs were defective!"), it allows defense counsel to respectfully clarify that there are two additional bridges that plaintiff bears the burden of proving. And, if plaintiff's counsel succeeds in proving two of the three bridges during the trial, it gives defense counsel the flexibility to focus on the third bridge during closing argument. Nothing is better than giving yourself the option of arguing that the prosecution/plaintiff "never gets past the first bridge."

Remember that the order of the bridges is important. During the 2010 *Nugent* trial, I started opening statement by identifying three bridges: (1) the officer's conducted electrical weapon (CEW) can cause cardiac arrest (general causation); (2) the CEW did cause cardiac arrest (specific causation); and (3) the officer's conduct was unreasonable. I chose that order because I knew the district attorney was going to assume that the CEW caused the victim's cardiac arrest (which it did not) and spend most of his opening statement arguing that the officer's conduct was unreasonable. The order of bridges I chose allowed me to start the trial by discussing the evidence of two bridges that the district attorney had largely ignored.

d. Use Classic Segues When Reviewing the Evidence

There is no excuse for having an "argumentative" objection sustained during your review of the evidence. If you are not comfortable walking the fine line between "being argumentative" and "persuasively reviewing the evidence," use the classic segues as a crutch and establish a consistent rhythm ("We will call . . . You will hear . . . We will call . . . You will hear"). The repetition itself will dissuade opposing counsel from objecting and increase the likelihood of the court's overruling any objection that is made. Table 6.4 shows a handful of the classic segues or introductions.

There may be times when a point is so important that a trial lawyer wants to sit down and plan how to make that point during opening statement without sounding argumentative. Table 6.5 shows some suggestions for avoiding argumentative objections.

e. Beware Using Trial Exhibits during Opening Statement

During opening statement, there is a difference between providing the jury with a roadmap of the evidence and showing that evidence to the jury. Some courts will instruct the jury that "what the lawyers say during opening statement is not evidence," and will prohibit counsel from

Table 6.4 Classic Segues and Introductions

Testimonial Evidence	"We will call . . ." "[The witness] will testify . . ." "You will hear [the witness] say/describe/report . . ." "The testimony will prove ..." "The testimonial evidence will establish . . ."
Physical Evidence	"We will show . . ." "We will introduce . . ." "You will see . . ." "You will observe . . ." "You will note . . ." "The [exhibit] will prove . . ." "The [exhibit] will establish . . ."
Videos	"We will play/show . . ." "You will see/hear . . ." "You will watch . . ." "The videos will establish . . ."
Demonstrations	"We will demonstrate . . ." "You will see . . ."
General	"You will learn . . ." "You will discover . . ."
Summary	"The physical and testimonial evidence will prove . . ."

Table 6.5 Avoiding Argumentative Objections

Will Draw an Objection	Less Likely to Draw Objection
"You heard counsel say that Sarah saw everything, but he was wrong. Sarah couldn't see anything because she was standing behind a tree."	"You heard counsel say that Sarah saw everything, but we will call John to the stand. John will testify that Sarah was standing behind a tree. We will show you photographs of the area, and you will see that the tree completely obstructed Sarah's view."
"The defense bases their case on the testimony of Dr. Smith, but Dr. Smith is not a cardiologist. He is not an expert on cardiac electrophysiology. He is not remotely qualified to testify . . ."	"The defense will call Dr. Smith, who is a forensic pathologist. You will learn that Dr. Smith is not board certified in cardiology. He never did a residency in cardiac electrophysiology and has never published in that field. In contrast, we will call Dr. Jones, who is a board-certified cardiac electrophysiologist . . ."
"Mr. Jenkins never cared about his employees or about safety. All he cared about was making money, and that was why didn't fix the floor, even when he knew it needed to be repaired."	"We will call Dr. Jenkins to the stand. He will admit that the floor was in disrepair. He will admit that employees asked him to fix it. You will see the estimate he was given for repairing the floor six months before this accident. You will learn that he chose not to spend the money fixing the floor for his employees."
"Dr. Jones is a psychiatrist who only spoke with the defendant for 30 minutes and couldn't possibly know whether the defendant could distinguish between right and wrong."	"You will learn that Dr Jones met with the defendant for only 30 minutes. You will hear her admit that she did not interview his family. She did not interview his coworkers. You will hear her admit that she administered no tests of any kind. In contrast, we will call Dr. Bravo, who met with the defendant, her family, her friends, her coworkers, and administered a battery of neuropsychological testing."

showing any trial exhibits because those exhibits have not been admitted. Other courts may, prior to opening statements, permit the parties to jointly admit *unopposed* trial exhibits into evidence. And some courts will rule on the authenticity and admissibility of a disputed trial exhibit prior to trial. But few courts (if any) will order that a disputed trial exhibit be admitted into evidence prior to opening statement when no physical testimony has been introduced regarding that exhibit and no foundation has been laid for its introduction.

Before you even think about using, enlarging, displaying, or playing an exhibit during your opening statement, make certain that (a) you absolutely need to use that exhibit during your opening statement and (b) the court has signed an order granting you permission to show the exhibit to the jury during your opening statement. When discovery ends, stop and consider whether any trial exhibits must be shown to the jury during opening statement. When in doubt, leave the trial exhibit out. Here are some of the right questions to ask:

- Will the jury be able to picture what happened without seeing the trial exhibit?
- Will the jury understand my review of the evidence without seeing the trial exhibit?
- Will the jury understand the physical and testimonial evidence that may be introduced (by either party) *prior* to the trial exhibit being introduced and published to the jury?
- Could jurors develop the wrong first impression of a party, witness, or legal issue if they do not see the trial exhibit during opening statement?
- Could seeing the trial exhibit cause some jurors to "make up their minds" during opening statement and affect the way they listen to the evidence?
- Will getting permission to show the trial exhibit dissuade opposing counsel from making certain prejudicial statements or arguments?
- Will the trial exhibit directly contradict what opposing counsel says/said during opening statement?
- Is there sufficient time to properly play/show/discuss the trial exhibit during opening statement?
- Could a demonstrative exhibit be used instead of the actual trial exhibit?

During the pretrial conference, always ask the court whether it allows the parties to show exhibits to the jury and confirm the correct process for introducing and/or stipulating to the introduction of the exhibit prior to showing that exhibit during your opening statement. Never assume opposing counsel will have no objection to your showing the video of the incident during your opening statement "because they know it's going to come in at trial" or "because their expert relies on it too." Never assume the court will have no objection to you showing a medical record during opening statement "because the parties have stipulated to its admissibility."

f. Be Selective with Demonstrative Exhibits

During the Golden Age of Lawyers, trial attorneys had limited technology and limited access to demonstrative exhibits (think chalk boards and easels). Back then, it was easier to select a demonstrative exhibit because there were so few options. Today, trial attorneys can present stunning computer animations, amazing graphics, detailed timelines, colorful charts, aerial drone footage, and PowerPoint slide presentations. Soon, every courtroom will be equipped with video displays directly mounted in the jury box, witness monitors, laptop connections, digital input connections, plugs in the right place, and wireless internet. The question is no longer "Can we do that for the jury?" The question is "Should we do that for the jury?"

Always be selective in the demonstrative exhibits. Never overwhelm the jury with so many graphics and charts that the jury is more confused *after* your opening statement. Never try to cram all your visual aids into an opening statement. Instead, as a mental exercise, pretend the court has limited each party to one demonstrative exhibit. Figure out what that one demonstrative exhibit should be and seriously consider how much more memorable that one exhibit would be if it was the only demonstrative exhibit used during opening statement.

Ask yourself what demonstrative exhibits would (a) most help the jury understand the evidence and (b) help the jury remember your theme best. For example, a timeline may help the jury understand the sequence of events, but a picture of the plaintiff's rear bumper showing no visible damage may be the visual anchor that the jury desperately needs throughout the trial. And when you've narrowed it down to two or three demonstrative exhibits, resist the temptation to use all of them. Try to picture yourself standing next to one demonstrative exhibit for your entire opening statement. Which exhibit would you place on the easel?

Whenever possible, limit yourself to only one of each type of demonstrative exhibit. Avoid presenting two timelines during the same trial. Avoid presenting two bar graphs or two pie charts during the same trial. During deliberation, when a juror mentions "the timeline," you want every juror to be picturing the same demonstrative exhibit. What you don't want is for other jurors to be silently struggling because their waiter brought them five timelines.

g. Consider Personally Writing and Drawing Exhibits

Once upon a time, when dinosaurs roamed the earth, students only paid attention when the teacher took the time and made the effort to write something on the chalkboard. If it was not on the board, it was not on the exam. Today, in a courtroom full of computers and monitors, jurors do not expect an attorney to take out a marker and (noisily) write or draw on a flip chart. But maybe that is exactly what we should do when something is truly important.

There is a scene at the end of the movie *Harry Potter and the Deathly Hallows Part I* where Harry decides to personally dig the grave for his friend Dobby. Harry is a wizard, and "a thumpin' good 'un." But instead of using magic, Harry chooses to put his wand away and dig the grave with a shovel. Harry wanted the task to take longer and to be physically more demanding because Harry wanted the task to mean more. And it did. Because it required time and effort.

Always consider going "old school" and personally (and imperfectly) writing or drawing to give the exercise greater importance and make it more memorable than displaying a completed table, chart, graph, diagram, or slide.

h. Consider Ways to Disguise Demonstrative Exhibits

Most courts require trial attorneys to exchange demonstrative exhibits prior to trial to allow counsel to object and the court to rule on the whether the demonstrative exhibit may be used during opening statement. As a result, attorneys are often reluctant to exchange detailed demonstrative exhibits before trial because it means that opposing counsel will have time to steal their thunder or prepare their response.

Consider the pros and cons of disguising your demonstrative exhibits. Instead of exchanging a completed timeline that includes specific dates (which will prompt opposing counsel to put those dates under a microscope), consider exchanging a timeline that includes only hashes and adding the dates to those hashes with a (noisy) marker during your opening. Instead of exchanging a completed timeline that includes needle icons to emphasize the date of each epidural steroid injection *before* the accident, consider ordering stickers (with the needle icons printed on them) you can add to the timeline during your opening statement. Instead of exchanging a completed pie chart that identifies each wedge, consider exchanging an unlabeled pie chart and telling the jury what the testimonial and physical evidence will reveal about each wedge ("You will learn that the smallest wedge is . . .").

Always check with the court to make certain that the court allows attorneys to mark previously exchanged exhibits and write or draw on flip charts during opening statements. During the *Fahy* trial, we painstakingly prepared a 99-slide PowerPoint presentation for opening statement. We tested the slides with focus groups until the 99 slides were perfect. When the plaintiff finished their opening statement, we asked the court for a few minutes to set up the PowerPoint presentation, and the judge promptly told us that demonstrative exhibits were not permitted during opening statement unless both sides consented, which the plaintiff's did not. When I advised the client, he asked me what I was going to do, and I replied, "I'm going to go talk to these people." Learn from my mistake. Never assume the court will allow you to use a demonstrative exhibit or slides the way you *want* to use them during opening statement.

i. Predict Turning Points and Distractions

Jurors often remember their initial impression (i.e., "I think plaintiff is right" or "I think the defendant did it"), but they rarely remember everything said about every witness and every exhibit during an opening statement. That is why a trial attorney should not be content with thoroughly reviewing all of the evidence.

Always consider calling the jury's attention to a key witness or a key question. If a boring but important videotaped trial perpetuation deposition will be played for the jury, consider telling the jury that the videotape is "incredibly boring, but incredibly important," and politely asking them to listen carefully for a specific question ("Please wait and watch for the moment when opposing counsel slides the first photograph to the witness and asks . . . You will hear . . .").

Consider calling the jury's attention to a specific examination. If you know that a witness will be persuasive during opposing counsel's direct examination, but you have excellent impeachment evidence, politely suggest they wait for your cross-examination ("During direct examination, you will hear the witness testify that . . . But during my cross-examination, you will learn . . ."). Consider the pros and cons of disclosing the important fact, admission, inconsistency, error, impeachment or testimony, especially when opposing counsel knows of its existence and could "steal your thunder" by disclosing it during direct examination.

Consider predicting and disclosing the turning point in the trial. Preparing the jury in opening statement can steal opposing counsel's thunder. Promising a turning point in the trial or calling the jury's attention to something they might otherwise overlook can create anticipation. Of course, the key is to never exaggerate during opening statement or make a false prediction regarding the physical or testimonial evidence (especially about "turning points").

Consider preparing jurors for a boring or unorthodox cross-examination and warning them not to "rush to any conclusions." If you have strategically decided to *only* solicit admissions from their expert during your cross-examination (saving the big reveal for your direct examination of your own expert), consider warning the jury that the purpose of your cross-examination may not be obvious and asking the jury to wait for your direct examination ("Yes, you will hear their expert testify . . . but you will also hear their expert make certain admissions, and, if you wait for our expert to take the stand, you will learn why those admissions are so important").

Consider preparing jurors for any foreseeable distractions. If there is a giant pink elephant in the room, find a way to address it during your opening statement. If there will be protests outside the courtroom, family members with matching T-shirts inside the courtroom, local media coverage, or an incredibly emotional "day-in-the-life" video, consider preparing the jury for that daily distraction or inevitable experience. Depending on the size of the pink elephant, that may require you to raise the issue during voir dire (preferably by asking the court to voir dire on the possible prejudice) and address the issue again during opening statement ("You will see an incredibly emotional day-in-the life video, and the plaintiff will be wheeled into this courtroom to meet you. As hard as it may be to remain objective after seeing him and learning about his daily challenges, you will be asked to determine his fault in causing the accident. We will call police officer . . .").

5. Remember the Alamo

The Alamo is where you make your last stand. It is the last 30 seconds to 60 seconds of your opening statement, and it should always be memorized because it allows you to end your opening statement with confidence and purpose. If you get lost or nervous, remember the Alamo! If your review of the evidence starts to lag, remember the Alamo! If you realize that you are running out of time, go immediately to your Alamo!

Having a brilliant Alamo for your opening statement is less important than having a brilliant Alamo for your closing argument. The Alamo for your opening statement serves the same purpose as a period at the end of a sentence. The Alamo for your closing argument should be an exclamation point. Keep your opening statement Alamo simple and direct. Do not make it too argumentative. Do not end your opening statement by soliciting an objection and having the court sustain that objection. Make sure you get the chance to end your Alamo by saying "Thank you."

Remember that the waiter should never delay the meal, and the jury is eager to start hearing the evidence. Always end your opening statement cleanly, quickly, and professionally. Table 6.6 shows two examples of Alamos that can be applied to most civil or criminal opening statements.

Table 6.6 Examples of Alamos for Opening Statement

Criminal Trial Example		
T	Teaser	*"Paul Brown was lying face down. Shot in the back. Bleeding to death. And that is the moment when John Smith [point to defendant] walked five feet closer to his victim. He aimed the hot muzzle at Paul's face, and pulled the trigger one more time."*
I	Introductions	*"Ladies and gentlemen of the jury, my name is ______ and I represent the State of Louisiana. This is the case of the State of Louisiana versus John Smith."*
A	Allegations	*"John is charged with the crime of second-degree murder, which is the killing of a human being when the offender has the specific intent to kill or do great bodily harm. At the end of this trial, you will be asked to determine whether the defendant (1) shot Paul Brown on February 2 and (2) intended to kill or do great bodily injury to Paul Brown."*
R	Review [By witness]	*"We will call Detective Ryan . . ."* *"We will call John Smith's ex-girlfriend, Sarah . . ."* *"We will call John Smith's best friend, David . . ."* *"We will call crime lab technician Andrew . . ."* *"We will call coroner William . . ."*
A	Alamo	*"When you have been presented with all the physical and testimonial evidence, the State of Louisiana will ask you to find John Smith guilty as charged of second-degree murder. Thank you."*
Civil Trial Example		
T	Teaser	*"There is nothing particularly interesting about the design of this ladder, except for the choice of metal. The metal this company selected was cheaper and weaker. That is why the ladder rung broke and Barbara fell. The cheaper metal renders this ladder unreasonably dangerous. The metal is the defect. The choice of metal is why we are here."*
I	Introductions	*"Ladies and Gentlemen of the jury, my name is ______ and [along with co-counsel, ______,] I represent the plaintiff, Barbara Johnson. This is the case of Barbara Johnson versus ABC Manufacturer."*
A	Allegations	*"This is a product liability action, in which my client claims that this ladder is unreasonably dangerous. At the end of this trial, you will be asked to decide whether the use of this type of metal (1) deviated in a material way from the manufacturer's own specifications and (2) made the ladder unreasonably dangerous."*

R	Review [By witness]	*"We will call Terrance, who worked for the defendant . . ."* *"We will call the president of the manufacturing company . . ."* *"We will call our ladder expert . . ."* *"We will call Barbara Johnson . . ."* *"We will call Barbara's treating physician . . ."* *"We will call Barbara's husband . . ."*
A	Alamo	*"When you have been presented with all the physical and testimonial evidence, you will know that defendant used the wrong metal for this type of ladder, that the ladder was defective, and that defendant chose to put profits over safety. We will ask you to hold the defendant 100 percent solely responsible, and we will ask you to fairly compensate Barbara for her injuries. Thank you."*

Chapter 7

Objections: How and When to Use a Loaded Crossbow

During the Golden Age of Lawyers, civil and criminal attorneys developed an impressive arsenal of objections, and that arsenal was put to good use. More trials meant more objections. More objections meant more rulings. More rulings meant more assignments of errors. More assignments of error meant more published opinions. More published opinions on the law of evidence from sundry courts . . . well, revealed a *profound* need for uniform rules of evidence. And so it came to pass on February 5, 1973, the United States Supreme Court submitted to Congress proposed Rules of Evidence for United States Courts and Magistrates.

The subsequently enacted Federal Rules of Evidence inspired states to codify their own rules of evidence and allowed trial lawyers everywhere to stand on the shoulders of giants. Suddenly, even novices could master the law of evidence and move past the threshold question of "Can I object?" to the *infinitely* more difficult question of "Should I object?"

Make no mistake. Some lawyers are born with natural trial instincts, intuitively knowing when to object and when to let the moment pass. Others develop their instincts through trial and error, slowly and painfully learning what judges and jurors dislike. But innate or learned, those trial instincts require the intestinal fortitude to refrain from objecting to every objectionable question. Which is harder than it sounds, especially when your client is sitting next to you.

It will always be easier to object and blame the court for an adverse ruling than to explain why you sat on your hands and failed to object, especially after an unfavorable verdict. But a good waiter knows when *not* to interrupt the conversation, and that is the discipline trial attorneys must somehow develop without the same jury trial opportunities.

It is the difference between knowledge and wisdom. Knowledge is like a loaded crossbow, ridiculously dangerous until the eager novice learns *when* and *how* to use the weapon. Similarly, knowing "every objection in the book" can be ridiculously dangerous until the eager attorney learns *when* and *how* to object.

During a jury trial, lawyers have a fraction of a second to decide *whether* to object and *what* to say when objecting. Courts require timely and specific objections to (a) require the objecting attorney to articulate the problem with the question; (b) give opposing counsel the opportunity to fix or withdraw the question; (c) give the court the chance to exclude the physical or testimonial evidence; and (d) give the court the chance to declare a mistrial or give a curative instruction, depending on the severity of the impermissible question or objectionable testimony. That is why a lawyer must enter the courtroom already knowing *how* to object and having some notion of *when* to object.

Practice does not *always* make perfect. Sometimes, practice with a loaded crossbow makes scar tissue. The following practical suggestions and charts are based on a career that has already produced far too many overruled, unwise, and unintelligible objections.

1. Learn the Four Steps for Making a "Perfect" Objection

It looks so easy on television. The attorney says "objection" and the court immediately says "sustained." Unfortunately, in the real world, judges are either unable or unwilling to read an attorney's mind. They insist that the attorney articulate the basis for an objection, which is why every lawyer needs to understand the right way to object.

The perfect objection starts with the correct "tag," which is the word or phrase commonly associated with the basis for that objection. Attorneys in movies often state only the tag in support of an obvious objection (i.e., "Objection: leading!"). Most objections start with the tag, but the "perfect" objection requires more than the tag.

The "perfect" objection involves four steps: (1) state the **T**ag for the objection; (2) cite the **A**uthority (i.e., article or case law); (3) repeat the relevant portion of the **R**ule; and (4) explain why the article **A**pplies. "TARA" can be a helpful mnemonic, and Table 7.1 shows a helpful chart.

By completing all four steps in the perfect TARA objection, an attorney can (a) start with the familiar tag, which identifies the general basis for the objection to the court; (b) direct the court to the correct Code of Evidence article, statute, or case law; (c) explain how the relevant article should be applied or interpreted; (d) emphasize to the court and to jurors

Table 7.1 The Perfect Objection

T	Tag	State the tag	"Objection. Hearsay."
A	Authority	Cite the article	"Article 803 ..."
R	Rule	Give the rule	". . . defines hearsay as an out-of-court statement offered to prove the truth of the matter asserted."
A	Apply	Apply the rule	"Counsel is asking this witness to repeat what he heard John say."

that the objection is based on the law; and (e) increase the chance (however remote) that the court will state reasons for its ruling, whether the court ultimately grants or denies the objection. When an attorney makes the perfect TARA objection, the impermissible question or inadmissible evidence will often be *Gone with the Wind*.[1]

2. Know When to Skip TARA Steps

Think twice before making the perfect TARA objection. High school mock trial judges may reward participants for repeatedly making the perfect TARA objection during competition. But real judges may not appreciate an attorney's unnecessarily defining "hearsay" for them (step 3), especially in front of the jurors. Picture the judge interrupting your objection and saying, "Let me stop you there, counsel. I know what hearsay is." Other judges may only want attorneys to state the **T**ag and will consider *anything* more to constitute a "speaking objection." In other words, the perfect objection should be saved for the perfect occasion.

Save the perfect TARA objection for those times when the legal basis for an objection is not obvious. On those rare occasions, do not be content to give *only* the **T**ag (step 1). Do not assume that the court will know the relevant code article or **A**uthority (step 2), will remember what the **R**ule states (step 3), and will correctly **A**pply the law to the facts (step 4).

For example, when a prosecutor asks the state's expert to identify the documents on which the expert based his opinion, and the state's expert relied on inadmissible evidence in reaching a conclusion, the criminal defense attorney should make the "perfect" objection (preferably outside the presence of the jury) by stating:

> Objection. Lack of Foundation. Article 705(B) specifically prohibits experts in criminal cases from referring to otherwise

1. Sorry, that movie reference was for my favorite Gray Hair.

inadmissible evidence during direct examination. This expert's report cites inadmissible evidence, which "shall only be elicited on cross-examination."

Most trial lawyers are capable of learning the rules of evidence and remembering how to make the perfect objection. But the real challenge comes *after* acquiring that knowledge. Not every trial lawyer is capable of *instantly* deciding which TARA steps to skip when objecting. But that is how you develop a rapport with the judge, avoid sounding like a broken record, and demonstrate to the jury that you are not a robot. Here are a few suggestions.

Never repeat the perfect objection. When the court sustains the perfect TARA hearsay objection, and opposing counsel immediately asks another hearsay question, be content to say, "Objection, hearsay" or "Same objection." Do not re-cite Article 801 (step 2), repeat the definition of "hearsay" (step 3), or repeat your explanation for why the specific question solicits hearsay testimony (step 4). Repeating the perfect TARA objection can drive the judge insane. It is a good way to get a gavel thrown at you. Or worse, go from hero to zero with the jury.

Stop after the **T**ag for obvious objections. When the basis for the objection is self-evident, an attorney can stop after stating the tag (step 1). For example, when opposing counsel asks an expert to "share with the jury how much she donated to charity last year," the court may not need more than the tag ("Objection. Relevance."). There would be no need for counsel to additionally cite Article 402 (step 2), define "relevance" (step 3), or explain why his or her charitable donations are not relevant to her qualifications, methodology, or opinion (step 4).

For example, when opposing counsel asks the plaintiff a question that calls for the witness to speculate as to *why* a defendant acted or *what* a defendant was thinking, the court may not need more than the tag ("Objection. Speculation."). There would be no need for counsel to additionally cite Article 602 (step 2), state that "a witness may not testify to a matter unless . . . he or she has personal knowledge of the matter" (step 3), or explain why the plaintiff could not have personal knowledge of the defendant's inner thoughts (step 4).

Stop after the **R**ule when the applicability of that rule is obvious. When the applicability of the rule is self-evident from the articulation of the rule, an attorney should stop after quoting or paraphrasing the rule (step 3). For example, when a prosecutor asks a fingerprint expert "So, are you saying the defendant is the murderer?," a criminal defense attorney could say, "Objection. Ultimate issue. Article 611(d) prohibits an expert in a criminal case from expressing an opinion as to the guilt or innocence of the accused." There would be no need for defense counsel to additionally **A**pply the rule (step 4) by explaining that "the expert's opinion on whether the defendant shot the victim would be an opinion as to the defendant's guilt." In that situation, the application of the rule is obvious.

3. Know the Proper Etiquette for Objecting and Responding

There is a right way to do everything, and there is a right way to practice law. For decades, Gray Hairs have been teaching and preaching the same rules for making and responding to objections. For decades, judges have known and enforced those rules. They are good rules. They show respect for the court and for opposing counsel. They absolutely belong in our playbook for the Age of Jurors.

Someday soon, judges with less trial experience may be less familiar with the proper etiquette for objecting and may be less inclined to enforce those "old fashioned" rules. When that day comes, trial lawyers will have to decide for themselves whether to push the envelope.

Let's resolve that we will never let "What can we get away with?" become our standard when objecting. Let's resolve that we will never breach the etiquette developed by our friends and mentors. Let's resolve that we will never rip those pages out of our playbook. It is not only the right way to practice law, but a great way to distinguish ourselves from those "lawyering lawyers" that jurors dislike and mistrust.

a. Standing and the Exception to Standing When Objecting

Trial advocacy classes often start with the first rule of objecting: "Always stand when addressing the court." That is a good rule. In fact, that rule should be expanded to: "Always stand when addressing the court *and* always be prepared to stand." When sitting down after conducting a direct examination, do not slide your chair forward. Leave yourself sufficient room to stand without having to first push your chair backwards (away from the table).

Remember that perception-reaction time varies. Every witness needs time to perceive (hear) an objection, process that objection, and respond to that objection (i.e., refrain from answering or stop talking). In practice, a trial lawyer may have only a fraction of a second before a witness answers an impermissible question or provides objectionable testimony.

That is why there is one exception to the first rule of objecting, and that exception applies to the word "objection." Do not wait until you are fully standing to say the word "objection!" Do not wait until you have *started* the process of standing to say the word "objection!" The moment you decide to object, say "objection!" whether you are standing, seated, or leaning over to pick up a dropped piece of paper. Say "objection!" and immediately stand up.

Some bells cannot be un-rung. When the question is impermissible *and* prejudicial, do not hesitate to object before counsel has finished asking the question. Here are a few of those occasions when an attorney should object instead of wait:

- When the witness is already nodding in agreement with the question, do not wait for opposing counsel to finish asking the question. In effect, the witness is contemporaneously answering by nodding.
- When the witness has been responding quickly to questions, do not wait for counsel to finish asking a question that is soliciting objectionable testimony. The record won't reflect what the jurors saw, and you can't ask the jury to unsee it.
- When your gut tells you that the remainder of the question will be prejudicial, do not wait for counsel to finish asking the question. Never wait for opposing counsel to finish the question when the question itself is prejudicial and objectionable.

No attorney has the right to finish a prejudicial question. Professionalism never requires you to allow opposing counsel to finish prejudicing the jury.

Do not take a "wait and see" approach. If you sit on your hands and wait for opposing counsel to finish the prejudicial question, the court may sustain your objection and grant your motion for a curative instruction (i.e., "The jury shall disregard that last question"). But jurors do not forget, and the damage may be done. The best way to prevent a question from prejudicing the jury is to make sure the jury never hears the prejudicial question.

Be prepared to be wrong and be willing to make a full *mea culpa*. When an attorney objects before opposing counsel finished asking the question and opposing counsel (truthfully or untruthfully) assures the court they "had no intention of finishing the question that way," immediately withdraw the objection, apologize to the court, and apologize to opposing counsel. Resist the temptation to respond to opposing counsel's assurances, even when your (interrupting) objection was the only reason counsel changed direction (i.e., "Your Honor, opposing counsel had every intention of going there"). Take the win. Apologize and sit down.

When the question itself is not prejudicial but could solicit inadmissible testimony, consider standing while opposing counsel finishes the question. The mere act of standing can (a) persuade opposing counsel to withdraw or rephrase the question; (b) cause the witness to hold off on answering; (c) distract jurors while the question is being asked; and (d) cause the judge to listen more carefully to the question. Sometimes, the mere act of standing can cause the judge to *sua sponte* instruct the witness not to answer and tell opposing counsel to ask another question. Nothing is better than standing during a question and having the judge flash you the "I know, and I got this" sign with his hand.

4. Only Address the Judge

If the first rule of objecting is to stand up, the second rule is "only address the court." Objections are always made to the court (not to opposing counsel) and responses to objections are always provided to the court (not to opposing counsel).

Never address opposing counsel during an objection. Do not ask opposing counsel a direct question (i.e., "That's ridiculous, Jane. How do you explain . . ."). Do not look at opposing counsel when making an objection or responding to an objection. In the same way that pretrial written motions *in limine* seeking to exclude evidence, along with supporting and opposing memoranda, are filed with the court (not opposing counsel), trial objections are directed to the court (not opposing counsel).

Resist the temptation to challenge opposing counsel (i.e., "I would ask opposing counsel to identify a hearsay exception" or "I haven't heard opposing counsel identify an exception to hearsay"). Never run the risk that the judge will instruct you to address your comments to the court, which is tantamount to the judge's calling you "unprofessional" in front of the jury. Instead, always address your comments or concerns to the court (i.e., "Your Honor, no specific exception to hearsay has been identified"), and let the court ask the specific question to opposing counsel (i.e., "That is true. What specific hearsay exception applies, counsel?").

a. Ask Permission before Responding to Objections

Most judges will allow an attorney to respond to an objection before ruling on an objection (i.e., "What is your response, counsel?"), but courts are not required to solicit a response or to permit a response before ruling.

That is why attorneys should resist the temptation to respond as soon as opposing counsel finishes stating the objection. Instead, when objections are being argued in the presence of the jury (an increasingly rare occurrence), an attorney should pause long enough to allow the court to request a response.

If the court does not immediately request a response, the attorney should request the court's permission to respond (i.e., "May I respond, Your Honor?" or "Brief response, Your Honor?") and wait for the court to grant that permission *before* addressing the objection. That show of respect can go a long way with jurors and possibly reduce the likelihood that the court will lose patience with you and interrupt you (i.e., "Enough! Your objection is overruled, counselor.").

Resist the temptation to say "please" when requesting permission to respond to an objection in the presence of the jury (i.e., "May I *please* respond, Your Honor?"). Adding "please" transforms your professional request into a personal request (i.e., "Do me this favor, judge"). More importantly, adding "please" may suggest to some jurors that the ruling is more harmful to your case than it actually is (i.e., "Please, Your Honor. I *really* need this, Your Honor!").

b. Never Thank the Court for Ruling on an Objection

There is no consensus on whether attorneys should thank the court for its ruling on an objection. Some attorneys thank the court for *every* ruling. Some attorneys thank the court for *favorable* rulings to emphasize that they "won" the argument. Some attorneys thank the court for favorable rulings, but respond "Yes, Your Honor" for *unfavorable* rulings, rather than just sit down. Other attorneys will follow opposing counsel's lead, not wanting the jury to wonder why *only* opposing counsel thanked the court after every ruling.

Different judges respond differently to being thanked for a ruling. I have heard judges call down excellent lawyers for thanking the court in the presence of the jury. I have also heard very good judges say that they like it when lawyers thank the court after a ruling. Whenever possible, find out the trial court's preference. During the pretrial conference, and in the presence of opposing counsel, ask the court whether it likes or dislikes when counsel thank the court for rulings. When in doubt, do not thank the court. The risk of aggravating a judge who hates being thanked outweighs the potential benefit of currying favor with a judge who loves it.

5. Always Win Your First Two Objections

The third rule of objecting should be "always win your first two objections." Trial lawyers should patiently wait until they are absolutely certain that the court will sustain their objection. And, after winning their first objection, trial lawyers should refrain from making another objection until they are absolutely certain the court will sustain their second objection.

Modern jurors do not like objections and bench conferences. They want to be trusted with all of the evidence. To them, trial objections are synonymous with trial interruptions. Making meritless "interruptions" at the start of the trial is one way to introduce yourself to the jurors as another "lawyering lawyer." Never start your trial that way.

The "always win your first two objections" strategy can become a self-fulfilling prophecy. Once adopted, the strategy can dissuade attorneys from starting the trial with petty objections. It can establish a high bar for objecting, which is exactly where the bar should be set.

Consider the alternative. Picture a lawyer losing his or her first two objections. What would starting the trial with consecutive adverse rulings (i.e., having an 0–2 record) suggest to jurors about that lawyer's ability? What would it suggest to the court? Would consecutive adverse rulings increase the probability the court overrules the losing lawyer's next objection? Would consecutive defeats cause the lawyer to hesitate before making their third objection, regardless of its merit? That is why, whenever possible, an attorney should wait and win the first two objections.

There is an important exception to the "win your first two objections" rule, and that exception is the appealable issue. To preserve a claim of error for appeal, an attorney must sometimes object, even though they know the court will overrule their objection. Whenever possible, avoid those occasions by filing pretrial motions *in limine* to solicit rulings on the admissibility of the evidence in advance of trial and to spare yourself from having to object (and lose) in front of the jury. When in doubt, make the objection and preserve the right to appeal.

6. Make Pre-emptive Objections and Pre-emptive Requests

An ounce of prevention is worth a pound of cure. When you know why opposing counsel is calling the next witness and you anticipate either impermissible questions or objectionable testimony, consider bringing it to the court's attention before the witness takes the stand.

Sometimes, the court will chastise you for failing to file a motion *in limine* seeking to exclude the testimony. And sometimes, the court will refuse to pre-emptively rule before opposing counsel has asked the specific question. But sometimes, making a pre-emptive objection can (a) solicit a promise or agreement from opposing counsel regarding the line of questioning; (b) dissuade opposing counsel from asking the questions; (c) bird-dog plaintiff's intention to ask those questions *and* the code article or argument on which plaintiff intends to rely; and (d) cause the court to pre-emptively rule on the issue. Here is how a pre-emptive objection might redefine the scope of an examination.

D. Atty: Your Honor, before the jury is brought back into the courtroom, I would like to put something on the record.

Court: Go ahead.

D. Atty: Plaintiff's next witness is John Doe, who has been plaintiff's best friend for many years. Mr. Doe is not a medical doctor. Mr. Doe is an accountant. But, during his deposition, Mr. Doe offered a number of medical opinions based on his personal medical history. If plaintiff's counsel intends to solicit any medical opinions from Mr. Doe, I would respectfully request that we address those questions now, outside the presence of the jury.

Court: Counsel, are you going to solicit medical opinions from Mr. Doe?

P. Atty: No, not medical opinions, but Article 701 permits opinion testimony by a lay witness. Mr. Doe has suffered two herniated discs in his lifetime, and he personally observed the way plaintiff was getting up from the table and walking. I intend to ask Mr. Doe, based on his personal perception, whether the plaintiff was moving around like he had a herniated disc.

D. Atty: That is a medical opinion, and we object to that line of questioning.

Court: I agree. That is not how Article 701 works. I am going to sustain the objection. Don't go there, counsel.

When the court has issued a favorable ruling limiting the testimony of a witness, it can be a good practice to pre-emptively request that opposing counsel or the court remind the witness of the ruling prior to the start of direct examination, especially if months or years have passed since the court's ruling.

P. Atty: Your Honor, before the jury is brought back into the courtroom, it is my understanding that defendant's next witness is Dr. Stretch, a local neurosurgeon. I have a copy of the court's ruling last month, in which the court ruled that Dr. Stretch is not allowed to offer an opinion on the speed of the vehicles or the angle of impact. In an abundance of caution, I want to confirm that the witness is aware of the court's ruling.

Court: Is Dr. Stretch in the courtroom?

D. Atty: Yes, Your Honor. He is seated in the first row, and he is aware of the ruling.

Court: He is nodding "yes." Good enough. Bring in the jury.

Of course, the court's willingness to entertain pre-emptive objections and conversations should always dictate whether an attorney makes pre-emptive objections and conversations. Some judges do not like to keep the jury waiting and will not welcome your attempt to resolve or avoid problems during direct examination. Read the room.

7. Make "Continuing" Objections Rather Than Repeated Objections

The primary purpose for objecting is to obtain a favorable ruling from the court that results in the exclusion of impermissible questions and inadmissible evidence. The secondary purpose for objecting is to obtain an unfavorable ruling from the court that preserves a claim of error for appeal.

After the court overrules a trial objection to physical or testimonial evidence, an attorney is not required to renew or repeat the same objection. Pursuant to Federal Rule of Evidence 103(b), "once the court rules definitively on the record—either before or at trial—a party need not renew an objection or offer of proof to preserve a claim of error for appeal." At least in theory, when the court denies a hearsay objection to a plaintiff repeating what an unknown bystander said, counsel is not required to repeat the objection after every question regarding that conversation.

That is why an attorney should not repeat the same objection and require the court to repeat the same unfavorable ruling, especially when the court requires counsel to approach the bench to discuss every objection. Neither the jury nor the court appreciates an attorney's repeatedly interrupting the flow of trial.

But a word of warning. Federal Rule of Evidence 103(b) requires the court to "definitively" rule on the record to preserve a claim of error for appeal, and no attorney wants to bear the burden of proving that the court's ruling on opposing counsel's first question was a "definitive" ruling on opposing counsel's fifth question.

Consider making a "continuing objection" to clarify that the court's ruling shall apply to subsequent questions. By making a continuing objection, an attorney can (a) take an additional step to preserve a claim of error for appeal; (b) avoid annoying the court and the jury by making repeated objections; (c) avoid giving jurors the impression that they are not objecting because they have "given up"; and (d) encourage jurors to "continue" thinking about the basis for your objection to the line of questioning. For example, when the court denies a "speculation" objection and permits the witness to speculate regarding the defendant's intentions, making a continuing objection can remind jurors that the *entire* line of questioning calls for speculation.

Always limit a continuing objection to a specific line of questioning. By making a "continuing objection *to this line of questioning*," an attorney can reserve the right to stand and make the same objection to the *next* line of questioning. Otherwise, there is a chance that jurors may not recognize the start of a new line of questioning and may not understand why the same attorney may need to make a hearsay objection only two questions later. By making a "continuing objection *to this line of questioning*," the jury will presume that a subsequent hearsay objection is being made in response to a different line of questioning.

Remember that the court must grant an attorney leave to lodge a continuing objection. Never declare that you are making a continuing objection (i.e., "In that case, make our objection a continuing objection, Your Honor"). Always ask the court for permission to make a continuing objection (i.e., "Your Honor, instead of repeatedly interrupting opposing counsel's examination, may we make our objection a continuing objection to this line of questioning?").

Remember that continuing objections can be waived. When the trial court grants a continuing objection regarding a particular class of evidence, an attorney is expected to remain silent during the subsequent admission of that class of evidence. For example, if the court grants a criminal defense attorney's continuing objection to evidence seized pursuant to a search warrant, that attorney could waive that continuing objection by saying "no objection" to *any* item seized pursuant to the warrant. Be consistent.

The bottom line is that continuing objections require vigilance. After making a continuing objection, an attorney must listen carefully to every question and answer. In a fraction of a second, an attorney must decide whether the impermissible question or inadmissible evidence (a) relates to a *different* class of physical or testimonial evidence or (b) requires a *different* evidentiary objection than the evidentiary objection the court made continuing.

8. Make Compound Objections, Not Consecutive Objections

Trial courts are granted the discretion to separately consider and separately rule on each articulated basis for an objection. Asking a compound question is always objectionable but making a compound objection is always appropriate and often necessary.

Compound objections require a slightly different approach. When there is more than one basis for objecting, an attorney should (a) start by providing the court with every applicable tag (i.e., "Objection. Hearsay. Hearsay-within-Hearsay. And calls for an expert opinion."); (b) explain the first stated ground for objecting (i.e., "First, the document itself is hearsay"); (c) explain the second stated ground for objecting (i.e., "Second, in the document, the author repeats what he heard a neighbor say, which constitutes hearsay-within-hearsay"); and (d) explain the third ground for objecting (i.e., "Third, the neighbor is not qualified to offer the medical opinions she shared with the author of the document").

Avoid making piecemeal objections. When an attorney recognizes two separate and distinct bases for objecting, that attorney should not wait for the court to overrule the first objection before making the second objection (i.e., "Wait. I have another objection, Your Honor!"). Some judges may incorrectly assume that attorneys will lead with their best objection. By waiting, an attorney can unintentionally give those judges (with that preconception) the impression that the second objection has less merit than the first. Otherwise, the attorney would have led with that objection. By waiting, an attorney can also give jurors the impression that he or she "just thought of another objection," which suggests the second objection is either "a reach" or the attorney initially failed to recognize the basis for the second objection.

9. Find Out How the Court Wants to Handle Objections

The proper method for objecting in a particular courtroom will always depend on the preference of the particular judge. Always ask the judge *before* the trial starts to explain how the court prefers to handle objections during direct examination and cross-examination. Here are three different ways a court can handle objections during a jury trial.

a. Object and Approach

The objecting attorney is only permitted to stand and say "objection." Nothing more. The court will then ask counsel to approach the bench, and the objection will be argued outside the presence/hearing of the jury (either on the record or off the record).

b. State the Tag and Wait for Further Instructions

The objecting attorney is permitted to object and identify the basis for the objection (i.e., "Objection. Hearsay."). The court will then decide whether to overrule the objection, solicit a response from opposing counsel ("Response, counselor?"), or ask counsel to approach the bench. When the court prefers this approach, do not expand on your objection. If the court wants you to explain your objection, the court will let you know.

c. Old School

Everything is said and done in open court (in front of the jury) unless an attorney asks to approach the bench.

Never assume that bench conferences will be on the record. If the court prefers to discuss objections at the bench (or in chambers), ask the court (a) whether those bench conferences will be recorded and (b) how those bench conferences will be recorded. Some courtrooms may be wired to record all bench conferences. Other courtrooms may require the court reporter to pick up the stenograph and join counsel where the objection is being heard.

10. Focus on the Purpose for Objecting, Not the Basis

Most lawyers decide on a strategy for voir dire, opening statement, cross-examining key witnesses, and closing argument. Few lawyers decide on a strategy for trial objections, but a strategy is exactly what an attorney needs in that fraction of a second before the witness answers. Adopting the right strategy can help an attorney answer the question "Should I object?"

The secret is to focus on the *purpose* for objecting, rather than focus on the *basis* for objecting. Lawyers have no obligation to object to every leading question and no obligation to object whenever a question solicits "non-relevant" testimony. Knowing whether you *can* object is less important than knowing whether you *should* object. Every trial lawyer should decide for themselves which of the following purposes justify interrupting the trial with an objection.

a. Objecting to Inadmissible and Prejudicial Evidence

Trial lawyers have a duty to object to physical evidence the jury should never see and testimonial evidence the jury should never hear. But today, the vast majority of evidentiary objections are made and ruled on *before* the trial starts.

In civil cases, courts have eliminated the need for many substantive trial objections by (a) requiring the listing and exchange of exhibits well in advance of trial, which allows the parties time to discuss, object, and file motions seeking the exclusion or redaction of trial exhibits; (b) requiring the parties to file motions seeking the exclusion of expert witnesses or expert testimony well in advance of trial, which allows the parties time to brief and orally argue objections to an expert's qualifications, methodology, and opinions; and (c) permitting written discovery and depositions, which allow the parties time to determine what witnesses will say at trial and file motions to exclude impermissible lay testimony.

Similarly, in criminal cases, courts have eliminated the need for many substantive trial objections by (a) requiring the listing and exchange of exhibits in advance of trial; (b) permitting pretrial hearings (absent indictment) to review the evidentiary basis or "probable cause" for an arrest; (c) permitting written discovery, albeit far more limited than civil discovery; and (d) permitting *Daubert* hearings regarding an expert's qualifications and methodology.

Even when a court rules on "big ticket" evidentiary objections before trial, attorneys need to be vigilant throughout the trial. When an attorney tries to solicit evidence that is inadmissible and prejudicial, it is time to object. When a witness volunteers inadmissible and prejudicial testimony, it is time to object.

b. Objecting to Stop Opposing Counsel's Coaching

People who are telling the truth have no need for coaching or leading questions. Only actors who forget their lines need prompting. That is why it can be important to call the jury's attention to attempts by opposing counsel to "coach" the witness. By pointing out that opposing counsel is coaching the witness, an attorney can call into question the witness's credibility and independence. After all, when a witness needs coaching, that witness could be acting, and the lawyer could be holding the script.

Three objections constitute the "Holy Trinity" of anti-coaching objections: (1) leading; (2) assumes facts not in evidence; and (3) asked and answered. These three objections reveal or highlight coaching in three different ways.

Making a "leading" objection is the most obvious and common way to stop coaching. Leading questions suggest an answer and lawyers who ask leading questions sometimes need to suggest an answer. Resist the temptation to object to leading questions when the facts being solicited are undisputed. Coaching doesn't bother the jury when the facts being solicited concern immaterial or background information (i.e., "You were born and raised right here in New Orleans, is that right?"). But when opposing counsel asks a leading question regarding a material fact (i.e., "So, you reasonably believed that you were in imminent danger of receiving great bodily harm?"), an attorney should help the jury see opposing counsel's fingerprints on the witness's answer.

Making an "assumes facts not in evidence" objection can also be an effective way to stop coaching, but its effectiveness almost entirely depends on opposing counsel's reaction and response. Savvy attorneys will immediately agree, thank counsel, withdraw the question, and calmly start a new line of questioning that eventually introduces the (assumed) fact into evidence *before* returning to the original question. Less patient and less experienced lawyers will immediately ask a single question that solicits a *verbatim* response regarding the fact. When that happens, the jury may focus on the repetition instead of on the fact being repeated.

Here is an example of how objections can shift the jury's focus from the significance of the testimony to the attorney and suggest coaching.

D. Atty: Where were you when the accident happened?

Witness: I was headed westbound. I was approaching the intersection, about four car lengths from the intersection.

D. Atty: With your clear and unobstructed view of the traffic light, please tell us, what color was the light when plaintiff's vehicle entered the intersection?

P. Atty: **Objection. Assumes facts not in evidence. Counsel has not established that the witness had a clear and unobstructed view of the traffic light.**

Court: Sustained.

D. Atty: Did you have a clear and unobstructed view of the traffic light?

P. Atty: Objection. Leading.

Court: Sustained.

D. Atty: What was your view?

Witness: Clear and unobstructed.

Be warned. Making an "assumes facts not in evidence" objection can backfire when a more experienced litigator responds to the objection by thanking counsel for the reminder and changing course with a line of questioning that solicits *facts* instead of agreement.

D. Atty: Where were you when the accident happened?

Witness: I was headed westbound. I was approaching the intersection, about four car lengths from the intersection.

D. Atty: With your clear and unobstructed view of the traffic light, please tell us, what color was the light when plaintiff's minivan entered the intersection?

P. Atty: **Objection. Assumes facts not in evidence. Counsel has not established that the witness had a clear and unobstructed view of the traffic light.**

D. Atty: That's true. I haven't. I withdraw the question. Do you wear glasses?

Witness: Yes.

D. Atty: What kind of glasses?

Witness: I am near-sighted, so I need glasses to see far away.

D. Atty: As your car was approaching the intersection, were you wearing your distance glasses?

Witness: Yes.

D. Atty: Were any trucks in your lane between the front of your car and the light?

Witness: No.

D. Atty: Were any cars or vehicles in your lane between the front of your car and the light?

Witness: No.

D. Atty: Were there any other vehicles on your road near the intersection?

Witness: No.

D. Atty: Were any tree branches hanging out over the intersection?

Witness: No.

D. Atty: Were there any trees near the intersection?

Witness: No.

D. Atty: Were you driving into a sunset?

Witness: No. It was noon.

D. Atty: Were there any office buildings at the intersection?

Witness: No.

D. Atty: Was there any glare from any source?

Witness: No.

D. Atty: Did anything **obstruct** your view of the light?

Witness: No. Nothing.

D. Atty: What was the weather like at the time of the accident?

Witness: It was sunny and **clear**.

D. Atty: How would you describe your view?

Witness: I could see everything. Plain as I'm seeing you right now.

D. Atty: With your [clear and unobstructed] view of the traffic light, what was the color of that light when plaintiff's minivan entered the intersection?

As the above example demonstrates, an "assumes facts not in evidence" objection can backfire when opposing counsel recognizes it as an opportunity to agree, apologize, and ask a series of questions that conclusively establish the "assumed" fact. By the time opposing counsel repeats the original question, the attorney may regret the objection, having succeeded only in calling attention to the "assumed" fact (i.e., the witness had a "clear and unobstructed view") instead of calling attention to any coaching.

Making an "asked and answered" objection can also stop coaching. When a lawyer wants a specific sound bite from the witness, the lawyer will try to solicit that sound bite even if the witness has already answered the question. For example, when a witness testifies that the defendant looked "angry," a lawyer might try to solicit a better sound bite (i.e., "Did the defendant look enraged?" or "Would you go so far as to say that the defendant looked furious?"). By objecting on the grounds that question has been asked and answered, you can reveal that the attorney is *trying* to solicit a different answer.

c. Objecting to Interrupt Momentum

Like a talented interviewer, a lawyer can help a witness tell their story during direct examination. By asking the right questions in precisely the right order, a lawyer can provide exposition, capture the jury's imagination, paint a scene, solicit sympathy, and build tension or suspense. It is unmistakable when a witness or a story hijacks your jury. The courtroom falls silent between questions, and the jurors become unnaturally still, hanging on every word.

A well-timed objection (that has merit) can break the spell by interrupting opposing counsel's line of thinking, rhythm, and momentum. When the court sustains the objection, opposing counsel must regroup while jurors shift in their chairs, check their watches, and glance around the room as if awakening from a trance. And even if the court overrules the objection, the moment is lost. Like an orchestra interrupted in the middle of Beethoven's Ninth Hallelujah Chorus, the lawyer must decide whether to start from the beginning of the line of questioning (and risk "asked and answered" objections) or awkwardly start with the last note.

Be warned. Jurors have more courtroom savvy than at any other time in history. Never make a meritless objection to interrupt emotional or moving testimony. When a well-timed objection is sustained, most jurors will forgive an attorney for interrupting opposing counsel's questioning of a tearful witness. But when a well-timed objection is overruled, jurors will recognize that the *real* purpose for the objection was to interrupt opposing counsel and the witness.

One meritless objection during emotional testimony can change the way those jurors perceive an attorney. That one meritless objection can also change the way those jurors listen to an attorney's subsequent arguments. Sometimes, it would be better to (sincerely and sympathetically) hand opposing counsel a box of tissues—which opposing counsel can then hand their witness—rather than make a meritless objection during emotional testimony. When in doubt, be decent not diabolical.

d. Objecting to Steal Opposing Counsel's Thunder

Most lines of questioning for direct examination and cross-examination are designed to build to a climax, whether that climax is a single fact, observation, admission, or opinion. If the court requires counsel to object and respond in the presence of the jury, there may be an opportunity to steal opposing counsel's thunder.

When an attorney recognizes where opposing counsel is headed with a particular line of questioning *before* the court and *before* the jury, a properly-timed "relevance" objection can prompt (a) opposing counsel to voluntarily disclose the end game (i.e., "This line of questioning is relevant because I intend to . . .") or (b) the court to demand that opposing counsel disclose their endgame (i.e. "Counsel, where are you going with this?"). Thus, even when the "relevance" objection is overruled, it can sometimes succeed in spoiling the surprise for the jury.

Some trial attorneys will default to promising the court that a line of questioning is relevant and asking the court for "latitude." But that tends to work better in movies, where an actor can't explain the relevance at the bench without ruining the surprise for the movie audience. That is why movie judges routinely overrule relevance objections based solely on the actor's assurance that the questioning is relevant. For example, in the movie *Legally Blonde*, Elle Woods does *not* respond to a relevance objection by asking to approach the bench. Instead of explaining the relevance of the Beta Delta Pi wet T-shirt contest where Tracy Marcinko was "completely hosed down from head to toe," Elle Woods assures the court that, "I have a point. I promise."

Similarly, in *A Few Good Men*, Lt. Danny Kaffee does *not* respond to a relevance objection by asking to approach the bench. Instead of explaining the relevance of asking Colonel Nathan Jessup whether he wore his dress uniform on the plane, Lt. Kaffee confidently responds, "I'm asking the court for a little latitude."

Of course, when the court permits bench conferences during the trial, a litigator can easily avoid the relevance trap. During a real trial, there is no need to respond to a relevance objection in open court, thereby warning the witness and ruining the surprise for the jury. Instead, the attorney who is conducting the examination need only ask to approach the bench (i.e., "May I disclose the relevance at the bench, Your Honor?"). By disclosing the relevance of a question or a line of questioning at the bench, an attorney can avoid "tipping off" a witness during cross-examination or prematurely making the "big reveal" during direct examination.

Be warned. Relevance objections can also backfire. Sometimes, relevance objections can be a gift to opposing counsel, and opposing counsel will jump at the chance to respond in the presence of the jury. When the relevance of the line of questioning is easily articulated, a "relevance" objection can be an opportunity to associate the line of questioning with a specific legal element or factual issue (i.e., "This line of questioning is relevant to the issue of notice, Your Honor"). When there is *any* chance that the jury may not understand the importance of the line of questioning, a relevance objection can be an invitation to give a closing argument (Your Honor, Plaintiff bears the burden of proving that the defendant had notice of the defect, and the jury has a right to know whether . . .").

e. Objecting to Rattle and Force Counsel to Go "Off-Script"

Some batters cannot hit curve balls, and some attorneys cannot handle certain objections. The same attorney who painstakingly typed open-ended questions and memorized responses to potential hearsay objections may have no earthly idea how to respond when opposing counsel objects to his last question ("What happened next?") because it "calls for a narrative."

The more brilliant the attorney, the longer they may stand there. "What code of evidence article prohibits questions that solicit a narrative?" they may wonder. "Don't most non-leading questions involve narration?" they might ask themselves. Neither question will help them formulate a persuasive and concise response to an unexpected "calls for a narrative" objection. Sometimes, to avoid responding to the curveball objection, counsel may volunteer to ask a different question. And, just like that, an attorney can rattle opposing counsel and force opposing counsel to go off-script.

To be clear, no attorney should make meritless objections to rattle opposing counsel or force opposing counsel to go off-script. But during the course of a long trial, there may be times when an attorney can legitimately make a relevance objection, a leading objection, or a calls for narrative objection. When deciding *whether* to make that objection, an attorney should at least consider the effect that objection may have on opposing counsel. Wink. Wink. Nudge. Nudge.

f. Objecting and Immediately Withdrawing the Objection to Wake the Jury

Objections can serve other purposes. When opposing counsel's examination is putting jurors to sleep, an attorney may want to do *something* to call the jury's attention to the question being asked. On those occasions, an attorney may not want to request a recess because that recess may give opposing counsel a chance to regroup or withdraw the important question. On those occasions, an attorney may not want to slam a book down on the table ("I'm sorry, Your Honor") or spill their water ("Oh no!") because the jury may still be looking at the book or thinking about the clumsy attorney while the important question is being answered. Instead, when the question is objectionable, an attorney may choose to stand and say "objection!" if only to wake the jury.

The problem with objecting for the purpose of waking the jury is that a sustained objection may cause the attorney to withdraw the question or shift to a new line of questioning. On those occasions, when an attorney *wants* to wake the jury and *wants* the jury to hear the answer to the question being asked, an attorney could say "objection!," stand up, reconsider, smile, and *immediately* withdraw the objection.

In theory, an attorney could also explain the reason for withdrawing the objection (i.e., "Objection. Wait. No, I want to hear this answer. Withdrawn."). Of course, adding that "I want to hear this answer" could suggest that the answer will be favorable to the client and could draw an objection from opposing counsel (i.e., "Objection. Counsel testifying!"). But that objection may also be welcomed because it would further rouse the jury and call more attention to the question.

To be clear, no attorney should make a meritless objection and immediately withdraw that objection solely to wake the jurors, even if the jurors desperately need to hear the next answer. But during the course of a long trial, there may be times when an attorney can legitimately make a relevance, leading, lack of foundation, or calls for narrative objection. When deciding *whether* to make one of those objections, an attorney should at least consider the effect that objecting and withdrawing that objection may have on the (sleeping) jurors. Wink. Wink. Nudge. Nudge.

g. Objecting to Opposing Counsel's Final Question

Sometimes, attorneys will intentionally broadcast that they are asking their final question by telling the witness "I have one more question." Other times, attorneys will unintentionally telegraph that they are asking their final question by starting that question with "in conclusion," or "to sum up," or "are you *absolutely* certain." Whenever opposing counsel reveals that they are asking their last question on direct examination or cross-examination, an attorney should listen carefully and strongly consider making an objection (that has merit).

Attorneys do not always save the best for last. Not every attorney prepares the perfect "Alamo" line of questioning to end an examination. Sometimes, the last question of a direct examination or a cross-examination is an attempt to get the witness to:

- Repeat an important fact (i.e., "One last question. Are you certain you saw the defendant . . ."), which can be susceptible to an "asked and answered" objection.
- Summarize the witness's testimony (i.e., "So, you never entered the grocery store, and you did not see the plaintiff slip and fall"), which can be susceptible to a "compound" objection and/or an "asked and answered" objection.
- Confirm what the witness meant (i.e., "So, your testimony is that the defendant did not have time to . . ."), which can be susceptible to a "leading" objection.
- Emphasize the legal effect of the witness's testimony (i.e., "So, in summary, your testimony is that the defendant was driving negligently"), which can be susceptible to a "leading" objection and/or a "calls for an expert opinion" objection.

Some jurors will only remember the beginning and end of an examination. When an attorney can legitimately object to the final question of an examination, an attorney should strongly consider making that objection. Nothing is better than having the court sustain an objection to opposing counsel's last question and watching opposing counsel sit down. Instead of ending the examination with a bang, help opposing counsel end their examination with a whimper.

11. Create and Use a "Common Objection" Cheat Sheet

There are three different types of objections: (a) substantive objections; (b) form objections; and (c) procedure objections. Entire law school classes and volumes of law books are dedicated to the law of evidence. What trial attorneys really need are good cheat sheets for the most common objections.

Cheat sheets can be specific to venue. A trial attorney in Louisiana could have a cheat sheet for Louisiana state courts, which cites the Louisiana Code of Evidence and the corresponding case law interpreting those articles, and a separate cheat sheet for Louisiana federal courts, which cites the Federal Rules of Evidence and the corresponding federal case law interpreting those rules.

Cheat sheets can be specific to criminal trials and tailored to the prosecution or the criminal defense. For example, a "Common Objections" cheat sheet for criminal defense attorneys could include everything from discussing anonymous phone calls to commenting on a defendant's failure to testify at trial.

Tables 7.2 through 7.6 are examples of generic cheat sheets that I have assembled and used during Louisiana federal court trials. They are solely intended to save our team from having to grab the Federal Rules of Evidence and flip through the pages looking for a specific article. Hopefully, these cheat sheets will provide you with a good starting point or template for your own. They are available for download at ambar.org/TrialAdvocacy.

Table 7.2 Common Objections (Federal Rules of Evidence)

1.	**Leading** Question suggests an answer. Does not apply to cross-exam or hostile witness.	611(c)
2.	**Vague and Ambiguous** The question is confusing and does not solicit a precise response.	611(a), 103(d)
3.	**Compound Question** Counsel is soliciting one response to two separate questions.	611(a), 103(d)
4.	**Calls for a Narrative** Answers must be given in response to questions to provide a chance to object.	611(a), 103(d)
5.	**Assumes Facts Not in Evidence** Question assumes a fact not established by physical or testimonial evidence.	611(a), 103(d)
6.	**Asked and Answered** Court may exercise reasonable control over questioning to avoid wasting time.	611(a)(2)
7.	**Counsel Testifying** Counsel is making a statement instead of asking a question.	611(a)(3)
8.	**Argumentative** Counsel is arguing, badgering, or becoming aggressive with the witness.	611(a)(3)
9.	**Relevance** The answer will not make a disputed material fact more or less probable.	401, 402
10.	**More Prejudicial Than Probative ("403 Objection")** Any probative value is outweighed by the danger of unfair prejudice, confusion of the issues, misleading the jury, undue delay, or waste of time.	403
11.	**Lack of Foundation** Failed to establish authenticity and admissibility (reliability and relevance) before introducing physical evidence or soliciting testimonial evidence.	601-602, 701-705, Art IX-X
12.	**Best Evidence Rule** Where the contents of a written document, recording, or photograph are being proved, an original must be offered absent a statutory exception.	1002

13.	**Speculation/Lack of Personal Knowledge** A witness may not testify to a matter unless evidence is introduced sufficient to support a finding that he or she has a personal knowledge of the matter.	602
14.	**Improper Lay Witness Opinion** Limited to opinions "rationally based on the witness's perceptions," "helpful to a clearly understanding the witness's testimony or to determining a fact in issue," and not based on scientific, technical, or specialized knowledge.	701
15.	**Calls for an Expert Opinion** Lacks requisite knowledge, skill, experience, training, or education.	702
16.	**Beyond the Scope of Expertise** The question requires the expert to be tendered in another field of expertise.	703
17.	**Opinion on Ultimate Issue (Criminal Trials Only)** Testimony in the form of an opinion . . . is *not* to be excluded solely because it embraces an ultimate issue . . . However, in a criminal case, an expert shall not express an opinion as to the guilt or innocence of the accused.	704
18.	**Beyond Scope of Direct/Cross-Examination** "A witness . . . is subject to redirect examination as to matters covered on cross-examination and, in the discretion of the court, as to other matters . . ."	611(b)

Table 7.3 Definition of Hearsay

"Hearsay is a **statement** other than one made by the declarant while testifying at the present trial or hearing, offered in evidence to prove the truth of the matter asserted."	801(C)
"Statement" is defined as "an oral or written assertion" or "nonverbal conduct of a person, if it is intended by him as an assertion."	801(A)

Table 7.4 Hearsay Exceptions (Availability Immaterial)

1.	**Present Sense Impression** "A statement describing or explaining an event or condition made while the declarant was perceiving the event or condition, or immediately thereafter."	803.1
2.	**Excited Utterance** "A statement relating to a startling event or condition made while the declarant was under the stress of excitement caused by the event or condition."	803.2
3.	**Existing Mental, Emotional, or Physical Conditions** "A statement of the declarant's then existing state of mind, emotion, sensation, or physical condition (such as intent, plan, motive, design, mental feeling, pain, and bodily health)" offered to prove then existing condition or future action.	803.3

4.	**Statements for Purposes of Medical Treatment and Medical Diagnosis**	803.4
5.	**Recorded Recollection**	803.5
6.	**Records of Regularly Conducted Business Activity**	803.6
7.	**Public Records and Reports**	803.8
8.	**Learned Treatises**	803.18
9.	**Reputation as to Character**	803.21

Table 7.5 Hearsay Exceptions (Declarant Not Available)

1.	**Former Testimony**	804.1
2.	**Statement Under Belief of Impending Death**	804.2
3.	**Statement Against Interest**	804.3

Table 7.6 "Non-Hearsay"

1.	**Admission by Party Opponent** Includes own statements, adopted statements, and authorized statements	801(D)(2) 801(D)(3)(a)
2.	**Prior Inconsistent Statements (Criminal Trials Only)** Only admissible after cross-exam attorney "fairly" directs the witness's attention to the statement and gives "an opportunity to admit the fact," and only when there is "additional evidence to corroborate the matter asserted."	801(D)(1)(a)
3.	**Prior Consistent Statement** Only when offered to rebut an express or implied charge of recent fabrication or improper influence or motive.	801(D)(1)(b)
4.	**Statement of Identification** Only when made after perceiving the person.	801(D)(3)

12. Choose the Right Strategy for Nonresponsive Objections

My understanding of nonresponsive objections has dramatically changed over the years. Straight out of law school, I thought: (1) the sole purpose for making a nonresponsive objection was to "keep the witness in line" during cross-examination; (2) the examining attorney should *always* object to nonresponsive answers during cross-examination; (3) non-examining attorneys had the same right to object to the responsiveness of an answer, especially when that answer is inadmissible and prejudicial;

and (4) the court was required to strike nonresponsive testimony. Today, I know that I was wrong on all four counts. My mistake was in thinking of nonresponsive objections as a request that the court *do* something about an evasive witness. In reality, nonresponsive objections are a request that the court *permit* an evidentiary objection by the examining attorney.

Nonresponsive objections are about the questioning attorney's *right* to object. When an attorney asks a question, that attorney has no right *whatsoever* to object to a responsive answer, even if that answer is inadmissible and prejudicial. If you open the door (even unwittingly) by asking a question that calls for inadmissible and prejudicial testimony, you have nobody to blame but yourself. No matter how ugly and prejudicial the responsive answer may be, you opened the door. As long as the answer that walked through the door was responsive, that ugly answer is *your* guest. No point in asking the court to kick him out. He's not going anywhere.

The bottom line is that an examining attorney's right to make an evidentiary objection depends *solely* on the responsiveness of the answer. No matter how many rules of evidence that answer may violate. No matter how prejudicial that answer may be. That is why it is so important to ask leading questions on cross-examination. That is why it is so important to know the answer before asking the question. Choices have consequences. And when a trial attorney chooses to ask an open-ended question *without* knowing the answer, that choice can have terrible consequences for that attorney's client.

Consider the cross-examination example of a criminal defense attorney who asks the arresting officer, "Why did you chase the defendant instead of the other suspects?" By choosing to ask that open-ended question, the defense attorney has opened the door for *any* responsive answer. If the officer truthfully responds, "Because I had previously arrested the defendant for selling cocaine on that same corner," the court may overrule the defense attorney's objection and deny the motion for mistrial, even though that answer constituted "evidence of other crimes."

In theory, the sole purpose for making a nonresponsive objection is to solicit a ruling from the court on whether the answer was responsive, and that ruling only affects the questioning attorney's right to object to the answer. Only the examining attorney is barred from objecting to responsive answers. Only the examining attorney needs to convince the court that they "didn't open the door with that last question." The non-examining attorney has no need to object to the responsiveness of the answer because he never lost the right to make an evidentiary objection.

That is why some courts only allow the examining attorney to make nonresponsive objections. In effect, those courts have taken the position that an examining attorney is not entitled to make evidentiary objections for *responsive* answers. In those courts, an examining attorney must make a nonresponsive objection, and the court must sustain that nonresponsive objection *before* the court will consider the examining attorney's evidentiary objection to the answer. Consider how those courts would handle the following objections:

D. Atty: On direct examination, you testified that you received an anonymous call. What did that anonymous caller tell you?

Officer: The anonymous caller told me that your client, Jon Smith, was selling drugs on the corner of Magazine and Julia.

D. Atty: Objection. Hearsay.

Court: Overruled. You asked the question, and the answer was responsive.

* * *

D. Atty: What time did you arrive at the corner of Magazine and Julia?

Officer: Well, I left the station at 0300 hours after an anonymous caller told me Jon Smith was selling drugs on the corner of Magazine and Julia.

D. Atty: Objection. Nonresponsive. Hearsay.

Court: Sustained. The answer was nonresponsive, and it constitutes hearsay.

D. Atty: Defense moves for a mistrial.

In practice, attorneys more commonly make nonresponsive objections to call the judge's and jury's attention to a difficult or evasive witness. Attorneys rarely provide more than the Tag (i.e., "Objection. Nonresponsive.") because the basis for a nonresponsive objection is self-evident. But the following three Federal Rules of Evidence arguably give trial courts the authority to interrupt, stop, and deter nonresponsive answers, regardless of who asked the question and whether or not the answer is relevant and otherwise admissible:

- Pursuant to Rule 102, the rules of evidence should be construed so as to administer every proceeding fairly and eliminate unjustifiable expense and delay "to the end of ascertaining the truth and securing a just determination." Nonresponsive objections can require the striking of testimony, curative instructions, and mistrials.

- Pursuant to Rule 103(d), "to the extent practicable, the court must conduct a jury trial so that inadmissible evidence is not suggested to the jury by any means." By sustaining nonresponsive objections, the court can deter future (inadmissible) nonresponsive answers.
- Pursuant to Rule 611(a)(2), the court should exercise reasonable control over the mode of examining witnesses and presenting evidence so as to "make those procedures effective for determining the truth" and "avoid wasting time." Every nonresponsive objection (especially those that solicit an objection) wastes the jury's time. And a single nonresponsive objection can result in a mistrial.

In short, the rules of evidence give the court the discretion to run the trial in a way that reduces the risk of introducing inadmissible and prejudicial testimony. Sustaining a nonresponsive objection and instructing the witness to "answer only the question asked" can be a means to that end.

That is why some courts allow the examining attorney *and* the non-examining attorney to make nonresponsive objections. In effect, those courts treat the nonresponsiveness of the answer as a separate and distinct basis for objecting to the answer. Even if the answer is relevant and reliable, and even if the answer is otherwise admissible, those courts will sometimes sustain a nonresponsive objection and (correctly or incorrectly) strike nonresponsive testimony.

Before the trial starts, every trial attorney should decide how they are going to handle nonresponsive answers depending on (a) who asked the question that solicited the nonresponsive answer and (b) whether the answer is relevant, admissible, and prejudicial. More specifically, every attorney should consider the following trial situations and fill out (for themselves) the chart in Table 7.7, which reflects one approach to handling nonresponsive answers.

a. During Direct Examination, Limit Nonresponsive Objections to Prejudicial Answers by Hostile or Independent Witnesses

There is no appropriate time for the examining attorney to make a nonresponsive objection in response to an answer given by a witness who that attorney called and prepped. During your direct examination of your client, your client's family/friends, or your expert, do not object to a nonresponsive answer, even if that nonresponsive answer is inadmissible

Table 7.7 Objecting to Nonresponsive Answers

Type of Nonresponsive Answer	During YOUR Direct Examination (Independent Witness)	During YOUR Cross-Examination	During THEIR Direct Examination or Cross-Examination
Not Relevant Not Prejudicial	Ignore	Ignore	Ignore
Not Relevant Prejudicial	Nonresponsive Objection + Relevance Objection + 403 Objection	Nonresponsive Objection + Relevance Objection + 403 Objection	Relevance Objection +403 Objection†
Relevant Not Admissible Not Prejudicial	Ignore	Ignore	Ignore or Evidentiary Objection†
Relevant Not Admissible Prejudicial	Nonresponsive Objection +Evidentiary Objection	Nonresponsive Objection +Evidentiary Objection	Evidentiary Objection†

†Note: When the court permits the non-examining attorney to objection to the responsiveness of the answer, consider adding a nonresponsive objection either to make the witness look bad or to explain to the jury why you didn't object to the question (which they may have missed or forgotten).

and prejudicial. You chose to put that family member or friend on the stand. You hired that expert. You are the sole reason why the jury is hearing from the witness, and you asked the question. Even if the answer is prejudicial to your client's case, you should not make a nonresponsive objection and move to strike the testimony. The judge will likely overrule your objection (i.e., "Overruled. You asked the question, and it is your witness.") and the jury will never understand your complaint. This rule is not negotiable. If you have a problem with the rule, do a better job of preparing your witness.

There are times when attorneys can and should make a nonresponsive objection to an answer given by an independent witness. During the direct examination of an independent witness (i.e., police officer, eyewitness, prior employer, ER doctor) or a hostile witness, the examining attorney has more latitude because the judge and jury know that the attorney has no control over the independent witness and had no opportunity to prepare or practice with the witness. Limit your nonresponsive objections to only prejudicial answers by these hostile or independent witnesses.

Prejudice should be the litmus test for making a nonresponsive objection during your direct examination of an independent witness. When a direct examination question to an independent witness solicits a nonresponsive answer that is relevant but inadmissible and prejudicial, make a compound objection that includes the evidentiary objection (i.e., "Objection. Nonresponsive. Hearsay."). When a direct examination question to an independent witness solicits a nonresponsive and prejudicial answer that also lacks relevance, make a compound objection that includes a relevance objection and a Rule 403 objection (i.e., "Objection. Nonresponsive. Relevance. More prejudicial than probative.").

For example, consider the following situation in which a plaintiff attorney calls the investigating police officer to the stand, asks a very specific factual question during direct examination, and receives a nonresponsive, inadmissible, and prejudicial answer:

P. Atty: What time did you arrive at the scene?

Officer: I arrived at 0300 hours.

P. Atty: Did you inspect the scene of the accident for skid marks?

Officer: Yes, sir. The defendant's vehicle left skid marks.

P. Atty: Did you measure the skid marks?

Officer: Yes, sir.

P. Atty: What was the length of the skid marks?

Officer: So, some guy on the corner told me that plaintiff hit his brakes for no reason back here by the telephone pole.

P. Atty: **Objection. Nonresponsive. Hearsay.**

Court: Response, counselor?

D. Atty: He asked the question, Your Honor.

Court: I disagree. He asked for the length of the skid marks. He didn't ask for anything else. The objection is sustained.

P. Atty: I move to strike that answer.

Court: Granted.

P. Atty: Let me repeat my question. What was the length of the skid marks?

Officer: I measured six feet of skid marks.

b. During Cross-Examination, Limit Nonresponsive Objections to Prejudicial Answers by Hostile or Independent Witnesses

Prejudice should also be the litmus test for making a nonresponsive objection during your cross-examination of an independent witness. During cross-examination, resist the temptation to object when *your* question solicits a nonresponsive but *not* prejudicial answer, even if that nonresponsive answer is not relevant or admissible. Some Gray Hairs will insist that attorneys should always "take control" of the witness during cross-examination by making nonresponsive objections early and often. But there is always the risk that jurors will perceive your nonresponsive objection as whining, complaining, tattling, or begging the court for help. The best way to "take control" during cross-examination is always to ask very specific and leading questions. And when the witness gives a nonresponsive (but not prejudicial) answer to your specific and leading question, stick with your question instead of sticking the judge with a nonresponsive objection.

During cross-examination, the examining attorney should always allow the jury to lose their patience with the witness first. Instead of "taking control" and claiming that the witness is being nonresponsive, let the jury reach that conclusion on their own. Consider how the following cross-examination might affect the way the jury thinks of the witness and opposing counsel.

D. Atty: Mr. Johnson, isn't it true that you were standing in line at the snowball stand when the accident happened?

Witness: I stopped on my way home. I work long hours, and I am responsible for 175 employees at work.

D. Atty: Mr. Johnson, isn't it true that you were standing in line at the snowball stand when the accident happened?

Witness: When the accident happened, I had a perfect view of the intersection. I could see everything, and your client ran the red light.

D. Atty: [Slightest sigh] Mr. Johnson, isn't it true that you were standing in line at the snowball stand when the accident happened?

Witness: What does it matter where I was standing? I know what I saw.

D. Atty: [Pause] Mr. Johnson, isn't it true that you were standing in line at the snowball stand when the accident happened?

P. Atty: Objection. Asked and answered.

Court: Overruled. The question has been asked, but it has not been answered. Mr. Johnson, please answer the question, sir.

Witness: What was the question?

D. Atty: Mr. Johnson, isn't it true that you were standing in line at the snowball stand when the accident happened?

Witness: Yes, I was. So what?

Remember that a nonresponsive objection may be made *before* the witness has finished answering the question. When a witness starts to provide information that is not responsive to opposing counsel's question, and an attorney has no idea where that nonresponsive answer is going or what the witness will say next, the attorney can make a nonresponsive objection to prevent the introduction of inadmissible evidence. Again, professionalism does not require trial attorneys to wait for the jury to hear inadmissible or prejudicial testimony.

The most awkward use of a nonresponsive objection is when, during cross-examination, an attorney asks a question and is compelled to interrupt the witness while that witness is still answering his or her question.

That is why Table 7.7 indicates that the cross-examining attorney should ignore nonresponsive answers that are "not relevant" and only object to answers that are prejudicial.

However, when a witness starts to volunteer information that is nonresponsive, inadmissible, and prejudicial, that witness is not entitled to finish his or her answer. Consider the following example of when an examining attorney should absolutely object before the witness finishes answering the question.

D. Atty: Isn't it true that you got out of your car without help?

Plaintiff: Yes, and some guy at the scene told me . . .

D. Atty: Objection. Nonresponsive. Hearsay.

Court: Sustained.

D. Atty: Move to strike everything except "Yes."

Court: Granted.

The pretrial conference is an opportunity to determine whether the court permits a non-examining attorney to make nonresponsive objections. When you have that answer, start filling out your chart. But again, the easiest strategy to remember and execute is to limit nonresponsive objections to only *prejudicial* nonresponsive objections solicited during cross-examination.

c. During Opposing Counsel's Direct and Cross-Examination, Make Nonresponsive Objections to Inadmissible and Prejudicial Answers

During opposing counsel's direct examination or cross-examination, resist the temptation to object to a nonresponsive answer when that answer is neither relevant nor prejudicial. When the witness wants to volunteer useless information, let that witness waste the court's time and alienate the jurors. Sit back, relax, and watch the jury get frustrated with the witness's answers.

During opposing counsel's direct examination or cross-examination, also resist the temptation to object to a nonresponsive answer when that answer is inadmissible but not prejudicial. Your objection might suggest that the answer hurt your case or helped theirs. Here is a good general rule: Never object to testimony that is not hurting your case or helping theirs.

There are exceptions to that general rule, and those exceptions depend on the *purpose* for your objecting. As discussed, there are times when any objection that has merit, including a nonresponsive objection, can be used to interrupt opposing counsel's momentum, rattle opposing counsel, or wake the jury. Also, whenever the judge or a single juror looks at you like "Would you please do something?" or "Are you asleep at the wheel?," wait for the witness to finish their (nonprejudicial) answer, and make the nonresponsive objection. If the jury or the judge are begging you to rescue them, get on your white horse.

d. Always Pair Nonresponsive Objections with an Evidentiary Objection

Attorneys should make an evidentiary objection *in addition to* the nonresponsive objection whenever moving to strike nonresponsive testimony or moving for mistrial, The nonresponsiveness of the answer is not sufficient grounds to exclude testimony, nor does it constitute a basis for a mistrial. Always make a *contemporaneous* evidentiary objection that calls the court's attention to why the nonresponsive answer is inadmissible.

The appropriate remedy for a nonresponsive answer depends on the prejudicial effect of the inadmissible portion of the nonresponsive testimony. When the inadmissible testimony is so prejudicial that it denies the client a fair trial, an attorney should move for a mistrial. And if the court denies that motion for mistrial, an attorney should move the court (in the alternative) to strike the prejudicial testimony and to give a strongly worded curative instruction.

Be careful when moving the court to strike a nonresponsive answer. Do not make a blanket objection to the whole answer (i.e., "I move the court to strike the answer as nonresponsive"). On appeal, the court's denial of a blanket objection to the whole answer may be upheld based solely on an attorney's failure to separate the admissible portion from the inadmissible portion of the nonresponsive answer. For that reason, only move to strike the inadmissible (and prejudicial) portion of the unresponsive answer.

Chapter 8

Foundation: The Steps and the Short List

During the Golden Age of Lawyers, there were no "technology-enhanced" courtrooms or "paperless" trials. Attorneys did not have laptops or iPads. Lecterns did not have integrated control panels. Jurors did not have video monitors. Witnesses never testified "live" via Zoom. Exhibits were never scanned or electronically filed. And judges could not click "witness preview mode." Consequently, trial attorneys had two options: (a) hand the physical evidence to the witness or (b) display the physical evidence (often on an easel) directly in front of the witness. Both options required the attorney to establish a proper foundation using only their wits and their bare hands.

Times have changed. A mere 25 years ago, as a new prosecutor in an old courtroom, I routinely practiced the same "tried-and-true" techniques for establishing a proper foundation. I learned from the best what to say, when to walk, where to stand, and what to ask before I should "offer, file, and introduce" the exhibit. But today, those old methods are not easily applied to new courtrooms. Whether standing at the "media cart" or sitting at "Table Video Source A2," the marked exhibit may be on your screen, not in your hand. And your witness may be "joining the call" from another continent. Which means you need to know more than lawyers knew in 1923 about laying a proper foundation.

The concept of "proper foundation" is simple: an attorney must establish the admissibility of physical and testimonial evidence *before* the jury will be allowed to see or hear that evidence. But what constitutes a proper foundation always depends on the type of evidence and the specific purpose for which that evidence is being admitted. And the proper technique for establishing that proper foundation may depend on the specific judge and the specific courtroom. That is why even the most experienced litigators might moan when asked to give the "Foundations" lecture during trial advocacy boot camps.

The bad news is that there is no proper foundation checklist that a trial attorney can easily apply to every type of evidence and to every purpose. Some teach that a proper foundation requires the two As: Authentic and Admissible. Others teach that a proper foundation requires the three Rs: Real, Relevant, and Reliable. Both general guidelines are helpful, especially for the introduction of physical evidence (i.e., the murder weapon) and documentary evidence, but neither is easily applied to testimonial evidence or to demonstrative evidence.

The good news is that litigators do not need a proper foundation checklist that can be applied to every possible piece of evidence and to every possible situation. Today, most attorneys stipulate to the authenticity of most exhibits prior to trial. Most judges rule on the admissibility of physical evidence, expert opinions, and controversial lay opinions prior to trial. And some judges spend the bulk of their pretrial conference systematically walking through the exhibit lists filed by the parties, admitting uncontested exhibits, and deferring their ruling *only* on those exhibits whose admissibility depend on the testimony solicited at trial. Consequently, attorneys have fewer opportunities to establish a proper foundation for physical evidence.

Moreover, thanks to pretrial motion practice and hearings, trial attorneys often know exactly what testimony the court wants to hear before admitting those exhibits. Exhibit-specific "foundation" roadmaps, which are based on the court's rulings (and comments), will always be more valuable than generic guidelines with alliterative appeal.

What litigators really need to know are (a) the general areas of questioning before tendering the witness as an expert; (b) the steps for establishing a proper foundation for physical evidence; (c) the steps for establishing a foundation for electronic exhibits; and (d) a short list of situations in which "lack of foundation" objection should be made.

1. Proper Foundation for Tendering the Witness as an Expert

Before soliciting an expert opinion from a witness, an attorney must first (a) establish the witness's knowledge, skill, experience, training, and education; (b) tender the witness in a specific field of expertise; (c) permit opposing counsel to question or "voir dire" the expert regarding their qualifications; and (d) have the court rule or "recognize" the witness as an expert in the field in which that expert was tendered.

This book dedicates an entire chapter to the direct examination of an expert witness, which includes tips regarding the tender of that expert. But with regard to establishing the proper foundation before tendering an expert witness, there are several standard areas of questioning that are commonly used to establish the knowledge, skill, experience, training, and education of an expert witness. Table 8.1 identifies 12 of those lines of questioning; it is available for download at ambar.org/TrialAdvocacy.

There is a difference between laying a proper foundation for the court to recognize a witness as an "expert" and laying a proper foundation for the admission of a specific expert opinion. After a witness has been tendered and recognized as an expert, the examining attorney is not required to additionally lay a proper foundation for each expert opinion. Federal Rule of Evidence 705 provides: "Unless the court orders otherwise, an expert may state an opinion—and give the reasons for it—without first testifying to the underlying facts or data. But the expert may be required to disclose those facts or data on cross-examination." Thus, while Federal Rule of Evidence 702 requires that an expert's testimony be based on "sufficient facts or data," Rule 705 does not require the examining attorney to solicit those "underlying facts or data" during direct examination, which is remarkable.

Never rely on Rule 705. Never solicit an expert opinion without first establishing the "underlying facts and data." Always ask your expert to share their methodology, the documents they review prior to reaching their opinion, and the facts upon which their opinion is based. Never be content to solicit only the opinion (i.e., "In your opinion, what was the speed of the defendant's truck at impact?") and immediately tender the witness (i.e., "80 mph. Awesome. I tender the witness for cross-examination.").

2. Proper Foundation for Physical Evidence

You are holding something in your hand. It is some type of physical evidence (i.e., a document, photograph, or other object). Before you can show or play that "real" evidence to the jury, it must be admitted into evidence and published to the jury. Here are the tried-and-true steps for establishing the proper foundation for admitting physical evidence.

a. Step 1: Mark for Identification Purposes Only

The trial transcript reflects what you say, not what you see. If you hand the witness whatever you are holding and ask, "Do you know what *this*

Table 8.1 Proper Foundation before Tendering an Expert

1.	Current Profession	What do you do for a living?
2.	Current Employment	Where do you work? How long have you worked there? What is your current job title/position/description? What are your current job responsibilities? Please tell us about a typical work week for you.
3.	Education & Training	What education prepared you for your current job? What training prepared you for your current job?
4.	Professional Experience	What work experience prepared you for your current job? How did that work experience prepare you?
5.	Organizations	Are you an active member of any professional organizations? Do you hold any titles/positions with those organizations?
6.	Literature	What textbooks on this subject have you published? What articles on this subject have you published?
7.	Teaching & Presentations	What classes have you taught in this subject? What presentations have you delivered on this subject?
8.	Awards & Honors	What professional awards and honors have you received?
9.	Cumulative Statistics	In total, how many years have you worked in this field? In total, how many [patients/clients/audits] have you performed?
10.	Prior Expert Tenders	Have you been tendered as an expert? How many times have you been tendered as an expert? In what field(s) have you been tendered as an expert?
11.	Prior Rulings	Have you been recognized as an expert in [that field]? What court(s) have recognized you as an expert in [that field]?
12.	Limited Testimony	Has any court ever limited your testimony?

is?," the trial transcript will not reflect what "this" is. That is why the first step is to mark the physical evidence as the next sequentially numbered exhibit but mark it as an exhibit "for identification purposes only."

Always remember to include "for identification purposes only." Do not mark the physical evidence as "Exhibit 37" because it is *not* the 37th exhibit until it has been admitted into evidence. Nothing is worse than saying, "I am marking this document as Exhibit 37," and having the judge reply, "No, you are not. It is not an exhibit until I say it is an exhibit."

Never identify or describe the physical evidence before it is admitted. For example, do not say, "I am marking *the police report* as Exhibit 37 for identification purposes only." Only sworn witnesses can identify physical evidence. Unless opposing counsel is asleep at the wheel, they will object to your identification as "counsel testifying," move to strike your statement, and succeed in leaving the jury with the impression that you don't know what you are doing.

Table 8.2 shows several examples of how to mark common types of physical evidence without inappropriately identifying or describing the physical evidence.

Table 8.2 How to Mark Common Types of Physical Evidence

Medical Record	"I am marking this *document* as exhibit 37 for identification purposes only."
Statement by Witness	"I am marking this *document* as exhibit 37 for identification purposes only."
Murder Weapon	"I am marking this *object* as exhibit 37 for identification purposes only."
Hair Fiber	"I am marking this *object* as exhibit 37 for identification purposes only."
Victim's Clothing	"I am marking this *item* as exhibit 37 for identification purposes only."
Surveillance Video	"I am marking this *item* as exhibit 37 for identification purposes only."
Photograph	"I am marking this *item* as exhibit 37 for identification purposes only."

b. Step 2: Ask Permission to Approach the Witness

Jurors want lawyers to show respect for the court, and nothing shows respect like asking permission. That is why an attorney should always ask the court's permission to approach the witness (i.e., "May I approach the witness, Your Honor?") *before* taking one step toward opposing counsel's table with a document, object, or item you want to admit.

c. Step 3: Show the Physical Evidence to Opposing Counsel

Opposing counsel should be given the opportunity to object *before* the examining attorney shows the physical evidence to the witness and *before* the examining attorney asks the witness any questions about that evidence. After the court grants permission to approach, the next step is to walk straight to opposing counsel's table and show the physical evidence to opposing counsel.

Sometimes, when the court permits an attorney to approach with physical evidence that opposing counsel does not need to inspect, opposing counsel will signal or gesture that there is no need for the attorney to show it to them before approaching the witness. But when opposing counsel does not wave you off, walk over to opposing counsel's table and physically hand the evidence to opposing counsel. Let the jury see you relinquish possession of the physical evidence. Take one step backwards. Relax your shoulders.

The longer opposing counsel spends looking at the physical evidence, the better. If opposing counsel spends too long reading the police report, more than one juror may wonder why counsel did not care enough to obtain and read the report prior to trial. If opposing counsel spends too long looking at the plastic bag containing the rock of crack cocaine, more than one juror may wonder why counsel is stalling. If opposing counsel spends too long looking at the evidence, more than one juror may become annoyed.

When opposing counsel forgets to show you the exhibit before approaching, think twice before objecting. Yes, an attorney should make sure that opposing counsel has not highlighted or annotated a document before entering that specific copy into evidence. Yes, an attorney should insist on seeing and inspecting impeachment evidence that opposing counsel never previously produced. On those occasions, even though you have a *right* to see it, respectfully request the opportunity to see it before it is shown to the witness. I always appreciated the way my mentor, Bob Kerrigan, would stand, smile, and calmly say, "May I please see it, Your Honor?" The court would always respond, "Yes, of course," and instruct opposing counsel to "show the exhibit to Mr. Kerrigan." Sometimes, opposing counsel would apologize while turning around and heading back toward our table. Bob's charming approach to pointing out opposing counsel's having skipped a step was much more effective than barking "objection!" It belongs in our playbook.

But sometimes, a trial attorney does not need to see the exhibit. Always ask yourself whether you really *need* to see the specific exhibit before objecting to opposing counsel's failure to show it to you. Is it sealed physical evidence (i.e., murder weapon or cocaine) that you have seen many times? Is it a deposition transcript and you already have a copy opened in front of you? When you do not need to see the exhibit, do not object. When the court *sua sponte* asks opposing counsel, "Did you show that to opposing counsel?" and you don't need to see the exhibit, politely reply, "No need, Your Honor. We have seen it." Always avoid being that whiny lawyer who insists on being shown a document that they produced to opposing counsel.

During the 2009 *Craige* trial, my co-counsel Josh grabbed a printed copy of the plaintiff's MRI imaging (the actual radiology film) and asked the court for permission to approach but did not show it to opposing counsel (skipping step #3) before walking toward the witness stand. Opposing counsel immediately jumped out of his chair, indignantly barked "objection!," and insisted on seeing the MRI image. Josh stopped, looked surprised, turned around, apologized, walked back, handed him the MRI, took one step backwards, and waited patiently. To justify his indignance, opposing counsel proceeded to fumble with the large, floppy MRI film.

After several seconds, opposing counsel in *Craige* actually held the film up above his head toward the overhead fluorescent light, as if he was trying to read the MRI. The absurd sight of a lawyer pretending to read an MRI caused jurors to smirk, laugh, and shake their heads. With one awful decision, opposing counsel forfeited his gravitas and his voice. It was almost as if we intentionally had Josh approach without showing opposing counsel because we knew he was so belligerent that he would lose his cool and object. Wink. Wink. Nudge. Nudge.

To be clear, no attorney should intentionally publish evidence to the jury before it has been admitted into evidence when there is *any* chance that the evidence will be excluded. Before taking your first step toward opposing counsel's table, consider (a) whether there is *any* chance that the evidence will be excluded and (b) whether it *could* be prejudicial for the jury to see the physical evidence before the court's ruling on its admissibility. Never take the chance that the court will exclude the physical evidence that you prematurely published and opposing counsel will move for a mistrial and sanctions.

As a practical matter, it can be difficult for an attorney to hide physical evidence from the jury while showing it to opposing counsel, while walking toward the witness stand, and while showing it to the witness. Fortunately, few judges (if any) will require an attorney to place the document marked as "Exhibit 37 for identification purposes only" inside a manila envelope *before* walking over and handing it to opposing counsel. That is because the unspoken standard is prejudice, and there is no real chance that jurors will be able to read the document as the attorney holding that document passes the jury box. But the court will not forgive an attorney who publishes the document on the courtroom's computer display system before that document has been admitted into evidence. Between those two extremes is a gray area that includes everything from the large plastic cup (that visually reveals the amount of alcohol the plaintiff who "drank four beers" consumed) to the five-year-old photograph of the accused holding a semi-automatic rifle. When in doubt, ask to approach and (outside the presence of the jury) ask the court how to proceed.

d. Step 4: Show the Physical Evidence to the Witness

After showing the physical evidence to opposing counsel, an attorney must show the physical evidence to the witness. The best way to do that may depend on courtroom technology and the type of physical evidence the witness must identify. In most courtrooms, you will be able to display the document, photograph, or diagnostic imaging on the witness's computer display, along with the computer displays for the court and opposing counsel (but not the displays mounted in front of each juror). In other courtrooms, you may have to hand the witness the document, photograph, or diagnostic image the same way you would hand the witness larger objects (i.e., the murder weapon).

e. Step 5: Have the Witness Identify the Physical Evidence

Federal Rule of Evidence 901 provides: "To satisfy the requirement of authenticating or identifying an item of evidence, the proponent must produce evidence sufficient to support a finding that the item is what the proponent claims it is." After showing the physical evidence to the witness, a trial attorney should establish that the witness has the knowledge, experience, position, or ability to identify the evidence and (if opposing counsel has not previously stipulated to the authenticity of the exhibit) to testify regarding its authenticity.

Toward that end, attorneys routinely ask the following three questions, in no particular order: (a) Do you know what this [physical evidence] is? (b) What is this [physical evidence]? and (c) How do you know what this [physical evidence] is?

f. Step 6: Offer, File, and Introduce the Physical Evidence

After establishing the proper foundation, an attorney must request that the evidence be admitted. Different states use different magic words. In Louisiana, it is traditional to say, "I offer, file, and introduce" the exhibit. Whatever those magic words are, resist the temptation to say, "Your Honor, I *want to* offer, file, and introduce Exhibit 37." Never run the risk that a snarky judge will respond, "Then, by all means counselor, do so." And, yes, that has happened.

g. Step 7: Request Permission to Publish the Exhibit

After the court admits an exhibit into evidence, the final step is for an attorney to publish that exhibit to the jury. Never publish the exhibit without first requesting the court's permission (i.e., "Let the record reflect that I am playing Exhibit 37 for the jury" or "Let the record reflect that I am handing the jurors a copy of Exhibit 37"). Always show the court deference by requesting permission to publish the exhibit (i.e., "Your Honor, may the defense play Exhibit 37 for the jury?" or "Your Honor, may the defense publish Exhibit 37 to the jury?").

Putting all seven steps together, here is an example of how a plaintiff attorney can lay the proper foundation before introducing the defendant's commercial trucking log:

P. Atty: What is a commercial log?

Owner: Our trucking company requires every driver to maintain a commercial log. That log records every arrival, unloading, and departure. It shows how many hours the driver has been driving and how many hours the driver has slept.

P. Atty: Is the log electronic or manual?

Owner: Our drivers do not have electronic logs. The log is a form that they fill in with a pen or pencil.

P. Atty: Does your company review the logs for its drivers?

Owner: Yes.

P. Atty: Does your company maintain the logs for its drivers?

Owner: Yes. We keep them for five years.

P. Atty: Your Honor, I am marking this document as Exhibit 37 for identification purposes only. May I approach the witness, Your Honor?

Court: You may.

[Attorney shows Exhibit 37 to opposing counsel.]

[Attorney shows Exhibit 37 to the witness.]

P. Atty: I am showing you what I've marked as Exhibit 37 *for identification purposes* only. Do you know what this document is?

Owner: Yes.

P. Atty: What is this document?

Owner: This is the defendant's log for the date of the motor vehicle accident.

P. Atty: Does that log record how long the defendant had been driving before the accident?

Owner: Yes, it does.

P. Atty: Your Honor, I offer, file, and introduce the defendant's log as Exhibit 37.

Court: Any objection?

D. Atty: No objection.

Court: Let it be admitted.

P. Atty: May I publish Exhibit 37 to the jury?

Court: You may.

[Attorney provides jurors with a copy of the log or displays the log.]

P. Atty: According to Exhibit 37, how long had the defendant been driving at the time of this accident?

Owner: According to this log, our driver had been driving for 17 consecutive hours.

The next time you have to introduce physical evidence, remember to "go to MASS" (think Church or Massachusetts). **M**ark the exhibit. **A**sk to approach the witness. **S**how the exhibit to opposing counsel (wait for opposing counsel). **S**how the exhibit to the witness. Ask the witness the questions needed to establish that the witness can authenticate and identify the exhibit. Offer the exhibit. Then publish the exhibit. Table 8.3 is a chart that some students have found helpful; it is available for download at ambar.org/TrialAdvocacy.

Table 8.3 Introducing Physical Evidence Without Courtroom Technology

Go to MASS		
M	Mark the exhibit	"I am marking this document as Exhibit 1 for identification purposes only."
A	Ask to approach	"May I approach the witness?"
S	Show exhibit to opposing counsel	
S	Show exhibit to witness	
Lay the Proper Foundation		
DO	"Do you know what this is?"	
W	"What is it?"	
H	"How do you know what it is?"	
O	Offer the exhibit*	"I offer, file, and introduce into evidence Exhibit 1."
P	Publish the exhibit	"May I publish Exhibit 1 to the jury?"
*Note: Always establish the relevance of an exhibit *before* you offer, file and introduce that exhibit into evidence. Otherwise, opposing counsel will either object to "relevance" or to "improper foundation" and you will be forced to explain to the court what you *intend* to establish or prove (i.e., "this exhibit is relevant because we are going to establish/prove/argue . . .").		

3. Proper Foundation for Electronic Exhibits in Technology-Enhanced Courtrooms

You are sitting at counsel's table, and there is an exhibit on the screen in front of you. Before you can "share" or "display" that exhibit to the jury, you know that you have to lay the proper foundation, and you recognize that "Go to MASS" is not easily applied to a technology-enhanced courtroom.

All courtrooms will someday be paperless. All courts will someday require all exhibits to be marked and submitted electronically. And most courts already rule on the admissibility of most exhibits before the trial starts.

Before the start of the 2021 *Lindale* trial, the court held a marathon pretrial conference. During that pretrial conference, the court admitted our 76 plaintiff exhibits and opposing counsel's 1,111 defense exhibits. Consequently, neither party had to lay a foundation before publishing and discussing *any* of the pre-admitted exhibits during the entire trial.

But trial attorneys will always need to know how to establish a proper foundation for an electronic exhibit (a) when the court deferred ruling on the admissibility of that exhibit "until trial" to allow the court to hear testimonial evidence (i.e., "The court is not convinced that this exhibit is relevant, but the court will defer ruling until the exhibit is offered at trial") and (b) when that exhibit is impeachment evidence that was never produced to opposing counsel, and an attorney needs to introduce that exhibit during cross-examination. The court will almost certainly explain the preferred procedure (when asked) during the pretrial conference. But, in general, here is how "Go to MASS" can be applied in a technology-enhanced courtroom to introduce exhibits that were *not* previously admitted into evidence.

a. Step 1: Mark the Electronic Exhibit

This step will depend on the court's preference and courtroom technology, but the challenge is always the same: How do you mark an electronic exhibit? If an exhibit sticker was added to the document before the document was scanned, identify the exhibit by that number (i.e., "Your Honor, I have *previously marked* the document/image on my screen as Exhibit 37 for identification purposes only").

If the document on your screen bears no exhibit sticker, but the courtroom technology allows attorneys to electronically mark documents, mark the document using that courtroom technology (i.e., "Your Honor, I *am marking* the document/image on my screen as Exhibit 37 for identification purposes only").

If the court requires attorneys to subsequently file or submit exhibits that were not pre-admitted, identify how the document will be marked (i.e., "Your Honor, I *will mark* the document/image on my screen as Exhibit 37 for identification purposes only").

b. Step 2: Ask Permission to Share Your Screen with Opposing Counsel and the Judge

In a technology enhanced courtroom, there is no need for an attorney to ask the court for permission to physically walk to where the witness is seated to hand the witness the exhibit (i.e., "May I approach the witness, Your Honor?"). Attorneys may only need to display the exhibit on the witness's monitor. But an attorney is still required to show the exhibit to opposing counsel before showing the exhibit to the witness to give opposing counsel the opportunity to object to the witness's seeing the exhibit.

After marking the exhibit, request permission to show the potential exhibit to opposing counsel *and* the court (i.e., "Your Honor, may I share my screen with opposing counsel and the court?"). That may mean different things in different courtrooms. It may mean requesting permission to "share your screen," or permission to "export the document," or permission to otherwise display the document on opposing counsel's monitor and the judge's monitor. In some courts, that may also mean requesting permission of the clerk, courtroom deputy, or whoever the court has designated to control of the courtroom's evidence presentation system. Always find out the court's preferred method for introducing electronic exhibits during the pretrial conference and request the opportunity to practice using the courtroom technology prior to trial. Imagine pressing the wrong button on Day 10 of a jury trial, accidentally publishing a prejudicial exhibit with the jury (before its admission) and causing a mistrial.

c. Step 3: Share the Screen with Opposing Counsel and the Judge

When the court has given permission, display the exhibit on opposing counsel's monitor and on the court's monitor (or request that the exhibit be displayed on those monitors). Most courts will dictate what happens next. Some will ask opposing counsel if they have an objection to the exhibit being shown to the witness. If the court has no protocol, consider letting opposing counsel (and the jury) know that you will wait for counsel's blessing before displaying the exhibit on the witness's monitor (i.e., "Counsel, please let me know when I may additionally share the exhibit with the witness"). Or wait an appropriate time before calmly asking, "Counsel, may I share the exhibit with the witness?" In a paperless courtroom, that is the equivalent of handing a physical exhibit to opposing counsel, taking a step back, and patiently waiting for opposing counsel to hand you the exhibit.

d. Step 4: Share the Screen with the Witness

When opposing counsel and the court have approved, share your screen with the witness. Always consider whether to provide an instruction or word of caution before displaying an electronic exhibit with the witness. Not all witnesses will wait for an attorney to ask a question when presented with an exhibit. Sometimes, the witness will immediately and intentionally comment on the exhibit (i.e., "Yeah. I've seen this photo. He smokes weed. Big deal."). Sometimes, the witness will unintentionally describe the exhibit (i.e., "Yeah. I knew David was arrested a few years back."). If there is any chance that an inexperienced or volatile witness will blurt out what the exhibit is or inappropriately comment on the substance of the exhibit (before a question is asked), consider telling the witness, "I am going to show you what has been marked as Exhibit 37 for identification purposes only. Please do not comment on the exhibit. Just let me know when you have had a chance to review it."

e. Remaining Steps 5, 6, and 7

The remaining steps are similar. Ask the witness the same questions needed to establish that the witness can authenticate and identify the exhibit. Offer the exhibit into evidence. Then, after the court has admitted the exhibit, ask the court to publish the exhibit by displaying it on the monitors in the jury box. Table 8.4 shows a modified chart; it is available for download at ambar.org/TrialAdvocacy.

Table 8.4 Introducing Electronic Evidence Using Courtroom Technology

Go to MASS		
M	Identify the exhibit	"The document on my screen which has as Exhibit 1 for identification purposes only."
A	Ask to share screen with opposing counsel and the judge	"May I share my screen with opposing counsel and the court?"
S	Share screen with opposing counsel and the judge	"Counsel, please let me know when I may additionally share my screen with the witness."
S	Share screen with the witness	
Lay the Proper Foundation		
DO	"Do you know what this is?"	
W	"What is it?"	
H	"How do you know what it is?"	
O	Offer the exhibit*	"I offer, file, and introduce into evidence Exhibit 1."
P	Publish the exhibit	"May I publish Exhibit 1 to the jury?"
*Note: Always establish the relevance of an exhibit *before* you offer, file and introduce that exhibit into evidence. Otherwise, opposing counsel will either object to "relevance" or to "improper foundation" and you will be forced to explain to the court what you *intend* to establish or prove (i.e., "this exhibit is relevant because we are going to establish/prove/argue . . .").		

4. Save "Lack of Foundation" Objections

A "lack of foundation" objection is a formal protest to the introduction of physical and testimonial evidence on the grounds that opposing counsel has not properly established the reliability and admissibility of that evidence. "Lack of foundation" objections are often misunderstood and misapplied.

"Lack of foundation" objections are not sufficient to preserve a claim of error for appeal. When making a "lack of foundation" objection, an attorney must additionally identify the "lacking" foundational element, and the need for that foundational element is often required by a specific Federal Rule of Evidence. For example, when the following common objections have merit, a "lack of foundation" objection will also have merit, and an attorney *could* make a compound objection.

a. "Relevance, Lack of Foundation"

Whenever an attorney can object to the "relevance" of physical or testimonial evidence in violation of Federal Rules of Evidence 401 and 403, that attorney could also object to "lack of foundation" because a proper foundation requires opposing counsel to establish the relevance of the evidence.

b. "Speculation, Lack of Foundation"

Whenever an attorney can object to a question as calling for speculation pursuant to Federal Rule of Evidence 602 because the witness lacks personal knowledge, that attorney could also object to "lack of foundation" because a proper foundation requires opposing counsel to establish the reliability of the testimony.

c. "Calls for Expert Opinion, Lack of Foundation"

Whenever an attorney can object to a question as soliciting an expert opinion from a lay witness in violation of Federal Rules of Evidence 701 and 702, that attorney could also object to a "lack of foundation" because a proper foundation requires opposing counsel to establish the reliability of the opinion.

5. When Not to Object to "Lack of Foundation"

Because "lack of foundation" objections can often be duplicative, and because the "lacking" foundational element is often required by a specific Federal Rule of Evidence, attorneys must decide (a) whether to always object to "lack of foundation" and (b) when to object to "lack of foundation" instead of making the evidentiary objection associated with the "lacking" foundational element. Here is one way of answering those two questions, which results in a very short list of situations in which a "lack of foundation" objection should be made.

a. Do Not Make a "Lack of Foundation" Objection When a Proper Foundation Does Not Exist

There is a difference between (a) making a procedural objection on the basis that counsel has not *yet* established a proper foundation and (b) making a substantive objection on the basis that "proper foundation does not exist."

"Lack of foundation" objections should *not* be made when a proper foundation can *never* be established. Some judges may interpret a "lack of foundation" objection as an attorney objecting because "counsel has not *yet* established a proper foundation," which can unintentionally suggest that a proper foundation *can* be established. When opposing counsel solicits additional testimony after the court sustains a "lack of foundation" objection, some judges will be less likely to grant a subsequent objection.

For example, when opposing counsel asks an obviously unqualified witness to offer an opinion that requires specialized knowledge (i.e., "Did the MRI scan reveal a subdural hematoma?"), an attorney should not object to a "lack of foundation." The attorney should object because the question "calls for an expert opinion" in violation of Federal Rule of Evidence 702.

b. Do Not Make a Compound Objection That Includes "Lack of Foundation" When the Lacking Element Is the Other Basis for Objecting

Do not make a "lack of foundation" objection when the resulting compound objection will be duplicative. For example, when opposing counsel tries to introduce an exhibit into evidence *before* establishing its relevance, do not make a compound objection (i.e., "Objection. Relevance. Lack of foundation.") because that compound objection will be duplicative. Picture the court denying your relevance objection and asking you to explain the "lack of foundation" objection. Picture yourself having to respond, "Counsel has not laid a proper foundation because he has not established . . . umm . . . the relevance." When the basis of your "lack of foundation" objection is the failure to establish relevance, only make a "relevance" objection.

c. Do Not Make a "Lack of Foundation" Objection When the Omitted Foundation Is Required by a Specific Evidentiary Rule

"Lack of foundation" objections should *not* be made when the underlying foundational element is a common objection or required by a specific Federal Rule of Evidence. Never make the more general "lack of foundation" objection. Inexperienced judges may deny a "lack of foundation" objection because they do not understand the basis for the objection and do not want to ask the lawyer to explain the "lacking" foundational element.

Specific evidentiary objections are always preferable to general "lack of foundation" objections because "lack of foundation" objections can educate opposing counsel on how to establish a proper foundation. For example, when the prosecutor asks a detective what a better camera angle—not present on the video in evidence—showed the defendant doing, defense counsel should object because that testimony would directly violate the "best evidence rule" established by Federal Rule of Evidence 1002. In that situation, defense counsel should not make a "lack of foundation" objection, which might require the defense counsel (upon questioning by the court) to identify the exceptions to Federal Rule 1002 and argue that the prosecutor "had not *yet* solicited the facts required to establish the foundation for one of those exceptions." Whenever possible, provide opposing counsel with a specific objection, not a roadmap for establishing a proper foundation.

d. Do Not Make "Lack of Foundation" Objections to Challenge an Expert's Methodology

"Lack of foundation" objections should *not* be made to challenge an expert's methodology. Before a civil or criminal trial, attorneys have the opportunity to file a motion *in limine* to exclude those opinions that are based on an unreliable methodology or "insufficient facts or data." But on occasion, during a jury trial, opposing counsel may solicit—or the expert witness may volunteer—an opinion that has not been addressed by the court. On those increasingly rare occasions, an attorney should make the more specific evidentiary objection to the expert's opinion. Consider the following circumstances:

- If the opinion is based on pure speculation (i.e., "Defendant probably had additional alcohol during the 30 minutes it took the police to arrive"), an attorney should object based on speculation.
- If the opinion is not based on sufficient facts or data, an attorney should object based on Federal Rule of Evidence 702(b), which limits expert opinions to those "based on sufficient facts or data."
- If the opinion is not based on a reliable methodology, an attorney should object based on Rule 702(c), which requires expert opinions be "the product of reliable principles and methods."
- If the opinion is not based on relevant facts or data, an attorney should object based on Rule 703, which requires expert opinions be based on facts or data on which "experts in the particular field would reasonably rely."

In each of these circumstances, the legal basis for objecting to the opinion is the expert's unreliable methodology, not opposing counsel's failure to establish the foundation for that opinion. Never bury the lede by making a "lack of foundation" objection when your real basis for objecting is an evidentiary rule.

e. Do Not Make a "Lack of Foundation" Objection When Opposing Counsel Fails to Establish the Underlying Facts or Data

Resist the temptation to object when an attorney asks an expert to share an opinion *before* establishing the facts and methodology on which that opinion is based. As discussed earlier, Federal Rule of Evidence 705 provides: "Unless the court orders otherwise, an expert may state an opinion—and give the reasons for it—without first testifying to the underlying facts or data. But the expert may be required to disclose those facts or data on cross-examination."

f. Save "Lack of Foundation" Objections for When a Proper Foundation Can Be Established but Opposing Counsel Has Failed to Establish It

"Lack of foundation" objections should be saved for when a proper foundation *can* be established but opposing counsel has failed to follow the proper steps, call the right witness, or ask the right questions to establish that proper foundation. Consequently, in practice, there are very few situations in which a trial attorney should make a "lack of foundation" objection. That list includes:

- When counsel fails to tender a qualified witness as an expert *before* soliciting an expert opinion.
- When counsel fails to establish that a lay witness has personal knowledge *before* soliciting facts that require personal knowledge.
- When counsel fails to call the right witness to authenticate evidence.
- When counsel fails to follow the proper steps *before* introducing physical evidence.

By limiting "lack of foundation" objections to these situations, a trial attorney can avoid suggesting that the evidence itself is not admissible. The sole purpose for making a "lack of foundation" objection should be to call the court's attention (and the jury's attention) to the need for opposing counsel to do more *before* introducing the evidence or soliciting the testimony.

i. When Counsel Fails to Tender a Qualified Witness as an Expert before Soliciting an Expert Opinion

Most direct examinations of an expert witness start with counsel asking questions to establish the skills, knowledge, experience, training, and education of the witness. Counsel then tenders the witness as an expert in a specific field. If opposing counsel does not immediately say "no objection," courts will typically permit opposing counsel the opportunity to question (or "voir dire") the expert regarding their skill, knowledge, experience, training, and education. After opposing counsel finishes questioning the witness, the court will either accept the witness as an expert, limit the scope of their expertise, or refuse to recognize the witness as an expert. Then and only then may counsel solicit an expert opinion from the witness. Rarely does a trial attorney have a reason to object to "lack of foundation" before an expert is tendered.

However, as jury trials disappear and experts grow bolder, it may become more likely that (a) opposing counsel will fail to tender the witness as an expert *before* soliciting an opinion or (b) the witness will volunteer an expert opinion *before* being recognized as an expert by the court. When the witness is obviously qualified and will eventually be recognized as an expert by the court, resist the temptation to object because the question or answer "calls for an expert opinion." Instead, make a "lack of foundation" objection and explain how counsel has failed to establish a proper foundation (i.e., "Objection. Lack of foundation. The witness has not yet been tendered or recognized as an expert witness.").

In this situation, the key is to make the "lack of foundation" objection like you are performing a public service. Just trying to protect the record. If the court permits counsel to state more than the tag, reveal your purpose when making the objection: "Objection. Lack of foundation. *As a matter of housekeeping*, the witness has not yet been tendered or recognized as an expert witness." When presented that way, the court and (a savvy) opposing counsel may thank you for the reminder. More importantly, no juror will wonder why you made a "calls for an expert opinion" objection when the witness is obviously an expert.

ii. When Counsel Fails to Establish That a Lay Witness Has Personal Knowledge before Soliciting Facts

Attorneys have an obligation to establish that a lay witness has personal knowledge of a matter *before* soliciting testimony from a lay witness regarding that matter. Federal Rule of Evidence 602 provides: "A witness may testify to a matter only if evidence is introduced sufficient to support a finding that the witness has personal knowledge of the matter." When opposing counsel fails to establish that the witness has personal knowledge, an attorney should make a "lack of foundation" objection.

iii. When Counsel Fails to Call the Right Witness to Authenticate Evidence

Attorneys have an obligation to authenticate every item of evidence. Federal Rule of Evidence 901 provides: "To satisfy the requirement of authenticating or identifying an item of evidence, the proponent must produce evidence sufficient to support a finding that the item is what the proponent claims it is." When opposing counsel fails to call the right witness to authenticate the item of evidence, an attorney should make a "lack of foundation" objection. For example, if opposing counsel fails to establish that the witness can reliably identify the exhibit or is not the right employee to identify the exhibit (i.e., the witness is not the custodian of records), object to lack of foundation.

iv. When Counsel Fails to Follow the Proper Steps for Introducing Physical Evidence

Attorneys have an obligation to establish a proper foundation before introducing an exhibit into evidence and before publishing that exhibit to the jury. When opposing counsel publishes an exhibit before introducing that exhibit into evidence, object to "lack of foundation." When opposing counsel forgets to introduce a document into evidence *before* asking the witness to read from the document, object to "lack of foundation." When opposing counsel forgets to introduce a video or audio recording into evidence *before* playing the video or audio recording, object to "lack of foundation."

An attorney's tone when making a "lack of foundation" objection is important. An attorney can lose credibility by objecting too passionately (i.e., "Objection! Lack of foundation!") about evidence that is later admitted. Why did counsel sound so angry? Why did counsel object to the item of evidence when it was obviously important and admissible? Remember that the jurors do not understand what "lack of foundation" means. That is why it is important for a purely procedural objection to *sound* like a purely procedural objection.

Table 8.5 lists four situations which justify a lack of foundation objection; it is available for download at ambar.org/TrialAdvocacy.

Table 8.5 Right Time for "Lack of Foundation" Objections

1.	Counsel fails to tender a qualified witness as an expert *before* soliciting an expert opinion.
2.	Counsel fails to establish that a lay witness has personal knowledge *before* soliciting facts that require personal knowledge.
3.	Counsel fails to call the right witness to authenticate the item of evidence.
4.	Counsel fails to follow the proper steps *before* introducing physical evidence.

Chapter 9

Direct Examination of Experts: Real Conversations and Realistic Jousts

During the Golden Age of Lawyers, courts got serious about excluding unqualified opinions and lawyers got addicted to expert testimony. Together, the courts and trial counsel created new professional opportunities for those with the requisite "skill, knowledge, and experience." Civil attorneys involved in personal injury lawsuits started routinely working with the same experts, including economists, certified life care planners, vocational rehabilitation counselors, and accident reconstruction experts. Prosecutors and public defenders started routinely working with the same experts, including forensic psychiatrists, ballistics experts, forensic toxicologists, handwriting experts, and forensic pathologists. Soon, expert witnesses had more trial experience than the lawyers questioning them.

Successful expert witnesses started shifting their professional focus to litigation services. Medical doctors started preparing more life care plans and treating fewer patients. Accountants started calculating more lost earnings claims for the courtroom and preparing fewer tax returns for the real world. Other experts earned a professional degree and went straight from the classroom to the courtroom. In an astonishingly short period of time, experts started catering to the legal profession, attending seminars, marketing their courtroom skills, seeking repeat business, and secretly coveting referrals as a "professional witness."

There were unintended consequences. Courtroom success begot attorney preferences. Attorney preferences begot professional relationships. Professional relationships begot reputations. Lines were drawn. Sides were chosen. Transcripts were saved. Right or wrong, lawyers became reluctant to hire experts who they might someday need to cross-examine, terrified of the possibility that future jurors (not to mention their clients) might learn they previously "hired and trusted" the opposing expert.

Soon, experts were estimating that the vast majority of their work came from one side of the aisle. In the blink of an eye, entire fields of medicine were subdivided. Your friendly neighborhood neurosurgeon was suddenly branded a "plaintiff neurosurgeon" or a "defense neurosurgeon."

A symbiotic relationship developed. Attorneys discovered the competitive advantages of having a stable of friendly experts. Experts discovered the financial advantages of charging their new friends to review documents, prepare reports, appear for depositions, and testify at trial. Both benefited in the short term. Neither imagined that their mutualism might someday displease jurors.

Not surprisingly, trial attorneys started thinking of expert witnesses as litigation support. Some lawyers started to expect favorable testimony from their experts. Others started to expect their expert to make them "look good" in court. Together, they drafted and perfected the attorney's questions for direct examination. They overhauled metaphors. They practiced with anatomical models. By the time trial started, the same lawyer who earned a C+ in high school chemistry sounded like a board-certified toxicologist.

Who can blame them? It is intoxicating for a lawyer to stand in front of the jury, ask brilliant questions, and bask in the glow of a smiling and nodding expert. Once Gray Hairs experienced that adrenaline rush, there was no turning back. Gray Hairs were no longer content with bringing the jury (like a good waiter) the more qualified expert and helping that expert persuade the jury. Now, Gray Hairs wanted to *also* sound like an expert. It was vanity, and it directly affected their approach to direct examination. Real conversations were replaced with well-rehearsed performances and meetings of the mutual admiration society.

Over time, jurors became suspicious of trial lawyers and their handpicked experts. Maybe jurors disliked the way experts had become dependent on litigation for their livelihood. Maybe jurors disapproved of the frequency with which the same lawyer hired the same expert. Maybe it was the way that books, television shows, and movies started portraying expert witnesses as "hired guns." Maybe too many lawyers bragged about their ability to "get an expert to say whatever they wanted." Maybe jurors lost respect for trial attorneys, and experts were guilty by association. Whatever the reason, jurors stopped seeing experts as independent resources and started seeing them as professional witnesses and paid advocates.

Let's change that perception, and let's start by changing the way we think about direct examination. Let's stop thinking of ways to impress the jury with our knowledge. After all, we are *never* going to persuade jurors that we know as much about cardiology as a cardiologist.

Let's write a new playbook for direct examination. Like a waiter calling for a sommelier, let's openly admit that we are not experts. Let's help our expert grab the jury's attention. Let's find ways to establish our expert's objectivity and independence. Instead of trying to earn the jury's admiration during direct examination, let's help our expert earn the jury's trust. Instead of asking our expert to help us win the trial, let's discover ways to help our expert win the trial. Ask not what your expert can do for you, but what you can do for your expert.

1. Don't Ask Leading Questions

During the Golden Age of Lawyers, Gray Hairs started telling law school students that the direct examination of an expert should be a "well-choreographed dance." That may have been good advice back then, but times have changed. Today, a flawless performance on direct examination emphasizes that the jurors are watching exactly that: a paid performance. It only confirms their suspicions about those lawyering lawyers and their hand-picked experts.

Stop thinking of your expert as your dance partner. Stop thinking of your direct examination of an expert as a well-choreographed dance. And stop asking leading questions of your expert. Leading questions are more suspicious and less effective than open-ended questions.

Imagine asking a waiter what wine would go well with your meal. The waiter recommends an expensive bottle but admits he is not an expert and calls the sommelier (who is a wine expert) over to your table. What should happen next? A good waiter flatters the sommelier ("She's the best in the business"), repeats the guest's open-ended question for the sommelier ("What wine would go well with their meal?"), steps aside, and allows the sommelier to answer the question. In contrast, a bad waiter tells the sommelier which bottle they personally recommended and asks a leading question like "Wouldn't that be the perfect pairing?" or "Don't you agree with me?" or "Don't you think it's worth the money?" You see where I am going with this.

Jurors do not want to hear your expert, in response to every question, reply "That is absolutely correct, counselor!" They want a real conversation, and the last thing that lawyers and their experts should give them is a rehearsed or choreographed performance. Trial lawyers must rethink their approach to the direct examination of experts or it will always be the most predictable, boring, and ignored part of the trial.

2. Deliver a Real Conversation

During your first meeting with the expert, you did not ask perfect questions and your expert did not give perfect answers. Your expert corrected you. Your expert suggested different questions or different approaches. Your expert explained why your metaphor was misleading. Your expert requested different photos or additional demonstrative exhibits. Your expert read something or drew something to help you understand. Somehow, your expert found a way to teach you, and you left that meeting impressed and persuaded. Let's recreate that conversation for the jury.

Remember that the goal of direct examination is not to raise the jury's level of understanding to your expert's level of understanding. The more realistic goal of direct examination is to take a juror's level of understanding and raise it to *your* level of understanding. And the best way to do that is to allow the jury to experience the same learning curve that you experienced. Never deprive jurors of mistakes and explanations that helped you. Never ask jurors to make a logical leap your expert never asked you to make. Do not start where you and your expert left off. Start where you and your expert started. Start at the very beginning. It's a very good place to start.

Make sure that your real conversation includes the questions jurors want answered, not just the questions you want answered. Imagine if the judge told the jurors to line up at the podium and allowed the jurors to question your expert *before* you started your direct examination. What questions would the jurors ask? Make no mistake. Some jurors are not listening to your questions. They are waiting for you to ask their question, and they are growing impatient with you. If you fail to ask their question, they will ask that question during jury deliberation—when neither you nor your expert will be in the room to provide the correct answers.

Stop focusing myopically on the verdict returned by focus groups and mock trials. Instead, make it a point to dissect and remember the strange questions asked during deliberation. Then ask those questions during your real conversation with your expert.

Every juror has a bias, prejudice, or misconception about some aspect of your trial (i.e., about a product, injury, diagnostic test, disease, etc.). When you identify that common misconception, do not try to disabuse the jury of it with a single, condescending question. Most misconceptions are based on a reasonable premise, fact, or metaphor. Some are based on something that a beloved parent, friend, or neighbor once said. Some are based on personal experience. Never ignore those misconceptions or insult those sources. Let the jury hear your expert agree with the truth of those premises, facts, or metaphors. Then ask why, if that premise/basis/metaphor is true, the common misconception is not also true. Let your expert correct you and explain it to you.

Never be sarcastic or belittling when asking a question. Never phrase your question in a way that suggests you know the answer is based on an incorrect premise, basis, or metaphor (i.e., "Would it be ridiculous for someone to think . . ."). Never phrase your question in a way that mocks opposing counsel (i.e., "What would you say if I told you that opposing counsel actually suggested . . ."). Always assume that at least one juror holds that misconception or was persuaded by the suggestion. Picture that juror thinking, "Hey, I was thinking the same thing," while your expert is agreeing with the premise or acknowledging the common misconception. Picture that juror thinking, "Oh, I see why that isn't true," while your expert explains where *you* (the trial lawyer) went wrong. Of course, that is easier said than done, and you must be sincere in your curiosity and questioning or the jury will recognize that the exchange was staged.

3. Let Your Expert Correct You

Gray Hairs would rather die than be corrected by their expert in front of the jury, but that vanity is depriving them of a golden opportunity. Nothing grabs the jury's attention like having your expert disagree with you. It is the absolute last thing that jurors expect from a "hired gun."

Every trial lawyer loves the movie *My Cousin Vinny.* It is brilliant. Since 1992, thousands of courses on trial strategy have included at least one hysterical clip. We all have our favorite scene, but it is worth remembering the real turning point in that trial was when attorney Vinny Gambini called his lovely fiancée, Mona Lisa Vito, to the stand. After the court recognized her as an expert, Vinny handed Ms. Vito a photo of the tire marks. Wisely, Vinny resisted the temptation to ask a leading question (i.e., "The defendant's car could not have made those tire marks, could it?" or "Isn't it true that these tire marks were left by a 1963 Pontiac Tempest?"). Instead, Vinny started by getting Ms. Vito to *disagree* with the defense theory and say that the defense is *wrong*—which immediately caused gasps of surprise. Vinny's gambit shocked every juror into listening carefully to what Ms. Vito said next (which, of course, exonerated Vinny's client). Here is that clever exchange from the timeless movie.

Vinny: Ms. Vito, it has been argued by me, the defense, that two sets of guys met up at the Sac-O-Suds, at the same time, driving identical metallic mint green 1964 Buick Skylark convertibles. Now, can you tell us by what you see in this picture, if the defense's case holds water?

[Lisa examines the picture.]

Vinny: Ms. Vito, please answer the question: Does the defense's case hold water?

Lisa: **No! The defense is wrong!**

Vinny: Are you sure?

Lisa: I'm positive.

Vinny: How could you be so sure?

Lisa: Because there is no way that these tire marks were made by a '64 Buick Skylark convertible. **These marks were made by a 1963 Pontiac Tempest.**

Let's include Vinny Gambino's gambit in our new playbook. If jurors expect agreement by our hand-picked experts, let's grab their attention by soliciting disagreement and constructive criticism during our direct examination.

Be careful not to take it too far. Remember that your questions should always be based on a common misperception, a reasonable assumption, a logical fallacy, or an understandable misinterpretation. The Greek philosopher Plato recognized the value of a good foil, but Plato did not want his students to play the fool. That is the fine line that trial lawyers should be walking during direct examination. Never play the fool, but never miss the opportunity to play the foil by asking the questions jurors want answered. Help your expert teach the jurors by allowing your expert to teach you . . . in front of the jury.

Resolve never to let a staged disagreement turn into a staged argument. Avoid asking follow-up questions that give the appearance you genuinely want the expert to change their answer (i.e., "But isn't there evidence . . ." or "But isn't it true . . ."). Picture a confused juror speaking up during deliberation and saying, "What I remember is that lawyer's own expert didn't agree with him!" Toward that end, always warn your expert before intentionally asking incorrect questions during direct examination. Remember that your expert trusts you. Tell your expert that you intend to ask certain questions to create an opportunity for the expert to correct you and educate the jury.

Resist the temptation to keep your expert in the dark. Always tell your expert which incorrect questions you will ask during direct examination. Before the 2010 *Nugent* trial, I decided it would be more realistic if I told my expert that it was "up to him" to listen carefully and catch my mistakes. I told him, in no uncertain terms, to correct every mistake, no matter how insignificant the mistake. My expert welcomed the challenge and took my instructions to heart. On the stand at trial, my expert challenged every number, metaphor, and statement I offered. My direct examination quickly became a wrestling match that caused (recorded) laughter among the jurors. Here is an excerpt from that trial transcript:

Q. I've shown a couple of witnesses this diagram, which shows the TASER X26 being applied to the chest of a person. Does this—is this a diagram that you have seen before?

A. I have.

Q. Do you believe it to be accurate?

A. It is.

Q. It shows the location of the two prongs on the chest of a person . . . This would be looking down like this at [the] person if we were to literally take a, uh, slice, one slice out like this and then we were to rotate it. That's what it would look like?

A. Yes. Your—

Q. Looking down?

A. Your diagram is [being held] a little low. You want to be a little higher, become more, uh, pectoral muscle there and a little more of the heart.

Q. Okay. I didn't hold it at the right height, but it's a slice—

A. Yes.[1]

* * *

Q. And the taser, the amount of energy is one-tenth of one joule. Is that right?

A. That's correct.

1. Transcript of Jury Trial at 32:29-34:18 of Day 5, State v. Nugent, No. 41475 (8th Jud. Dist. Ct., Winn Parish, La. 10/27/10).

Q. So if we're—if you heard the expression, that the dose is the poison—

A. I've heard that expression.

Q. . . . [i]f you say well, one Tylenol is not poisonous but if you were to have 200 Tylenols, that could be poisonous?

A. Actually about 15 will kill you.

Q. Right. Now, I—but I—okay. But we're—

[Court reporter note: **Laughter in the courtroom**.]

A. And that's if you're not alcoholic.

Q. I'm gonna lose this battle. I'm gonna try. All right. **Work with me. You're my witness. All right?**

[Court reporter note: **Laughter in the courtroom**.]

Q. All right. I've been waiting how long to call a witness?[2]

Fortunately, the *Nugent* trial resulted in an acquittal for our client, and the direct examination (somehow) succeeded in persuading jurors to trust our expert, perhaps because *nobody* thought he was being paid to agree with me.

But, in retrospect, I crossed a line. I took it way too far. Instead of helping my expert impress the jury with his intelligence and independence, I suggested to jurors that my expert was annoying and nitpicking. Instead of shining the spotlight on my expert, who was a true pioneer in the field of bioelectricity, I cast myself as the protagonist and my expert as comic relief. Instead of being content to play the interested student, I portrayed my expert as the eccentric teacher. Do not make the same mistake. Always tell your expert what mistakes you plan on making and share with your expert why you are creating each teaching opportunity.

4. Make It More Complicated

Gray Hairs preach "Keep It Simple Stupid." In general, that is good advice, and the acronym KISS is certainly easy to remember, but lawyers can forget the reason behind the rule and make the mistake of *only* presenting the simplest explanations and the simplest exhibit. Those trial lawyers can learn

2. Transcript of Jury Trial at 30:24-31:10 of Day 5, State v. Nugent, No. 41475 (8th Jud. Dist. Ct., Winn Parish, La. 10/27/10).

the hard way that, by "dumbing down" the material, you can unintentionally "dumb down" your expert and "dumb down" your argument. Or worse, you can commit the cardinal sin of appearing to talk down to your jury.

Jurors know more about science and medicine (and everything else) than at any other time in history. They know there is more to the story, and they will be suspicious of your expert's folksy explanation. They do not want your expert to take the stand and read them *Shakespeare for Dummies*. They want your expert to take the stand and read them Shakespeare in the original Elizabethan dialect . . . and then read them *Shakespeare for Dummies*.

During every trial-prep meeting, ask your experts how they would explain the most critical concepts or opinions (1) to their most learned peers; (2) to college students studying in their field; and (3) to their next-door neighbor. Also ask the expert to create or describe three demonstrative exhibits for those three very different audiences.

During the trial, solicit all three explanations and present all three demonstrative exhibits. Use the first explanation and exhibit to demonstrate your expert's degree of understanding and experience (i.e., the "he's smart" exhibit). Use the second explanation and exhibit to make the concept more accessible to the jury (i.e., the "that makes sense" exhibit). Use the third explanation and exhibit to convince the jury your expert is correct (i.e., the "he's right" exhibit). Remember that you are asking the jury to trust your expert and base their verdict on your expert's testimony. Do not make the mistake of asking the jury to trust the simplest explanation and to base their verdict on a single metaphor.

Never omit the simplest explanation or demonstration. During the *Nugent* trial, we had the challenge of explaining to jurors the path of electrical current during a drive-stun by a TASER Conducted Electrical Weapon (CEW). Contrary to what the opposing expert said, the current did not travel all over the body like lightning. It only traveled between the two contact points at the tip of the device, and it did not travel very far beneath the skin.

When we met with our expert in bioelectricity, we asked him to show us the most accurate exhibit, and our expert showed us a finite element model, which looked a lot like an atmospheric infrared image of earth and a little like the Imperial Death Star. We asked him for a simpler explanation, and he showed us a visual graphic depicting the layers beneath the skin and using arrows to identify the path. But what we found the most persuasive was our expert's willingness to nonchalantly drive-stun a metal soda can *while holding* the can. At trial, we provided the jury with all three explanations and exhibits: the finite element model, the skin-layer graphic, and a photograph of the expert tasing the metal can while holding it (Figure 9.1).

Figure 9.1

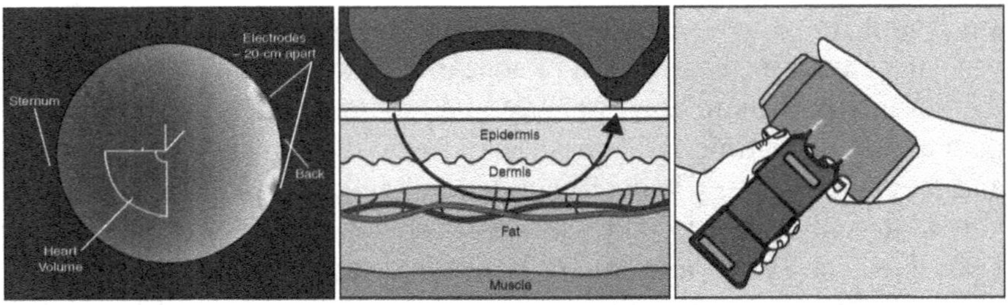

During the next break in the *Nugent* trial, the bailiff walked up and said, "I figured you were right for the past week, but I didn't really get it until I saw that can." That comment opened my eyes. While the more complicated explanations impressed the bailiff and made it clear that the witness knew more than *anyone* in the courtroom, the bailiff was no closer to understanding or believing our expert's analysis. The bailiff needed to see the demonstration. That is why a trial attorney must do both: make it simple, but do not keep it simple.

5. Start with Agreement and Concessions

Gray Hairs can be reluctant to ask their expert if they "agree with" something the opposing expert said or did because they do not want to "lend credibility" to the opposing expert. Let's stop thinking that way. Let's stop being afraid of agreement.

Jurors want you to tell them specifically where the two roads diverge in the yellow wood before you ask them to choose a road (to travel by). If you do not tell them, jurors may try to figure it out for themselves during jury deliberation. And nobody wants that.

Start your direct examination by soliciting agreement. Discuss with your expert the undisputed basic facts, assumptions, and definitions. Give your expert a chance to impress the jury with his knowledge of opposing counsel's methodology and conclusions. Encourage your expert to share with the jury the points on which both experts agree. Then, and only then, ask your expert to explain how and why he or she reached a different conclusion. By employing this technique, you can reduce the chances that your jury will start deliberation with the impression that the two experts passed like two ships in the night.

That line of questioning does not write itself the day before trial or the night before your direct examination. Always bring the opposing expert's report and deposition transcript to your meeting with your expert. Show your expert everything their expert said and find out what premises, assumptions, calculations, and opinions are 100 percent accurate and complete.

6. Show "Textbook" Examples

When you are sitting at a blackjack table, the dealer (who is an expert at blackjack) does not tell you his or her opinion, they tell you whether "the book says to hit." And you do not hit 15 because Gina from Little Rock, Arkansas told you to hit 15. You hit 15 because the book says to hit 15. Similarly at trial, give jurors a reason to believe your expert by reading textbook passages and showing them textbook examples that support your expert's opinions.

Before the 2010 *Nugent* trial, I noticed that the forensic pathologist cited a textbook in support of his autopsy finding. When asked, the forensic pathologist told me that he physically took a book off his bookshelf, found an image (microscopic photography), and saw that the textbook example was identical to what he saw on the deceased's histology slides. I asked him to bring that textbook and that slide to trial, and it made all the difference in the world. During our examination, the jury heard the following exchange, which allowed us to refer to the death as a "textbook case" for the rest of the trial:

Q. And did you bring that textbook with you?

A. Yes, I did.

Q. Can't help but notice that you did. I see it. It's right here. We can't miss it. It's huge . . .

A. Uh, the title of it is Spitz and Fisher's . . . uh, Medical, Legal Investigation of Death. This is the fourth edition published in . . . 2004.

Q. Please tell me that they talk about packing and stacking there of the sickled red blood cells.

A. Uh, they do and this is the reference that I used in my autopsy report . . .

Q. So, literally, literally what you saw in microscopic examination is a textbook example of the sickling of red blood cells before death?

A. Uh, that's correct with the exception of the degenerative changes . . . which didn't have time to occur. Death occurred so rapidly.[3]

Always ask your expert to show you what a "textbook" example looks like, especially when textbook examples do *not* support the opposing expert's conclusions. Picture showing your expert "textbook" MRI images of acute trauma, and having your expert physically point to the edema in the MRI. Now picture your expert showing the plaintiff's MRI images, and physically pointing to where there is *no* edema. Proving that the present case is not a "textbook" case can be half the battle.

7. Explain How Their Case Could Be Better

Today, jurors know that only the "really good" and the "really bad" cases go to trial, and they want to know which type of case they are deciding. They want to know where on a scale of one to ten a specific claim, defense, argument, or injury ranks. Teach them by telling them what a *better* claim would be. Show them what a *more severe* injury would have been.

In a traumatic brain injury trial, have your expert respond to "gloom and doom" testimony about a mild concussion by explaining more severe injuries (that did not happen) like those involving gross abnormalities (i.e., mass effect, midline shift, edema, contusion, or subarachnoid hemorrhage). In a slip-and-fall case, have your expert respond to a defendant's argument that the lighting inside the restaurant was "reasonable" by showing jurors examples of better lit rooms. Teach the jury what a much better claim or defense *would have been*, and the jury will learn why the current claim or defense is inadequate or untenable. That trial strategy starts during the meeting with your expert. When you meet with your expert, find out what facts or circumstances would have made opposing counsel's claims or defense much better.

8. Get Your Experts Out of Their Seats

Today, jurors have shorter attention spans and have become more visual learners. They crave movement and sound. They need visual reinforcement. Instead of asking your expert to describe the location of L5-S1 on

3. Transcript of Jury Trial at 18:20-19:20 of Day 3, State v. Nugent, No. 41475 (8th Jud. Dist. Ct., Winn Parish, La. 10/25/10).

the lumbar spine, tell your expert to stand up and point to it on a model of the lumbar spine, or on an MRI, or on your back.

Find a way to let the jury see your expert doing her job. Do not be satisfied telling the jury that your expert has been practicing for 20 years. Let them see and hear 20 years of experience. If a finding from a physical examination is critical (i.e., finding of muscle spasm), have your orthopedic surgeon stand up and demonstrate on you how they routinely administer a physical exam. Let the jury see and hear how professional and routine a physical examination is for your expert. If a field sobriety test is the key to the case, let the jury see and hear the officer administer one to you. Watching your witness do what your witness does every day reminds the jury that your witness is an expert and makes it easier for jurors to trust that expert's opinion.

9. Make Sure They Act Normal (for Them)

During an hour-long meeting, you cannot change your expert's personality and you should not try. Jurors do not expect genius to tolerate stupidity, and jurors do not expect hardened professionals to be warm and cuddly. If anything, jurors will be suspicious of brilliant experts who flatter ordinary (mere mortal) lawyers. The real challenge is to discover your expert's real personality and disabuse your expert of any ridiculous notions they may have about themselves. You know that friend of yours who *thinks* he is funny? How about that friend who *thinks* he knows everything? Or that friend who *thinks* he is a lawyer? Well, you need to figure out which one your expert is. Our job is to help our experts become who they are.

Before the 2006 *Swain* trial, we retained a gray-haired cardiologist who was unbelievably patient and kind (truly grandfatherly) toward me, but an absolute nightmare to opposing counsel. During the cardiologist's deposition, it was difficult to watch him bully opposing counsel with one-word answers, pained facial expressions, and openly hostile criticism of well-intentioned questions. I quickly realized that the jury would almost certainly dislike and be suspicious of his Jekyll-and-Hyde routine. When I shared my concerns with him, he assured me that he could be "folksy" on the stand. I told him, "You don't have that club in your bag."

Before my curmudgeon took the stand during the *Swain* trial, I made an executive decision. I asked him to be cantankerous to *both* attorneys. I told him not to suffer foolish questions from either of us. I encouraged him to treat both lawyers like the dumbest cardiology students he had ever met (which we absolutely were). My expert nodded his head and smiled. Freed from having to pretend to be Dr. Nice Guy, he took the stand at trial, relaxed, and answered questions like they were being asked by lazy medical interns. The jury loved him and agreed that the accident did not cause the plaintiff's subsequent heart problems.

Turns out that a difficult witness is a trustworthy witness, and a little hostility (or disagreement) can go a long way in persuading jurors that your expert is objective and that the conversation they just witnessed was real.

10. Tell the Jury What Your Expert Does All Day

Jurors often define *who* an expert is by *what* that expert does. Do not treat your expert's *curriculum vitae* like a roadmap for the start of your direct examination. It is neither interesting nor sufficient to have your expert list their degrees, certifications, organizations, prior employers, published materials, and current titles.

Make sure the jury can picture what your expert does by asking your expert to tell you what a typical day or a typical week is like in their practice. During the 2010 *Nugent* trial, we tendered our witness as an expert "in the field of emergency medicine" and "on the physiological effects electronic control devices on the human body." Because our expert had conducted so many articles on the same product, we were concerned the jury would get the impression he was a "lab geek" or (worse) a "hired gun" who worked for the manufacturer of the products he tested. To make sure the jury understood what he did (and who he really was), we solicited the following testimony about a typical week in his life:

> Q. If you would, please tell the jurors about your actual practice, what you do in the course of a week?
>
> A. Uh, several things. I wear many hats. Uh, in the course of a week I spend approximately 24 to 25 hours, uh, actually taking care of patients in the emergency department. Uh, I probably spend, uh, 20 to 25 hours, uh, doing what's called EMS, medical direction. So, I provide, uh, administrative and medical director services to, uh, some of the law enforcement and, uh, fire department paramedic programs that are around our area, and I spend an additional 20 to 25 hours on, uh, research activities. So, my typical work week is about seventy hours or so.[4]

4. Transcript of Oral Argument at 7:15–24 of Day 6, State v. Nugent, No. 41475 (8th Jud. Dist. Ct., Winn Parish, La. 10/28/10).

As you can see, our expert's answer did not sound rehearsed (go back and count the "uhs"), and his description of his typical week emphasized he was neither a "lab geek" nor a "hired gun." We interviewed some of the jurors after the favorable verdict. It was clear that those jurors realized our expert was a hard-working doctor who helped people every day, which is precisely why they gave his testimony great weight and acquitted our client.

Similarly, during the 2009 *Craige* trial, which involved a paralysis claim, we asked our defense neurosurgeon to tell the jury about the surgeries he had performed and the patients he had seen within the past 72 hours. As the jury listened to the specific surgeries and learned about the volume of patients he had treated, they realized that our neurosurgeon was not a "hired gun" or a "defense expert." If anything, they got the impression that our expert would much rather be in an operating room than a courtroom. In stark contrast, the plaintiff's neurosurgeon had performed no surgeries during the same period and had almost exclusively examined other plaintiffs (referred by plaintiff attorneys).

Always interview your experts so you can choose the right question to ask (i.e., typical day versus typical month) and prompt your expert if he forgets an important detail. Be careful not to practice or rehearse how your expert will respond.

11. Let Experts Name Their Field of Tender

Do not assume that you can tell the proper field in which to tender an expert based solely on your expert's *curriculum vitae.* Make sure your expert agrees with the exact wording of every field in which he or she will be tendered as your expert witness. Your expert will always be the best judge of whether the field is too broad or too narrow.

Avoid tendering an expert as an expert in *doing* something. There is a difference between tendering your witness as an expert "in the field of cardiology" and tendering that same witness as an expert "in open heart surgery." There is a difference between tendering your witness as an expert "in the field of economics" and "in calculating the present value of future medical expenses." There is a difference between tendering your witness as an expert "in the field of human factors" and "in analyzing the rise and run of stairs."

Courts are more willing to recognize a witness as an expert in a specific field than in a specific task. Once the court recognizes that your witness is an expert in a specific field, and you have established that a particular task is routinely performed by that expert (and by other experts in the same field), opposing counsel will be less likely to object to the expert's testimony regarding that particular task.

12. Know Whether the Internet Agrees

During the Golden Age of Lawyers, Gray Hairs did not have to worry about jurors going home and researching online. It was a magical time. There was no risk of a juror fact-checking experts, researching products, or investigating witnesses. No chance of a juror reading an abstract, article, website, or blog about a specific disease or injury. No danger of a juror discovering evidence excluded by the court but still available online.

Always assume that at least one juror will ignore the court's instruction not to go home and conduct online research. Prior to meeting with your expert, perform relevant internet searches regarding that expert, the opposing expert, and the relevant testimony (i.e., regarding the injury, illness, product, or accident).

Never allow the outcome of your trial to be determined in a basement apartment by a juror wearing pajamas and reading Wikipedia. Learn what Wikipedia says and learn what your expert would say about any contradictory or controversial Wikipedia entries. Maybe the Wikipedia entry discusses an earlier model of the product. Maybe the Wikipedia entry contains factually incorrect statements. Maybe the Wikipedia entry cites an inapplicable or discredited medical study. Discuss with your client the pros and cons of handing that Wikipedia page to your expert during direct examination and letting your expert "set the record straight." Never introduce a Wikipedia entry for the sake of attacking a Wikipedia entry during direct examination unless you are certain your expert can absolutely crush it. When in doubt, leave the inadmissible prejudicial material out!

13. Steal Their Thunder about Your Expert

There is a reason why politicians and corporations want to get ahead of bad press. Jurors will never forgive you for hiding something unfavorable about your expert during direct examination. You must be the one to bring it up. You must ask the tough question that opposing counsel was going to ask. And your expert must answer directly and honestly.

Do your homework. Before meeting with your expert, research them like you had to cross-examine them next day at trial. That way, when you meet with them, you can (gently) discuss the issues that may come up about them and their testimony.

Always give your expert the benefit of the doubt. They may not know their skeletons are out there on the internet or in published opinions. They may not fully understand how those skeletons could negatively affect the way jurors listen to their testimony. And they may be (unwisely) expecting you to object and the court to sustain your objection. Always show your expert what you found and find out what your expert would want you to ask about that issue (during direct or redirect) Make sure your expert is comfortable with your approach.

Yes, it can be difficult to walk the line between "preparing" your expert and "scaring" your expert into not wanting to testify at trial. Never play devil's advocate so aggressively that you anger or alienate your expert. Always approach the issue as if you are simply trying to make sure your expert's side of the story comes out at trial.

Before the 2015 *Crayton* trial, we realized that the plaintiff's neurosurgeon and the defense neurosurgeon had both omitted from their expert reports the existence of swelling (edema) in a lumbar MRI taken one year after the car accident, even though that edema was critical evidence of recent (subsequent) trauma. When we met with our expert, we showed him the MRI film, selected specific views to enlarge for the jury, and respectfully asked him the obvious question (i.e., "Why didn't you mention the edema in your report?"). Only after hearing his perfectly reasonable answer, and only after forcing him to defend his omission of the edema, did we decide (a) to raise the issue during my cross-examination of their neurosurgeon and (b) "steal thunder" during my direct examination of our expert by raising his failure to include the edema in his report.

Chapter 10

Cross-Examination of Experts: Pin, Don't Punch

During the Golden Age of Lawyers, attorneys prepared for cross-examination like they were preparing for combat. Since birth, Gray Hairs had been fed a steady diet of stories about trials won during cross-examination. And, in law school, they feasted on the poor souls who played "expert witnesses" during mock trials. By graduation, they were foaming at the mouth to do the same to a *real* expert in front of a *real* jury during a *real* trial. They pictured themselves deftly revealing the expert's embarrassing mistake or catching the expert in an outright lie. In their heart of hearts, they truly believed that the right combination of words would force the expert to recant their testimony and change their opinions on the stand. They imagined themselves returning victorious to their table after the "perfect" cross-examination, knowing *they* had just won the trial.

Not surprisingly, Gray Hairs developed a bad habit of swinging at every mistake and every perceived weakness during cross-examination. They confronted experts with overlooked test results. They waived around ignored peer-reviewed articles. They read aloud misquoted and misread documents. They highlighted errors in methodology. They snickered at the absurd consequences of the expert's reasoning. And they demanded admissions and apologies. For some, victory became synonymous with humiliation. But as experts became more experienced, and trials less frequent, those types of victories became increasingly rare.

Pride perpetuated the myth that "great lawyers" always defeated "great experts." When frontal assaults against experts failed, Gray Hairs told nobody, thinking it reflected poorly on their cross-examination skills rather than their cross-examination strategy. But when they succeeded, Gray Hairs proudly repeated the story for anyone who would listen. And so, the same handful of stories about the same handful of times that the same handful of partners at the firm "crushed" experts inspired decades of young lawyers to admire and follow their example. Few realized that repetition was the canary in the coal mine. Cross-examination stories were getting older because there were no new tales to tell.

Times changed because expert witnesses changed. These are not your grandfather's experts. These experts have more trial experience than the attorneys questioning them. They are smarter, tougher, faster, and stronger. They have joined organizations and attended seminars. They know our deposition strategies and trial tactics. They know how we are going to attack, and they know how to defend their opinions, their qualifications, and their methodology. Do not kid yourself. They know the questions you are going to ask before you ask them.

These courtroom veterans look forward to cross-examination. They welcome the opportunity to be questioned in their field of expertise. They will happily discuss every article and every study you want to show them on the stand. They can't wait to discuss *your* expert's assumptions, definitions, methodology, and opinions. They will politely punish you for every mispronounced word, faulty premise, incorrect fact, misunderstood concept, illogical conclusion, and inappropriate metaphor. At night, they kneel by their beds and pray for long, meandering cross-examinations that give them the chance to demonstrate their knowledge and expertise.

The Greeks called it *hubris*, but jurors call it vanity. Asking a lawyer to cross-examine a cardiac electrophysiologist in the field of cardiac electrophysiology is like asking a high school student to cross-examine J.D. Salinger on *The Catcher in the Rye* based only on the CliffsNotes. It is not a fair fight, especially *after* J.D. Salinger has been cross-examined by other smart students, in other classrooms, on countless other occasions. So let us chisel in stone a sacred new rule for cross-examination:

You don't win a trial with their expert. You win a trial with yours.

Let's embrace this new philosophy. Let's shift our focus. Let's stop picturing ourselves winning the trial and start picturing our expert winning the trial. Instead of trying to "land the big punch" during cross-examination, let's resolve to pin their experts down and let our experts do the honors. Let's stop trying to shine the red-hot spotlight on ourselves during cross-examination and start shining that spotlight on our expert during direct examination. Let's dedicate ourselves to the monumental challenge of tackling these slippery suckers. Let's use cross-examination to catch a cloud and pin it down.

1. Pin Don't Punch

Experts do not fear contradictory evidence or contradictory opinions. What experts fear most is that opposing counsel will reveal their mistakes *after* they leave the courtroom. Above all, experts desperately want the chance to respond to whatever evidence they omitted or overlooked. Show them an ignored test result, and they will happily explain why that result was neither conclusive nor reliable. Show them a contradictory article, and they will quickly recall the professional criticism that article received. Show them a devastating statistic, and they will share personal experiences and anecdotal evidence proving your statistic is misleading or wrong. Show them a highlighted transcript page, and they will calmly explain why that testimony does not change their opinion. So, here's an idea. Let's stop obliging them.

The next time you stand at the crossroads, choose to pin the expert (by clarifying their opinion) rather than take a swing at an expert (by confronting the expert with your game-changing evidence). Before you try to land the knockout punch, ask yourself:

- Why give their expert a chance to address my evidence?
- Why give their expert a chance to respond to my logic or argument?
- Why give their expert a chance to change their opinion?
- Will the point that I so desperately want to make sound better coming from my expert (in the same field of expertise) or from me (a paid advocate)?

During the 2009 *Craige* trial, the plaintiff's neurosurgeon either missed or was never provided with the results of testing that conclusively proved plaintiff's paralysis was caused by an unrelated (non-traumatic) inflammation of the spinal cord called transverse myelitis, not by the car accident. During direct examination, plaintiff's neurosurgeon lamented the fact that a cerebrospinal fluid (CSF) cell count and differential was not performed because it was the "conclusive test" and *would have shown* that plaintiff's spinal fluid protein (SFP) was normal, ruling out transverse myelitis. Remembering our sacred new rule for cross-examination, I resisted the temptation to confront the plaintiff's neurosurgeon with the favorable results of that laboratory testing. After all, why should I give their expert a chance to argue that the SFP level was normal, borderline normal, or not conclusive? Why give their expert a chance to criticize the reputation of the lab that performed the testing? As we say in Louisiana, why give their expert a chance to crawfish on their testimony?

Instead, I took a flip chart and solicited the following admissions during my cross-examination, which I calmly (but noisily) wrote with a black marker:

- CSF = conclusive test
- CSF *not* performed
- SFP *would have* been normal
- Normal SFP = no transverse myelitis
- High SFP = transverse myelitis

Betraying nothing, I thanked the plaintiff's neurosurgeon for his time, tendered the witness for redirect, and suppressed a smile as I watched the expert walked out of the courtroom, none the wiser. Then, after the plaintiff rested her case, my co-counsel Josh called our defense neurosurgeon to the stand, placed the flip chart in front of him, turned to same page, and solicited the following testimony:

- Yes, CSF = conclusive test
- Yes, normal SFP = no transverse myelitis
- Yes, high SFP = transverse myelitis
- No, plaintiff's expert is mistaken. The test *was* performed.

As surprised jurors glanced at plaintiff's red-faced counsel, Josh provided the expert with a paper copy of the testing and asked him to share with the jury the results of that testing. "The SFP was abnormally high, consistent with transverse myelitis," our neurosurgeon explained. Josh then gave our expert the opportunity to explain (at length) the testing itself and the importance of the results. By the time Josh tendered our neurosurgeon for cross-examination, we were loving our decision to "pin, not punch" plaintiff's neurosurgeon during my cross-examination. Like good waiters, we had brought the jury the "conclusive" test results *and* the testimony of the only expert who had the benefit of reviewing those results.

Pick your sports analogy for remembering to "pin, not punch" their expert. Picture your flip chart page bearing their expert's assumptions and opinions as an archery target that you paint during cross-examination and place in front of your expert during direct examination. Or pretend you are that professional wrestler whose duty is to put the opponent in a head lock while your tag team partner climbs the ropes. Whatever works for you. But make no mistake. Your new mission in life is to give your experts a clean shot.

2. Test Ability to Define Terms and Concepts

Experts are often moving targets, effortlessly changing their opinions and the basis for those opinions. That is why experts fear definitions. Definitions are handcuffs. Before trial, demand an expert's definitions and test that expert's understanding of basic concepts. An entire cross-examination can be based on an incorrect or incomplete definition.

Preparation is the key. Start every deposition or pretrial hearing by asking an opposing expert to define the medical or professional terms in their report. Ask the orthopedic surgeon to define "herniated disc" and "bulging disc" before you let them open their file and see what the MRI or CT scan of the plaintiff showed. Taking this approach, we have learned that some orthopedic surgeons define "herniated disc" as "any bulging disc that causes pain" and diagnose a herniated disc based solely on a plaintiff's complaints of pain. Remember that an incorrect, inappropriate, or circular definition may not result in an expert's exclusion, but it can cause the jury to ignore that expert's conclusions.

During a deposition or pretrial hearing, never be content with *only* soliciting the expert's definition. Ask the expert to provide real-world examples of what does and does not satisfy that definition. Ask the expert to produce reports where the expert found the definition applicable and not applicable. Ask the expert to compare definitions and explain differences. Create as many opportunities as possible for the expert to volunteer more information and insight.

Use definitions to expose an expert's lack of knowledge. Before the 2010 *Nugent* trial, I deposed the elected coroner who was determined to offer his opinion in the fields of cardiac electrophysiology and conducted electrical weapons. Rather than asking the coroner to admit he was not an expert in either field, I started his videotaped deposition by asking 50 basic electrical questions. The elected coroner quickly became defensive, as the following excerpts from the first 18 pages of his deposition transcript confirm:

Q. Am I correct in saying that you cannot define ampere for us?

A. No.

Q. Okay. What is your definition of ampere?

A. I don't have one. I'm not going to try to do that.

Q. What is your definition of coulomb?

A. I'm not going to try to define—to give you a definition of coulomb either.

Q. What is your definition of ohm?

A. I'm not going to do that.

Q. What is Ohm's Law?

A. I'm not prepared to answer electrical engineering questions.

Q. I mean, do you know what Ohm's Law is?

A. No, I do not.

* * *

Q. Okay. What is your definition of electricity?

A. It's a—I don't—I don't have a specific definition of my own of electricity.

Q. One volt represents the amount of force required to do what?

A. I—I—I'm not competent to answer that question for you.[1]

The coroner's inability to define and discuss basic electrical concepts was so pronounced that the Louisiana Second Circuit Court of Appeal limited his testimony in the parallel criminal prosecution, and the district attorney chose not to call him during the *Nugent* manslaughter trial, which resulted in a "not guilty" verdict for our client. What the Second Circuit and the district attorney both realized was that an expert who is incapable of defining and discussing basic concepts in a field of expertise is not qualified to offer an opinion in that field—which is something that jurors would have realized after the third unanswered question.

3. Test the Use of Legal Terms and Opinions on Probability

Experts have started appropriating and incorporating legal terms in their opinions and expert reports. Sometimes, those experts cannot define basic legal concepts and do not understand the proper legal threshold. Their misconceptions can be fertile ground for cross-examination.

Always ask an expert to define legal terms. And, if an expert balks at defining a legal term like "defective" because "I'm not a lawyer," ask the expert for their personal definition of that legal term. What does that

1. Transcript of Deposition of Williams at 15:23-16:14, 17:23-18:05, Thomas v. City of Winnfield, No. 1:08-CV-1167 (W.D. La. 8/28/09).

legal term mean to them? What did they mean when they used that legal term in that specific sentence of their report? By asking those questions, you will discover that some experts have given very little thought to common legal terms and concepts. Picture a mechanical engineer defining "unreasonably dangerous" as "capable of causing injury," even though every product (including a pencil) can cause injury, depending on how it is used. That cross-examination writes itself.

Many expert reports end with a boilerplate sentence like "I hold these opinions to a reasonable degree of [professional] probability." Always ask the expert to define "reasonable degree of [professional] probability." Always request that the expert identify a *specific* percentage, and do not accept a generic answer like "more than 50 percent." Force the expert to either identify the specific percentage ("Is it 51 percent or 52 percent?") or admit they cannot identify a specific percentage. Force an expert to admit there is no peer-reviewed or published rate of error for their opinion on probability. When an expert admits they cannot give a specific percentage for probability *and* their opinion is "not subject to a rate of error calculation," the judge and/or the jury may conclude that expert's opinion is not scientific.

During a deposition or pretrial hearing, discuss with the opposing expert the relationship between probability and rate of error. Provide them with a real-world example to establish a baseline for probability and certainty. For example, if studies show that only 15 percent of women with metastatic breast cancer live five or more years after diagnosis, a medical expert could testify with a reasonable degree of medical probability that a patient with metastatic cancer (tragically) will more likely than not die within five years. If pressed, that same medical expert could testify that there is an 85 percent likelihood that a patient diagnosed with metastatic cancer will die within five years and cite the rate of error established by those peer-reviewed and published studies.

Using that baseline, force the expert to admit that their opinion cannot be offered with "the same degree of professional certainty" or "the same degree of professional probability" as an opinion on the survival rate of metastatic breast cancer. Obviously, an orthopedic surgeon's opinion that a plaintiff's neck stiffness yesterday morning was more likely than not caused by a car accident seven years earlier (a) is not based on a peer-reviewed and published study; (b) cannot be supported with similar statistical evidence; (c) cannot be offered with the same degree of professional certainty; and (d) is not subject to a calculable rate of error.

During the 2006 *Cole* trial, which involved a negligent care claim brought by a former inmate, the Chief of Infectious Diseases Section at a prominent medical center testified during direct examination that the detention center "more likely than not" could have stopped the spread of group F streptococcus (which caused an induced coma and amputation) if antibiotics had been started by a certain date. During cross-examination, I insisted that the expert identify a *specific* percentage, and the expert identified a *different* percentage than he identified during his deposition. When pressed, the expert admitted he could cite no source for either percentage. The trial court immediately excluded his testimony regarding percentages and subsequently found the detention center was not negligent. On appeal, the Louisiana Third Circuit Court of Appeal affirmed the zero verdict, stating the following about that expert's testimony:

> Dr. Martin went on to testify in his deposition that he thought starting antibiotics between the 15th and the 28th when swelling showed up would have prevented progression of the infection beyond the sinuses. He stated that one can say that antibiotics on the 20th perhaps would give him a better than 50 percent chance of containing the organism or avoiding the complications. Then he said, probably, antibiotics some time between the 15th and the 25th, more likely than not, would have prevented his complications on the 26th. Dr. Martin then followed with, "He would have had a better chance if he had been started on antibiotics on the 26th but I'm less comfortable with that as being a time that antibiotics and decongestants or whatever, would have worked." Dr. Martin changed his testimony at trial, and his percentages were ultimately rejected by the trial court.[2]

Some experts will refuse to give a percentage to support their opinions. Some will calmly testify that some opinions are not susceptible to a rate of error. And others will default to testifying that their opinion is based solely only on personal experience. But these types of admissions can be half the battle during cross-examination.

4. Attack Assumptions

Experts frequently base their opinions on factual assumptions, but they rarely volunteer *why* they made those assumptions or explain *how* changing those assumptions would affect their opinions. Never underestimate the risk that jurors will incorrectly conclude that the expert personally

2. Cole v. Acadia Par. Sheriff's Dep't, 2007-1386 (La. App. 3 Cir. 11/5/08); 998 So. 2d 212, 219, *writ denied*, 2008-2875 (La. 2/6/09); 999 So. 2d 784.

investigated and verified the facts (versus assuming those facts to be true). Design a line of cross-examination questioning that makes it clear that the accuracy of the expert's opinions 100 percent depends on the accuracy of the expert's factual assumptions. Garbage in, garbage out.

That line of cross-examination will always depend on the specific facts of your case. But, in general, harvest the necessary information from expert reports and use opportunities to question the expert under oath (i.e., depositions or pretrial hearings) to:

- Identify each factual assumption (force the expert to say "I assumed . . .").
- Identify when (on what day) the expert decided to assume each fact.
- Identify what the expert knew and did not know when he made each factual assumption.
- Identify what steps the expert could have taken to verify each fact (instead of assuming).
- Confirm the expert failed to take those steps to verify the fact.
- Confirm the expert did not verify and is not personally vouching that any of the factual assumptions are correct.
- Determine whether the expert disregarded or ignored any evidence contradicting the factual assumption.
- Identify the source for each assumption (especially if opposing counsel *instructed* the expert to assume that fact).
- Confirm how the factual assumption factored into the expert's methodology and affected the expert's calculations or conclusions.
- Confirm that the accuracy of those opinions depends on the accuracy of the assumptions.

Economists are a good example of how attacking assumptions can be used to undermine an expert's opinion. When calculating a plaintiff's claim for lost future wages, an economist must rely on multiple factors or factual assumptions, including the plaintiff's annual base salary, fringe benefits, future work expectancy, and projected salary increases. Sometimes, an economist will be instructed by the hiring attorney to assume certain facts. Sometimes, the hiring attorney will not send the economist all the relevant employment, wages, and tax documents. But in every case, the accuracy of the economist's calculations completely depends on the accuracy of the factual assumptions. Consequently, a good cross-examination solicits the testimony you need to paint that economist as nothing more than a calculator, as demonstrated by the following deposition excerpt:

Q. And you're not verifying or approving the accuracy of the information given to you by plaintiff's counsel?

A. Correct.

Q. Your role is to take the information that you were given and your methodology is essentially *like a calculator*, you take all of that information, and you get to an end result figure, is that correct?

A. That's right.

Q. So if another expert or another individual were to give you different information or different numbers, does your methodology change?

A. No, sir.

The same can be true for other expert opinions. If the plaintiff's certified life care planner assumed that every recommendation by the plaintiff's neurologist was medically necessary, establish the fact that the life care planner did nothing more than price the items listed by the neurologist. Never let the jury think that a (non-medical) life care planner is qualified to offer a medical opinion or *independently* determined the plaintiff's future medical needs. Make it clear to the jury that a life care planner who priced items within a certain radius was nothing more than a "bargain shopper."

If the defendant's accident reconstruction expert assumed that the defendant's account of the accident was accurate (and the plaintiff's account was inaccurate), find out whether defense counsel *instructed* the expert to assume their client's testimony was truthful. Determine how changing that assumption would change their calculations, reconstruction, and opinions.

The same can be true for medical experts. If the plaintiff's neurologist assumed the plaintiff truthfully reported loss of consciousness, find out how that assumption affected the neurologist's determination that the plaintiff sustained permanent brain damage. If the plaintiff's orthopedic surgeon assumed the plaintiff truthfully reported that cervical pain started immediately after the accident, find out how that assumption affected the orthopedic surgeon's opinion that the accident caused a disc herniation. Always determine how changing factual assumptions (especially assumptions based on the plaintiff's subjective complaints or the defendant's self-serving statements) would change their expert opinions regarding medical causation and damages.

5. Visually Connect Admissions to Opinions

For decades, Gray Hairs have correctly embraced and emphasized the need for verbal signposting, the art of letting the jury know that you are finished with one line of cross-examination questioning (i.e., "Let's talk about the accident" or "Let's shift to your opinion on medical care"). But the attention span of jurors has decreased, and verbal signposting is no longer sufficient. Today, the risk is too great that jurors will miss your five-word segues to the next line of questioning and the relevance of your next line of questioning will be lost.

Let's start giving jurors visual signposts during cross-examination. Create charts that group related questions and solicit "yes/no" or "true/false" answers from the expert. Make certain the jury can follow along and understands the importance of each factual admission by visually connecting that admission to one of their specific opinions.

An effective cross-examination could involve nothing more than filling in three "yes/no" charts separately addressing the expert's three opinions. During the 2021 *Lindale* trial, we argued that the contract entitled our client, Lindale Pipeline, LLC, to be the "sole and exclusive water provider and pumper on the pipeline." Fortunately, the original parties to the contract specifically defined "pipeline" and even went to the trouble of attaching a map showing the wells located "on the pipeline." Nevertheless, the defendant hired an "expert" in the oil and gas industry, who testified that the contract only required the defendant to purchase water from Lindale if the water was delivered "through the pipeline." During my cross-examination, I displayed and completed the chart shown in Table 10.1 to attack their expert's opinion that "on the pipeline" should be interpreted as "through the pipeline."

The chart allowed the jury to "keep score" and follow along as I collected each important admission from the opposing expert. The jury knew exactly why I was asking each question, and the jury knew exactly how many more questions I was going to ask on this critical contractual issue.

The chart magically encouraged the expert to answer more directly. Everyone in the courtroom could see what I was doing. Everyone in the courtroom could *see* the relevance of the line of questioning. Everyone in the courtroom could see that I wanted a "yes" or "no" answer regarding each carefully worded fact. After answering the first question, the expert realized that resistance was futile.

Table 10.1 Through the Pipeline

		YES	NO
1.	Parties chose unique language in Section 4.		
2.	"Through" has different meaning than "on."		
3.	"Through" refers to movement into one end and out another.		
4.	"Through the pipeline" refers to physical act of water traveling inside the pipeline.		
5.	All 11 uses of "through the pipeline" outside the exclusivity provision refer to the physical act of water traveling inside the pipeline.		
6.	"Through the pipeline" has different meaning than "on the pipeline."		
7.	"On the pipeline" refers to a geographical position relative to the pipeline.		
8.	"On the pipeline" only appears in Section 4's exclusivity provision.		
9.	"On the pipeline" cannot be used interchangeably with "through the pipeline" in Section 4.		
10.	Replacing "on the pipeline" with "through the pipeline" would violate Section 1 of the contract.		

The chart itself discourages evasiveness. Instead of interrupting or responding to a long-winded or evasive answer with a "non-responsive" objection, I could sigh and wait patiently, leaving the tip of my pen hovering over "yes." And, when the expert finally finished her answer, I could seek the exact clarification that my chart required and every juror wanted by asking, "Is that a 'no'?" or "May I check 'no' on my chart?" No lawyering lawyer here. Just a waiter trying to get these answers for the jury.

An effective cross-examination could also involve nothing more than writing down the bullet points you want to address with your expert. During the 2010 *Nugent* trial, the court allowed me to write on a flip chart during cross-examination. Every cross-examination started with my writing the witness's name at the top of the flip-chart page. Every time the witness made a critical admission, I grabbed my marker and (noisily) wrote the quote or added a bullet point to his page. During closing argument, I flipped to that witness's page to remind and reassure the jury that the witness *really did say that* during my cross-examination.

Pinning down their expert is the right strategy for cross-examination, even if you don't have an expert, and you have to "take the punch" yourself during closing argument. In the *Lindale* trial, I wanted to nail down their expert's Big Four Opinions, so that I could pull them up during closing argument, remind the jury how extreme those four opinions were, and address each opinion without the jury wondering if I was misstating those opinions. The chart shown in Table 10.2 and some checkmarks did the trick.

Table 10.2 Four Opinions Chart

		YES	NO
1.	Pipeline Agreement is limited to water delivered "through the pipeline."	√	
2.	Wells and well pads are NOT included in the definition of Pipeline.	√	
3.	On day Lindale finished investing $1.2 million & brought Brigham pipeline "online," Brigham was not obligated to purchase a drop of water from Lindale.	√	
4.	Brigham's obligations are "almost nonexistent" under the contract.	√	

Some courts may (incorrectly and stubbornly) refuse to recognize your cross-examination chart as a demonstrative exhibit, refuse to allow you to publish the empty chart to the jury, and/or refuse to give you time to fill in the blanks during your cross-examination. I have encountered and had to deal with all three rulings.

During the 2011 *Wiltz* trial, we defended our client against the plaintiff's claim that the store sold alcohol to minors who were involved in a car accident eight hours later that killed three minors and caused severe brain damage to a fourth. During every cross-examination, we asked the same two questions to the minors who were on the trip: (1) "Did you personally purchase alcohol or beer from my client that was taken on the tubing trip on Sunday, August 21, 2005?" and (2) "Did you personally see a minor purchasing alcohol or beer from my client on Sunday, August 21, 2005?"

During cross-examination, we wanted Lions on the jury to *see* the same two questions and to *watch* us write down the responses of every minor who testified. I pictured placing a page full of "no" on the projector at the start of our closing argument. Instead, the first time I placed the paper with the two questions on the overhead projector, and asked the court to turn on the projector (which the court controlled from the bench), the court immediately asked, "Is that in evidence?" My answer was "no," and the piece of paper was never shown to the jury. Inexplicably, that judge refused to permit us to display two questions, *even though* Gray Hairs have been free to write those two questions on a flip chart for decades.

Always find out whether the court will allow you to write down responses during cross-examination. When a court refuses to allow you to publish your chart, you should still complete the chart and use that completed chart during cross-examination. If possible, find a way to call the jury's attention to the fact that you are filling out a chart, perhaps by walking back to the table, retrieving that single piece of paper, placing it in front of you, using a verbal signpost ("Let's talk about your opinion on . . ."), and making sure the jury sees you write down *something* after each question. Resist the temptation to pause too long and never flourish your pen as dramatically as the *Tonight Show*'s Jimmy Fallon did between Thank You Notes. Avoid soliciting an objection.

Remember that "yes/no" and "true/false" charts are not the only way to allow jurors to "follow along" with your questions. Place a timeline in front of the jury and check off events on that timeline as you review the plaintiff's medical treatment. In preparation for the 2021 *Friedley* trial, we timely produced the "pre-accident medical timeline" shown in Figure 10.1, culminating in the impact with the plaintiff's trailer (which was insufficient to damage the trailer hitch shown on the timeline). The case favorably settled during jury selection, while the court was handling hardship requests. But, had the *Friedley* trial not settled, we planned on showing the jury Figure 10.1 during opening statement and checking off every event on that timeline during our cross-examination of plaintiff's experts.

Figure 10.1 Timeline before the accident.

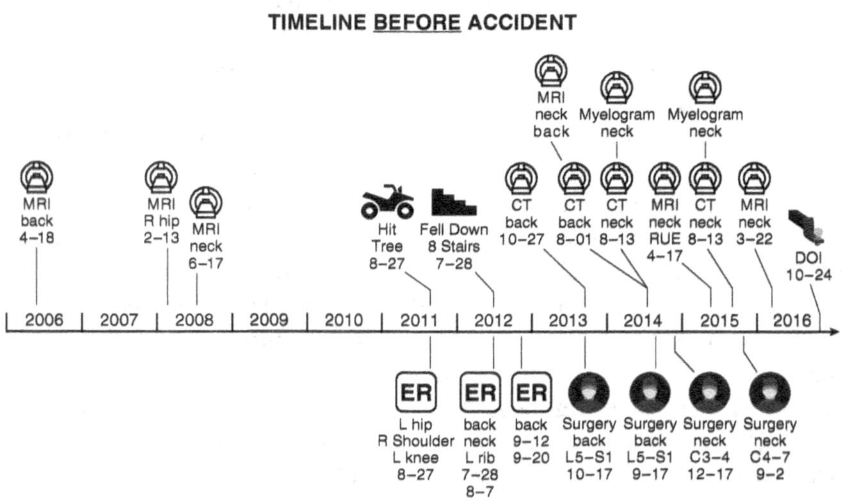

What we recognized was that the plaintiff's pre-accident medical treatment was so extensive that we needed some way of *constantly* reminding jurors that multiple MRIs, doctor visits, and procedures all occurred *before* the date of the incident (DOI) for which plaintiff was suing our client.

6. Establish What They Read, Received, and Requested

Expert witnesses may fail to read, receive, or request critical evidence (documents, transcripts, or video) that undermine their expert opinions. When that happens, do not confront the expert with the missing evidence during cross-examination. Do not insist they admit the evidence changes everything (it doesn't) or demand they recant their opinion (they won't). Instead, consider the following alternatives during your cross-examination.

Consider forcing their expert to admit each item they did *not* read, receive, or request (soliciting three "no" responses for each item). Grab an easel and noisily write each item on the list. Resist the temptation to comment on opposing counsel's failure to send the evidence to the expert or the expert's failure to request the evidence. And resist the temptation to ask their expert how that evidence *might* change their opinion. Instead, wait until your direct examination of your expert. With your expert on the stand (and their expert on a plane home), flip to the page of their expert's unread/unsent evidence and ask your expert: (a) whether they received and reviewed the listed evidence; (b) whether they relied on any of the listed evidence in forming their opinions; and (c) why that evidence was important.

Alternatively, consider making a list of the evidence their expert *did* read, receive, and request. Let their expert leave the courtroom *still* not knowing what you and your expert know. Picture yourself standing in front of the flip chart and asking your expert: "Did you review any important evidence that does not appear on this list?" That should get the jury's attention.

Consider more visually effective ways to show the jury what the expert did *and* did not read, receive, or request. Sometimes, I want the jury to see how many pages of deposition testimony the opposing expert did not read. One by one, I will hold up bound deposition transcripts and ask the exert "Did you read this deposition?" I create a stack of depositions the expert read and a separate (hopefully much taller stack) of depositions the expert was not provided or did not read. When I am finished with that line of questioning, the jury can see for themselves that the expert read only a fraction of the deposition testimony, and the jury looks forward to learning what the expert missed. Always resist the temptation to call the expert's attention to any testimony in the "unread" stack. Instead, wait for the direct examination of your expert to show the jury what your expert found in their expert's stack of unread depositions.

Should that magical day arrive when an opposing expert denies the knowability of a known fact, and you can't resist the temptation to confront the expert with the document containing that fact, remember that it doesn't matter whether the expert ignored the document (which makes the expert look bad) or never received the document (which makes opposing counsel look bad).

During the 2010 *Nugent* trial, the prosecutor's forensic pathologist incorrectly testified that it was "impossible" to know a key fact because that fact had not been included in any police report. The expert placed a stack of documents on the witness stand and openly dared me to find where that key fact appeared in any of the documents. When I saw that the police officer's typed statement was not in the stack, I asked "Is that all of the documents you received?" The expert replied that he had more documents in his luggage, and I calmly asked the court for a recess to allow the bailiff to retrieve (but not open) the expert's luggage.

Back on the stand, the doctor charmingly apologized "in advance" to the jurors in case his "boxers fell out" of his luggage. The expert then opened his luggage, retrieved the additional stack of documents, and handed it to me. There, among those luggage documents, was the overlooked police report that specifically included the "unknowable" fact. Unable to resist, I handed the document to the surprised expert and had him read the sentence containing the unknowable fact. As the jurors smiled, I launched into a line of questioning that forced the expert to admit: (a) nothing was underlined or circled on the document; (b) nothing was highlighted anywhere on the document; and (c) there were no annotations, writings, or marks anywhere on the document. I finished the line of questioning by asking; "Is there any evidence you even read this document before issuing your report?" The expert turned to the jury and smugly answered, "Only my eyeball prints." No juror laughed, and the smug expert's opinion was ignored.

7. Establish What They *Physically* Did Prior to Issuing a Report

Experts know how to defend their methodology. If permitted, an expert will impress the jury with a long-winded answer that lacks any meaningful detail. They will tell jurors how they "analyzed" and "assessed" and "weighed" and "deconstructed" and "matriculated" and *whatever.* They will make their methodology of reading the documents sent by opposing counsel and dictating a report sound like the gold standard in their profession. Always clarify for the jury what the expert *physically* did before dictating a report.

Consider stretching out the point by identifying what the expert did *not* physically do (before confirming that he "only" read the materials sent). Use your deposition to prepare a list of actions that their expert did not take, and use your cross-examination to establish that their expert in forensic pathology:

- Did not physically examine the patient.
- Did not physically examine the product.
- Did not physically crack a book in the expert's library.
- Did not physically pick up the phone and consult with any other expert.
- Did not physically take any tissue samples.
- Did not physically touch any diagnostic images.
- Did not physically download or pull-up any electronic images.
- Did not physically look at anything under a microscope.
- Did not physically run any tests on anything.
- Did not physically perform any calculations on a calculator.

Resist the temptation to ask the expert "Why not?" Resist the temptation to ask the expert how it is possible to reach a conclusion without performing certain tests or calculations. Resist the temptation to confront the expert with the additional steps that your expert took because that will only provide the expert with an opportunity to comment on the need for those additional steps (i.e., "it wasn't necessary to . . ." or "that test is not applicable because . . ."). Whatever answer you think you are going to get, you are not going to get it.

Just collect the "no" and go!

8. Expose Bias Demonstrated by Factual Omissions

In their reports, experts are rarely content to list the evidence (documents, depositions, videos, etc.) they reviewed. Instead, experts often feel compelled to include a section summarizing that evidence. Sometimes, experts include that section to impress counsel with their "command of the facts." Sometimes, experts include that section to help themselves prepare for deposition or trial (because they have no intention *whatsoever* of re-reading *anything*). Whatever the reason, that section of an expert report can be a gold mine.

Always make a list of facts that their expert omitted from their summary of the evidence, focusing on any facts that are inconsistent with the expert's opinions or undermine that expert's opinions ("unfavorable facts"). What you do with those omitted unfavorable facts will always depend on the following circumstances.

When the expert omitted a *critical* unfavorable fact because the expert was never provided the document containing that unfavorable fact, remember our sacred rule (you don't win a trial with their expert, you win a trial with yours), and resist the temptation to confront the expert with that document during your cross-examination. Instead, as discussed, pin the expert down on what he was (or was not) provided and wait for your direct examination of your expert to reveal and review the document they never gave their expert.

When the expert omitted a *critical* unfavorable fact that was contained in a document the expert reviewed, (again) remember our sacred rule (you don't win a trial with their expert, you win a trial with yours) and resist the temptation to confront the expert with that fact during your cross-examination. Instead, as discussed, pin the expert down on what he was (or was not) provided and wait for your direct examination of your expert to reveal the fact their expert omitted.

However, when the expert omitted unfavorable facts that (individually or collectively) only establish the expert's bias and prejudice, confront the expert with those unfavorable facts and ask the expert whether they "missed or intentionally omitted" each fact from their summary." That is *not* something you can do during the direct examination of your expert, who can only speculate as to whether their expert missed or intentionally omitted each fact. Remember that it doesn't matter whether the expert missed the unfavorable fact (proving the expert is not diligent) or intentionally omitted the unfavorable fact (proving the expert is biased).

Few experts are willing to admit that they missed a fact, even when they absolutely, positively, undeniably, missed that fact. Instead, most experts will calmly and confidently tell the jury that they intentionally omitted that fact and immediately volunteer one of the following specific reasons for their omission: (a) the unfavorable fact was not important; (b) they only reviewed the "abnormal" or "normal" findings (depending on the expert); (c) they only included in their summary those facts on which their opinion was based; (d) they can't include every fact in their report; or (e) they knew that the opposing expert would cover the unfavorable facts in their summary. Be prepared for each potential response.

Always start that portion of your cross-examination by getting the expert to generally agree that an expert witness: (a) should be fair and objective; (b) should not cherry pick their facts; and (c) should not hide from the jury evidence that is inconsistent with their opinions. Asking these set up questions will cause anticipation to build. Jurors will immediately assume that you are asking these questions for a reason. They will sit up. They will pay attention. They will get excited. Any expert asked about cherry picking facts *must be* guilty of cherry picking facts, and any expert asked about hiding inconsistent evidence *must be* guilty of hiding inconsistent evidence. Take your time. Set the stage.

After securing these general admissions, establish that each unfavorable fact was omitted from the expert report and force the expert to admit that he or she either missed or intentionally omitted each unfavorable fact. Remember the following steps:

1. Show them the document they reviewed.
2. Confirm that they reviewed the document.
3. Call their attention to the omitted fact in the document.
4. Force them to admit the omitted fact is not included in their summary.
5. Force them to admit the omitted fact is not included *anywhere* in the report.
6. Ask them whether they missed or intentionally omitted that fact.

Resist the temptation to ask the expert *how* they could have missed such an unfavorable fact or *why* they intentionally omitted that fact. When the expert omitted several unfavorable facts, consider (noisily) writing down a list. If you are defense counsel, wait for the direct examination of your expert to (a) confirm that all the omitted facts either undermined or were inconsistent with the expert's opinion and (b) comment on the importance of the omission.

Similarly, if you are plaintiff's counsel, wait for the testimony of your rebuttal witness or wait for your closing argument to (a) confirm that all the omitted facts either undermined or were inconsistent with the expert's opinion and (b) comment on the importance of the omission.

9. Smash Microscopic and Telescopic Approaches to Literature

Experts only want to talk about those articles, studies, and papers that (they believe) support their opinion. They will force the jury to look at a single article under a microscope, hoping to make a single chart or finding appear much bigger and more important than it really is. They will hold a telescope up and ask the jury to look back in time at a single article and pretend that article is the only article the jury needs to see. Do not be content to spend your cross-examination attacking the single article or the single chart that the expert discussed on direct examination.

Time equals importance during jury trials. If you spend your entire cross-examination discussing an unimportant article or the expert's misinterpretation of that article, the takeaway for some jurors will be that the article is very important, and the expert's interpretation is a game changer. Instead of focusing on the article their expert wants the jury to focus on, find a way to help jurors look up from the expert's microscope or put down the expert's telescope. Show them all the literature that the expert ignored.

During the 2012 *Fahy* trial, plaintiff's expert focused the jurors' attention on a study that the expert believed was sufficient to prove my client knew (actual knowledge) or should have known (constructive knowledge) when they sold the product that it could cause cardiac arrest. Instead of discussing the one pig study their expert wanted to discuss, I marked a large box "yes" and another large box "no."[3] I showed printed copies of other pre-sale studies to the expert and forced him to admit whether he had read the article, physically placing the stapled article into the corresponding box.

The exercise itself educated the jurors during the *Fahy* trial. It forced them to put down the telescope that the plaintiff's expert had held to their eyes. They were no longer myopically focused on the one pig study relied

3. Proper credit should be given to Michael Brave, Esq., who had the idea of using boxes to emphasize how many documents the expert had ignored during the *Fahy* trial.

on by the expert. Now, they wanted to know what the studies in the "no" box said, and whether the expert had unintentionally missed or intentionally ignored the results of studies in the "yes" box. The line of questioning had minimized the importance of the one pig study and perfectly set the stage for the direct examination of our expert (who was prepared to discuss articles in both boxes).

10. Use an Expert Comparison Chart

Nothing is more effective than filling out a chart comparing your expert's qualifications with their expert's qualifications. Days later, jurors may not recall what each row said, but they will remember seeing a column of "yes" for your expert and a column of "no" for theirs. If you want that visual seared into a juror's mind (and you do), you must select the right qualifications to list on your chart.

Always meet with your expert and discuss what qualifications your expert has that their expert lacks or likely lacks. Together, you can create a draft Expert Qualification Chart that lists only those qualifications for which you will be able to write "yes" in your expert's column. Whenever possible, hold that meeting with your expert before you depose their expert or question their expert during a pretrial hearing. That way, you can ask their expert (under oath) whether they do or do not have each qualification that your expert has.

Do your best to maintain the element of surprise. Try not to tip off opposing counsel. When deposing an expert, do not whip out your draft Expert Qualification Chart, place it on the table, and start writing "yes" or "no" as their expert answers each question. Bury the questions somewhere in your deposition outline. Avoid soliciting a string of "no" responses by cleverly including questions about qualification that both experts share (and you have no intention of including in the Expert Qualification Chart). Show no interest in their expert's answers to any of your qualification questions.

Decide, before trial, whether you are going to (a) physically write "no" on the Expert Qualification Chart during the cross-examination of their expert and "yes" during the direct examination of your expert or (b) be content to ask the exact same qualification questions (in the exact same order) of both experts and wait until closing argument to present the jury with a filled-in chart showing a column of "yes" and a column of "no."

There are advantages and disadvantages to both approaches. Using a pen to (noisily) write "yes" or "no" can be very effective, but it can also be time consuming and/or draw an objection. Only asking the questions during direct and cross-examination will save time and avoid objections, but it requires the jury to remember or trust the accuracy of the filled-in chart you subsequently show them during your closing argument.

Be prepared for experts to get squirrely if you choose to place the Expert Qualification Chart on an easel during cross-examination. When opposing experts see the chart and realize that they lack the listed qualifications, they will not want to let you ask them each question, nor will they want to watch you write "no" next to each qualification. After answering your first question, some experts will interrupt you and volunteer that "my answer is 'no' to all of those questions up there, counselor." Some experts will comment that the listed qualifications are not important. Some will explain why they do not have that qualification. Other experts will criticize you for intentionally omitting the qualifications that they do possess.

During the Golden Age of Lawyers, Gray Hairs developed methods for proactively or reactively handling an expert's refusal to answer "yes" or "no" to a direct question. Those methods included: (a) at the start of cross-examination, asking the expert to agree that they will try to answer only the question asked (i.e., "Can we agree that I will do my best to ask one question at a time, and you will do your best to answer only the question asked?") and (b) while the expert is volunteering additional information, objecting to the expert's answer as non-responsive and moving to strike everything the expert said after "no."

Both methods are likely to draw an objection from opposing counsel. Both will make you look like a lawyering lawyer, especially if the court sustains opposing counsel's objection or overrules your "non-responsive" objection. So, let's rip both pages out of our playbook.

Let's agree to wait for an expert to finish their answer (instead of interrupting the expert) and then politely remind everyone that you only asked whether the expert held that qualification: "I'll ask my question again . . . are you board certified?" In so doing, without objecting or interrupting like a "typical" lawyer, you can remind the jury that the expert is being defensive, difficult, or evasive.

Trust your instincts. If the expert's answer is obnoxiously non-responsive, consider responding with a more aggressive question that solicits an admission by the expert: "In fairness, I only asked you *whether* you were board certified, I did not ask you *why* you are not board certified, did I?" Let opposing counsel object to your question as "argumentative." Let the court sustain that objection. Let the expert continue to play games and refuse to answer directly. The jury will feel your pain, and the jury will not like the expert.

Be prepared for their expert to change their answer from the "no" they told you during their deposition to the "yes" they want to tell the jury. After watching opposing counsel write "no" for the first five listed qualifications, some experts will crack. They will forget that they previously admitted under oath that they did not possess the next qualification. They will exaggerate or outright misrepresent their experience. Anticipate that moment. Make certain you have what you need to immediately impeach the witness. Do not approach the podium or start your cross-examination without having (in hand) a certified copy of the transcripts containing the expert's highlighted admissions, the expert's *curriculum vitae*, or whatever documents prove the expert lacks that qualification (and should have answered "no").

During the *Ricks* trial, plaintiff's expert in cardiac electrophysiology admitted that he did not have the first seven qualifications listed on our Expert Qualification Chart. Then he panicked and said "yes" to the eighth and tenth question. When he answered the eighth question "yes" (despite answering "no" during his deposition), the jury was treated to this exchange, which emphasized that the expert was exaggerating his experience:

Q. Had you ever researched the effect of a conducted electrical weapon?

A. Yes.

Q. Prior to being retained in this case?

A. It was part of published data that I had seen.

Q. When articles came out, you'd read them from time to time. Had you ever done a research project?

A. I read the medical journals.

Q. Had you ever done a research project?

A. No.

The *Ricks* trial ended with a directed verdict for the defense, and we never had to call our expert in cardiac electrophysiology. But, if the trial had continued, the jury would have watched us start the direct examination of our expert in cardiac electrophysiology by writing "yes" in every row of our expert's column during direct examination. The completed Expert Qualification Chart would have looked like Table 10.3.

Table 10.3 Expert Qualification Chart Showing Knowledge of Conducted Electrical Weapons (CEWs)

When Hired:	**Kerwin**	**Swerdlow**
Served on Scientific and Medical Advisory Board for TASER International, Inc.?	**NO**	**YES**
Served on board for any CEW manufacturer?	**NO**	**YES**
Published (first author) a peer-reviewed CEW scientific paper?	**NO**	**YES**
Published (senior author) a peer-reviewed CEW scientific paper?	**NO**	**YES**
Published *any* peer-reviewed CEW scientific paper?	**NO**	**YES**
Written *any* peer-reviewed CEW scientific paper?	**NO**	**YES**
Retained as an expert in a CEW lawsuit?	**NO**	**YES**
Researched effects of CEWs?	**"YES"**	**YES**
Touched a CEW?	**NO**	**YES**
Seen in real life a TASER M26 CEW?	**"YES"**	**YES**
In the broadest possible sense, did you have any exposure or experience with TASER CEWs?	**NO**	**YES**

Remember that expert qualification comparison charts can serve as the perfect back drop for closing argument. If your case is a "battle of the experts," prominently display your completed chart (containing a column of "yes" for your expert and a column of "no" for theirs) throughout closing argument as a visual reminder that "objectively" the jury should give greater weight to your expert's testimony than theirs.

An Expert Qualification Chart can be effectively used during cross-examination even when opposing counsel calls the only expert to the stand. During the 2021 *Lindale* trial, I used an Expert Qualification Chart to call the jury's attention to *their* expert's lack of experience writing and interpreting exclusivity provisions in the oil and gas industry, even though we had no expert in that field (because the expert deadlines had passed before we enrolled). Table 10.4 shows the chart I completed for the jury, with every answer being checked "no."

Sometimes, the real reason why jurors should listen to your expert's opinion and ignore their expert's opinion is your expert's superior methodology. If your expert's methodology is more reliable than theirs, use an Expert Methodology Comparison Chart listing all the steps your expert took before reaching an opinion. In some cases, their expert's failure to take just one step (that your expert took) can make all the difference in the world. During closing argument, you can circle that row and explain why objectively your expert's methodology is more reliable and your expert's opinion should be given greater weight.

Table 10.4 Expert Qualification Chart Showing Lack of Experience

When hired by Equinor in 2020:	**Yes**	**No**
Lawyer?		√
Graduated from law school?		√
Attended law school class on contracts?		√
Published any peer-reviewed articles on interpretation of terms in contracts?		√
Submitted for publication any articles on the interpretation of terms in contracts?		√
Hired to write a contract?		√
Written an exclusivity provision?		√
Recognized as an expert in *writing* contracts by a state or federal court?		√
Recognized as an expert in *interpreting* contracts by a state or federal court?		√
Offered as an expert in *writing* or *interpreting* contracts by a state or federal court?		√

Resist the temptation to ask "why" an expert does not hold a credential, did not obtain certain experience, or did not perform a specific step in your expert's methodology unless: (a) the expert has already answered that question under oath; (b) you need or want the jury to hear that answer; and (c) you have the answer highlighted in a certified transcript. Otherwise, let opposing counsel ask the expert *why* he failed to obtain the additional experience or failed to perform the additional step(s) in your expert's methodology. The mere act of opposing counsel's asking rehabilitation questions will tell jurors that their expert *needs* rehabilitation.

Avoid the temptation to sound judgmental. Do not betray your contempt for the expert's lack of qualifications with your tone or with unnecessary words (i.e., "You didn't even get your doctorate in . . . ," "You never even treated a patient with . . . ," or "You didn't even perform a Google search for . . ."). Resist the temptation to scoff or shake your head as you write "no." Just get the answer. You can stress the importance of each qualification with your expert during your direct examination of your expert (i.e., "Why did you feel it was important to get a doctorate?" or "What have you learned by actually treating patients with . . . ?").

Just get the "no" and go!

Chapter 11

Direct Examination of Lay Witnesses: The Great Disappearing Act

During the Golden Age of Lawyers, trial attorneys wisely decided that direct examination of a lay witness should shine the spotlight on the lay witness who was answering the questions, not on the attorney who was asking the questions. This was the one area of trial advocacy in which attorneys were openly encouraged (like good waiters) to do nothing more than bring the testimony of a lay witnesses to the jury. No commenting on the evidence. No distracting jurors with bravado or braggadocio. During the perfect direct examination of a lay witness, jurors would forget the lawyers were in the courtroom.

For many years, Gray Hairs have taught techniques for focusing the jury's attention on the witness and the testimony during direct examination. Most of those techniques helped attorneys "disappear" during direct examination, and those techniques absolutely belong in our new playbook for the Age of Jurors. The challenge is to identify the handful of techniques that should be abandoned or modified to keep this area of trial advocacy moving in the right direction.

1. Have a Checklist for Your Trial Preparation Meeting

Most trial attorneys understand the importance of meeting with a lay witness (i.e., plaintiff, defendant, brother, friend, neighbor, coworker, supervisor, eyewitness) before that lay witness testifies under oath. Civil attorneys meet with lay witnesses before their deposition. Prosecutors and criminal defense attorneys meet with lay witnesses before they testify during a hearing or trial. Those meetings can be the difference between the witness being ignored and adored.

Trial preparation meetings can be factually and emotionally overwhelming. Ask the witness to tell you *everything* they remember and fasten your seat belt. Suddenly, the witness starts remembering facts they forgot and reliving every emotion they experienced. For the attorney responsible for preparing the witness, it can be intellectually challenging to help a lay witness sort through and organize their memories. And it can be emotionally exhausting to help that same witness process, articulate, and explain their feelings.

No matter how many times you have prepared a witness, you can become disoriented. Maybe their crying compels you to end the trial preparation meeting early. Maybe their remembering a "new" fact compels you down the rabbit hole of reviewing the witness's deposition, dissecting discovery responses, and deciding on whether/when the "new" information should be produced to opposing counsel. That is why every attorney should develop their own checklist for what they want to cover during that meeting with a lay witness.

Table 11.1 shows a sample agenda for a trial preparation. It is intended only as a starting point or a skeleton outline for identifying specific questions for your specific case.

Table 11.1 Lay Witness Prep Checklist

1.	What testimony can the witness offer the jury?
2.	What is that testimony based on (i.e., observation, documents, hearsay)?
3.	What questions would solicit desirable and admissible testimony?
4.	What questions would solicit undesirable or inadmissible testimony?
5.	What is the best order for asking questions?
6.	What exhibits can/should be introduced with this witness?
7.	What facts would establish proper foundation for introducing each exhibit?
8.	What exhibits would refresh the witness's memory (if they forget)?
9.	What demonstrative exhibits would help the witness explain testimony?
10.	What demonstrative exhibits would help the jury remember the witness's testimony?
11.	What facts would help jurors respect or like the witness?
12.	What facts would help jurors give greater weight to the witness's testimony?

2. Avoid Rehearsing the Witness's Testimony

Jurors are interested in and moved by testimony, not by recitals. That is why a trial attorney has to be careful when preparing a lay witness for trial. The challenge is to learn what the witness would say when asked specific questions, without having the witness memorize (or try to memorize) specific responses to specific questions. Never practice your direct examination of a lay witness to the point that the witness knows exactly what you are going to ask and exactly what they should say word-for-word. Rehearse with the lay witness, but not to the point that the testimony sounds rehearsed—which is easier said than done.

This happens all the time in high school mock trial competitions because the same direct examination is repeatedly delivered throughout the tournament. When a direct examination is too rehearsed, the question-and-answer rhythm takes on a "see-saw" quality. There are no pauses during the question or the answer. The witness stops using inflection or varying pitch. Instead of processing the answer, the attorney immediately asks the next question. There is no feeling or passion or spontaneity. The witness does not hesitate, stumble, or search for the right words. It sounds rehearsed because it was rehearsed. Mock trial judges will deduct points. Real jurors would disregard the testimony as coached and contrived.

The ultimate red flag for jurors is when witnesses correct themselves (i.e., "That is when the defendant showed . . . I mean . . . *threatened* me with . . ."). That moment tells the jurors that the testimony is scripted, and the jurors will assume that the questioning attorney wrote the script and is directing the performance. When that happens, do not blame the lay witness, blame the trial lawyer who prepared that witness. Self-corrections only happen when witnesses feel pressured to say specific words, worry that they have made a mistake, and want to start over. Like a young piano player who forgets the next note and must start the whole song over from the beginning, the lay witness may even start the sentences over (i.e., "I put the gun on the . . . I mean . . . I put the gun on safety and *then* I put the gun on the table"). That is when the jury knows that the witness has been practicing, and that the jury is being played.

Another red flag for jurors can be the quick production of an exhibit. This happens all the time on late-night talk shows. The host asks when the guest first started acting, and the guest blushes and mentions an embarrassing television advertisement. Instantly, the host reaches under the desk and produces a screenshot of that embarrassing advertisement, and the guest half-heartedly complains, "I can't believe you found that!" Whenever that happens, I am reminded that the entire exchange was planned, and the spell is broken for me. Similarly, during the trial, when the witness mentions something obscure, like a social media post, do not reach under the podium and immediately produce it. Consider turning to co-counsel and asking, "Can you find that?" Let co-counsel find the exhibit and bring it to you. If you don't have it with you at the podium, the exchange and the moment *must have been* unscripted.

3. Do Not Taint Testimony with Legal Terms or Expressions

Lay witnesses always have questions before trial. Plaintiffs will want to know whether they could win or lose. Defendants will want to know what the plaintiff is required to prove. Friends and family will want to know whether their testimony will help or hurt. And the more tangential the witness, the more that witness will want to know why their testimony is relevant. Young lawyers answer these questions without hesitation, eager to prove that they know the law and know what they are doing. But with every legal answer given to a lay witness, there is risk.

Jurors do not want to see a lawyer's fingerprints on the testimony of a lay witness. By explaining the law to a lay witness, you run the risk that the witness will repeat the legal term or legal standard on the witness stand. And the less-educated the witness, the more a legal term or standard will sound out of place to jurors. Always consider how the use of a legal term could suggest coaching. In the below example, the lay witness's attempt to remember the importance of "actual or constructive knowledge" could ruin otherwise persuasive testimony and cause the jurors to distrust an otherwise likeable witness.

Q. Did you know the railing was rotten?

A. No, sir. I had no idea.

Q. Did any inspection reveal that the railing was rotten?

A. No, sir. We hire a contractor to inspect our property twice a year. His name is Dan. Dan is a contractor and an engineer. He has been doing this for most of the businesses in our city for the past 30 years. Dan did not find it. You can check his inspection reports. You won't see it.

Q. Did any tenant in your apartment building tell you the railing was rotten?

A. No, sir. We record all of our tenant complaints in a daily log book. We saved that book. You can check it. Rotten balcony railing ain't nowhere in there. I can tell you that with 100 percent certainty. I checked it a dozen times since this lawsuit was filed.

Q. Did anyone at any time ever tell you the railing was rotten before this accident?

A. No, sir.

Q. Are you absolutely certain?

A. **I am. We had no actual or constructive knowledge of this defect.**

There is no way of knowing what words a lay witness will remember or advice a lay witness will take to heart during your trial preparation. That is why it is so important to avoid using legal terms and standards. Instead of teaching lay witnesses the law, focus them on what is important about their testimony, using the *same* words that the witness used while talking with you. Instead of introducing a lay witness to the term "defect," tell the lay witness that the jury has to decide whether the wood was "rotten." Instead of explaining the importance of "actual knowledge," emphasize how important it is that the witness "had no idea." Instead of using a term like "constructive knowledge" (which would be a red flag if repeated) or asking the witness whether he "should have known" (which the jury will hear you say in opening statement), ask the witness if there were any "clues" that the wood was rotten before the accident.

Every lay witness has their own way of answering and explaining. They have their own words, expressions, similes, and metaphors. During your first meeting, discover their different ways of answering the same questions and explaining the same concepts. Write them down on your legal pad and weed out the words that could cause confusion or concern. Always think twice before suggesting or substituting your words for theirs. Make sure that you would be comfortable hearing your witness repeat on the stand whatever you are about to say.

4. Do Not Steal Quotes, Similes, or Metaphors for Opening Statement

Trial attorneys know great quotes and metaphors when they hear them. Sometimes, during trial preparation, a lay witness will use an expression (i.e., "That dog don't hunt!") or the perfect metaphor (i.e., "Our security guards are like toll booth operators, they check the construction workers' identification. But they don't tell nobody nothing about how to do their jobs."). When that happens, the skies will part and Beethoven's Ninth Symphony will erupt in all its glory, filling your heart with joy and hope.

Suddenly, all of those lonely days spent searching for the right words will be behind you. At last, you will know exactly what you want to tell jurors during your opening statement. But here's the thing: you can't.

Never steal your own lay witness's thunder. Never deprive the jury of the same experience you had. Always let them hear that soundbite, simile, or metaphor from your witness, and in his own words, accent, tone, and pacing. Even though "Ode to Joy" is still playing in your head, you must stand up for your opening statement and somehow resist the temptation to sing a few bars.

Using an anticipated quote during your opening statement will backfire. Never promise the jury that "Dan will take the stand, and Dan will tell you . . . that dog don't hunt!" If you do, when Dan takes the stand and says, "that dog don't hunt," it will not have the desired effect. Instead of that genuine "Dan moment" that made you smile during your first meeting, jurors will be treated to hearing Dan repeat what his lawyer said during opening statement.

Using an anticipated simile or metaphor during your opening statement will also backfire. Never promise the jury that "the evidence will prove your client's security guards are like construction site toll booth operators. They just check identification." Save it for Dan. Picture Dan turning to the jury in the middle of his cross-examination and saying, "Look here, our security guards ain't nothing more than toll both operators checking badges. They don't tell nobody nothing!" That is when the quote will be most effective. If you save the simile for Dan, jurors will look back at Dan, smiling and nodding. If you steal Dan's thunder, the jurors will neither smile nor nod because they heard it before. Dan is just towing the party line.

5. Do Not Warn Your Lay Witness If You Want an Honest Reaction

Everyone at the surprise party can tell whether the birthday boy was genuinely surprised, usually while they are yelling "surprise!" You might think that you can act surprised, but few of us have that kind of acting ability. It is almost impossible to re-create your unique startle response. The instantaneous transition from fear to fun on your face. How wide your eyes open. The way your cheeks get flushed. How quickly your head sweeps a room full of screaming friends. The only way to make sure that your guests—who went to the trouble of showing up early and parking five blocks away—see a surprised birthday girl is to actually surprise the birthday girl.

Similarly, if you want to solicit genuine surprise from a lay witness, do not share that surprise with them before trial. Carefully consider whether showing the altered document, playing the surveillance video, or sharing the false testimony with your client will solicit the same degree of surprise, indignation, frustration, anger, or disappointment. Like a good waiter, deliver a surprised witness to the jury by surprising the witness.

During the 1998 *Allen* trial, I called the victim's wife, Miss Bertha, to the stand. I asked her to identify the man who had shot her wheelchair-bound husband, entered her bedroom, and shot her in the eye. Miss Bertha pointed at the defendant and identified him as the man who had been smoking marijuana with her husband earlier that evening before deciding he wanted all of the disability money and tried to kill them both. During cross-examination, opposing counsel showed Miss Bertha the tall stack of medical records from her long stay at Charity Hospital in New Orleans. Pulling a single piece of paper from that stack, opposing counsel confronted Miss Bertha with the fact that the history section on one record indicated that Miss Bertha had said "three strangers" entered her house and shot her. That trial ended with a hung jury, and the judge was forced to declare a mistrial.

Before the 1999 *Allen* retrial, I chose not to share with Miss Bertha what we had subsequently found in those medical records from Charity Hospital. Instead, I performed the exact same direct examination. Opposing counsel stood up, grabbed the exact same piece of paper, and asked the exact same questions about the Charity Hospital note suggesting Miss Bertha had blamed "three strangers." But this time, during re-direct examination, I grabbed a second piece of paper from the tall stack of medical records. I told Miss Bertha, who had never seen the piece of paper I was holding, that I was now going to ask her the most important question of the trial. I then asked Miss Bertha whether she was black or white.

Completely confused, Miss Bertha responded as if I had lost my mind, saying "Honey . . . I'm black." I then showed her the Charity Hospital medical record indicating that she was white, and asked her, "Should we believe *you* when you tell us that you are black, or should we believe this piece of paper from Charity Hospital?" Unprompted, Miss Bertha turned, looked at the jurors, showed them her arms, and matter-of-factly said, "Believe me. I am black." That is when I grabbed the other exhibit and asked Miss Bertha, "Should we believe you when you say the defendant shot you, or should we believe this other piece of paper from Charity Hospital?" Miss Bertha replied, "You should believe me. That man shot me." This time, the defendant was convicted of second-degree murder and sentenced to life imprisonment. And while I will never know whether my sharing that piece of paper with Miss Bertha before trial would have resulted in a second hung verdict, I do know that it would not have solicited the same response.

6. Introduce the Witness with Facts, Not Compliments

The best direct examinations do not always take place in a courtroom. They often take place during daytime and nighttime talk shows, where the host has the distinct challenge of asking the right handful of questions to get the studio audience to fall madly in love with their guest. Even with the benefit of "applause" signs, that can be difficult to do when the host has only minutes to introduce the guest, and one false note can break the spell. The best interviewers prepare for the interview and discover that one fact or story that will tell the audience everything they need to know about the guest.

Jurors do not want to be told what to think, especially by the advocate who called the lay witness to the stand. Always start direct examination by soliciting facts that will help the jury decide for themselves what to think about the witness. It is the difference between telling jurors what is obvious and providing them with the facts they need to reach the obvious conclusion. Like a good waiter, deliver the perfectly prepared meal and let the jurors decide it is delicious for themselves. Never tell your customers what they should think about the meal. For example, there is a right way and a wrong way to establish that the witness is a hard worker who would do anything for her children.

a. Wrong Way

Q. How hard did you work before this accident?

A. I worked hard.

Q. How many jobs did you work?

A. I worked two jobs.

Q. Did you work two jobs because you loved working *two* jobs?

A. No, not really.

Q. [Turning to look at jurors.] What was the *real* reason you worked so hard?

A. My children.

Q. Are you the kind of mom who would do *anything* for your children?

COUNSEL: Objection. Leading.

COURT: Sustained. Rephrase.

Q. What would you do for your children?

A. Anything.

b. Right Way

Q. Please tell jurors about a typical work day before this accident.

A. Well, I would wake up early to make their breakfast and their lunches.

Q. What do you mean when you say "early"?

A. I set my alarm for 4:15 a.m.

Q. Whose breakfasts and lunches were you making?

A. I am a single mother. I have five children. So, I would make five lunches. Put them in brown bags on the table. Then, I would make breakfast for everyone. Then, I would get ready for work.

Q. Where did you work?

A. I worked at the coffee shop. My shift started at 6:00 a.m., and I had to leave at 5:15 a.m. to get there for 5:45 a.m. So, I would wake the children at 5:00 a.m. so they could eat their breakfast while it was hot.

Q. Did you get to spend any time with them in the morning?

A. No, I would wake them and walk out the door. My oldest was 16. She would make sure they were ready for the bus to pick them up outside at 6:30 a.m.

Q. How did you get to work?

A. I would drive. The same car I was driving at the time of this accident.

Q. How long was your shift at the coffee shop?

A. We all worked six-hour shifts. I worked from 6:00 a.m. until noon.

Q. Would you go home then?

A. No, I had a part-time job at the hotel across the street. I would clean the rooms, change the beds, vacuum the lobby, clean the public bathroom.

Q. When would that job end?

A. I worked from 12:00 to 5:00 p.m. Then, I would drive home. I would get there at 5:30 p.m. Make dinner. Help them with their homework. Make sure they bathed and brushed their teeth.

Q. How old were your children.

A. Well, the oldest, Katie, was 16. Molly was 14. Maggie was 12. Abbie was 9. And the baby, Danny, was 7.

Q. What time would you call it a day?

A. Katie and Molly could stay up as late as they needed to finish studying. But I had the youngest ones in bed by 10:00 p.m.

Q. What would you do then?

A. There was always something. Laundry. Dishes. Clothes that needed a button. Either Katie or Molly would need to talk. And I had to pay the bills. That was usually the last thing I did before I went to sleep.

Q. When would you call it a night?

A. Most nights it was midnight when I set my alarm for the next day. Do it all again.

Q. How may days did you work a week?

A. Seven days a week at the coffee shop. But I did not work at the hotel on Sundays. I always spent Sunday afternoons with my kids.

There will always be a fact or story that demonstrates how dedicated the lay witness was to their job, or how good a friend the witness was to the plaintiff, or how honest the witness is, or how well the witness served their country in the armed forces. Find the facts or stories that properly introduce the witness and be content to serve those facts and stories to the jury. As difficult as it may be, especially for plaintiff attorneys, never inject your argument or agenda or opinion into the question. After incredibly moving testimony about how the plaintiff suffered at a plant, every plaintiff attorney must choose whether to ask, "And when did you start working at the plant?" or "And for how long did you *suffer* for the owners of that plant?" Make the wrong choice, and you could solicit an "argumentative" objection from opposing counsel or distract jurors with your advocacy. Make the right choice, and the spotlight stays on your witness. And you stay invisible.

7. Do Not Distract Jurors by Commenting or Soliciting Agreement

Trial attorneys know when their witness is scoring points. And that can be a wonderful feeling, especially when you have waited days or weeks to hear this witness deny a statement made by opposing counsel said during opening statement or correct a statement made by an earlier witness on the stand. At that moment, you will want to do *something* to acknowledge or emphasize the importance of the testimony. Resist that temptation.

Never comment on the testimony. During the 2015 *Crayton* case, we wanted the jury to like our former driver. During direct examination, my co-counsel Paul asked our driver about his employment. Our driver proceeded to describe the different jobs that he works in the course of a week. As soon as our driver finished answering, Paul commented, "Hmm. Three jobs. Impressive."

Fortunately, opposing counsel did not object (i.e., "Objection. Counsel testifying!"), probably because they didn't want to call more attention to the testimony. But it was an unnecessary risk. The jury was already impressed with our driver, and the jurors loved Paul, whose local charm was (and is) undeniable. Why comment on the testimony? Why shift the spotlight to yourself? Why take the chance that the court will sustain the objection? Instead, Paul should have been content to pause and let that testimony sink in before starting the next line of questioning.

Never solicit agreement from the witness. There will be times that a lay witness's testimony will conclusively prove what you said during opening statement and conclusively refute what opposing counsel said during opening statement. When that happens, every fiber of a trial attorney's being will crave some acknowledgment that they were right and opposing counsel was wrong. Every trial attorney is genetically predisposed to act whenever action will increase their credibility with a jury or decrease opposing counsel's credibility. It is not in our nature to show restraint, but restraint is what we must show during direct examination.

Never shift the focus from the witness to yourself by soliciting agreement (i.e., "So, when I told jurors during my opening statement that you saw the whole accident, was I correct?"). Similarly, never shift the focus away from the witness by soliciting criticism of opposing counsel (i.e., "So, if *somebody* told this jury during opening statement that you didn't arrive until after the accident, would that person have been correct or incorrect?"). Be content to wait until your closing argument, when the spotlight is on you, to point out how this one lay witness proved opposing counsel was absolutely wrong during opening statement.

Once again, we can learn from waiters. When a customer says, "I really enjoyed the special, thank you for recommending it," a good waiter will reply, "I am so glad you enjoyed it." A good waiter will never shift the focus from the meal to himself by obnoxiously declaring, "I told you! Didn't I tell you? Aren't you glad you listened to me? How great am I?" Similarly, let's resist the temptation to take a bow during the direct examination of a lay witness. That is neither the time, nor the place.

8. Forget Your List of Questions and Listen to the Answers

The best interviewers always listen to the witness's answers. They don't ask a typed question, wait for the guest to respond, and then ask the next typed question. When a guest responds, "I have been fighting depression for the past year," Oprah Winfrey listens, nods, and asks, "What has that fight involved?" When a guest responds, "I have good days and bad days," Barbara Walters listens and asks, "What does a bad day look like for you?" When a famous actor volunteers that they hope their children don't go into showbusiness, Johnny Carson leans forward and asks, "Why do you say that?" Somehow, the truly great interviewers always find way to help the guest tell their story *without* telling that story for the guest.

Similarly, during direct examination, it is so important for an attorney to listen to the lay witness's answer. Ask the witness to explain what they meant. Ask the witness to explain why they chose a particular expression. Ask the witness why they hesitated before answering. Never ignore the answer and move on to the next question. Never ignore an opportunity to help the witness tell the story. And never ignore natural segues to the next question or the next line of questions.

There is a difference between listening and waiting to talk. In this regard, direct examination is not unlike the dinner table. You can always divide your dinner guests into those who are listening to the story and those who are waiting to tell theirs. The people who are waiting to talk are easy to spot. As soon as the story is finished, they immediately spring into their own story. Often, their only segue is "that's nothing, one time . . ."

To teach our daughters how to act at the dinner table, we started the "keep it going" game. The goal of the game was to listen to the guest's answer and keep their story going *without* their realizing what you were doing.

Dad: How was your dinner last night with your neighbor?

Guest: It was so good.

Katie: Where did you go?

Guest: We went to Clancy's.

Molly: We love Clancy's. What did you order for an appetizer?

Guest: I had the crabmeat salad.

Katie: That's mom's favorite. What did your neighbor order?

Guest: She had the turtle soup.

Molly: Did she give you a taste?

Unfortunately, our daughters soon got tired of the game and objected to the game itself. They thought it was mean because the guest was not in on it. Of course, they were right, and we discontinued the game. But the point of the exercise was not to trick or mock the guest. The point of the exercise was to listen to the guest's story and (quickly) think of a question that would help the guest share more about their story. It required them to think of potential questions, but always let the guest's answer dictate the next question. The same can be said of a good direct examination.

9. Never Ask a Question to Which You Don't Know the Answer

There may be times when trial attorneys should ask questions that they don't know the answer to during cross-examination, but that should never happen during direct examination. When the lay witness says something that could use clarification, but you have no idea what the witness will say, let opposing counsel ask the question. That is another absolute rule. If you don't like the rule, prepare your witnesses better.

Before the 1998 *Baloney and Burns* trial, in which the defendant was charged with attempted second-degree murder, I asked the eyewitness what the defendant beat the victim with, and the witness told me a hammer. At trial, I saved that question for my last question of the trial. I asked the eyewitness what the defendant beat the victim with, and she responded, "a hammer . . . or a golf club." Like a deer frozen in the headlights, I stood there, knowing those two objects did not look the same and wondering what I should do. Several seconds (or possibly years) later, I decided to ask a question to which I did not know the answer: "How can a hammer look like a golf club?" The eyewitness responded, "It was the bottom part of a golf club. They snapped it in half and pretended it was a gun to rob people." Defense counsel shot out of his seat, objected, and moved for a mistrial, which was granted. As the jurors filed out of the courtroom, they all patted me on the back and lamented that they would have convicted both defendants. But one year later, after the 1998 *Baloney and Burns* retrial, the jury found the defendants not guilty, and I blamed myself. Lesson learned.

10. When Appropriate, Have Second Chair Directly Examine a Client

Gray Hairs look forward to the direct examination of their clients, and their clients fully expect that lead trial counsel will be asking them questions. For some Gray Hairs, you would have to pry those direct examinations from their cold, dead hands. But sometimes, allowing second chair to perform the direct examination is absolutely the right strategy, especially when lead counsel has a much stronger personality than the witness.

Actions speak louder than words. Want to send the message that your client does not need to be coddled or coached? Want to send the message that you, as lead trial counsel, have absolute confidence in your client's testimony? Let the jury watch your second chair stand up, call your client to the stand, and start asking questions. Nothing shifts the spotlight from lead counsel to the client more effectively than lead counsel not performing the client's direct examination. Nothing says, "my client does not need me" like staying in your seat. Suddenly, jurors do not have to worry about your coaching the witness. It is tantamount to the head coach of a football team grabbing a box of popcorn and watching the game from the owner's luxury suite.

No, this strategy is not always appropriate. You have to trust your second chair to ask the right questions during direct examination. You have to be certain your second chair can handle objections during opposing counsel's (often vicious) cross-examination of your client. And above all, your client has to agree with the strategy. Make no mistake. Your client is expecting the attorney they hand-picked and hired to be defending them, not that attorney's associate. But when all the moons align, this strategy can be incredibly effective.

11. Do Not Change the Way You Conduct the Examinations

Gray Hairs often teach that the direct examination of a client or a (friendly) lay witness should not be conducted from the podium whenever the court permits attorneys to "move freely about the courtroom." Instead of standing at the podium and drawing attention away from the witness, Gray Hairs encouraged students to stand inconspicuously at the end of the jury box. In theory, by standing at the edge of the jury box, an attorney could (a) force jurors to stop looking back at the attorney and (b) have the witness be looking *toward* the jury when answering questions. The logic behind the technique was sound.

During COVID, the practice of standing so close to the jury box ended abruptly. During the 2021 *Lindale* trial, the jury was seated in the gallery, and the witness was seated in the back row of the jury box. Pursuant to the court's instruction, trial counsel wore face shields, remained seated at their table while questioning the witness, and only left their table to approach the witness. Since COVID, people are more aware of their personal space, and trial attorneys should think twice before standing in close proximity to the jury box. Instead of helping jurors focus on the witness, standing too close could distract (and possibly offend) some jurors.

The world is quickly returning to the point where no jurors enter the courtroom wearing masks *and* there is no possibility that standing too close to the jury box will distract the closest juror. When that day finally comes, trial attorneys should *not* return to the practice of leaving the podium and standing by the jury box. It is time to retire that particular technique.

The goal of direct examination is for the attorney to disappear. Stepping away from the podium often has the opposite effect. Invariably, some jurors continue to look back at the attorney to listen to the next question. When the witness is seated near one end of the jury box, and the attorney is standing at the opposite end of the jury box, those jurors are forced to whip their heads back and forth like they are watching a tennis match. Moreover, leaving the podium calls attention to the examining attorney. It is an unnecessary aberration, a departure from the norm. For some jurors, it is not unlike when a restaurant dims the lights, and someone says, "ooh, ambiance." Why take the risk that even one juror will find your different approach to be cheesy, melodramatic, or theatrical? Go to the podium and ask your questions. If you ask the right questions, and your witness has important information, you will disappear soon enough.

12. Do Not Steal Thunder the Way You Do with Experts

Whereas trial counsel should always steal thunder when performing the direct examination of an expert witness, trial counsel should hesitate before stealing thunder during the direct examination of a lay witness. There are a number of factors to consider. One reason is perception. When a trial attorney confronts a lay witness with an unfavorable fact, opinion, allegation, or event, and solicits a favorable explanation, it can appear staged and contrived. For another, there is no "good time" to interrupt your direct examination by raising unfavorable evidence (only to refute that evidence). And if you choose to end the direct examination by stealing thunder (i.e., "Oh, before I sit down, let me ask you about this . . ."), you are choosing to end your direct examination on a terrible note.

Yes, a trial attorney should steal opposing counsel's thunder regarding facts or documents that are absolutely 100 percent going to be raised during cross-examination and that the jury would hate you for hiding. Give your client a chance to admit that he has a prior felony conviction when it has nothing to do with his subsequently being rear-ended by the defendant. Let your client explain how the company initially thought that the document had not been retained (which is why he denied it existed in his deposition) and how they subsequently found the document. But do not steal thunder when you do not know whether opposing counsel will confront the lay witness with the fact, document, or exhibit you fear. When in doubt, do not steal thunder with a lay witness.

During the 2021 *Lindale* trial, I had to make the difficult decision of whether to confront my client, the co-owner of Lindale Pipeline, LLC, with a series of unflattering facts and unfavorable documents during my direct examination *solely* to steal opposing counsel's thunder. I literally lost sleep that night trying to decide. I knew my client was prepared to answer the tough questions, but I didn't want to shift gears and spend my direct examination going through those (irrelevant) documents and (irrelevant) facts. It would ruin the tone of my direct examination, and the jury would almost certainly conclude that his answers were coached because they would be in response to *my* questions during *my* direct examination. The next morning, I decided not to steal opposing counsel's thunder, and it was the right decision. For whatever reason, opposing counsel chose to confront my client with only a handful of the emails and none of the unflattering facts. My client handled the cross-examination exceptionally well, and the jury awarded $26 million.

13. Have an Alamo for Your Direct Examination

Every direct examination of a lay witness should end with a single question or a series of questions that (a) will not draw an objection; (b) will make an important point; and (c) will end the direct examination on a good note. We call this question or line of questioning an "Alamo," and it is as important a part of direct examination as it is cross-examination. Never take the risk that your direct examination will end on a sustained objection or a whimper. If you do not have an Alamo for your direct examination, you are not prepared to start your direct examination.

The right Alamo for direct examination will always depend on the specific case and the specific witness. But factual questions are always better than questions that solicit opinions or conclusions. For example, if plaintiff's counsel spent direct examination methodically and chronologically walking the plaintiff through her treatment following an accident, the following could be good and bad Alamos.

a. Bad Single Question Alamo

Q. Is there any doubt in your mind that the motor vehicle accident on January 2nd is responsible for all of your current pain and suffering?

Counsel: Objection.

Court: Sustained.

Q. Then . . . umm . . . no further questions. I tender the witness for cross-examination.

b. Good Single Question Alamo

Q. Prior to the accident on January 2nd, had you *ever* treated with *any* doctor for *any* neck pain?

A. No. I never had any neck pain.

Q. No further questions. I tender the witness for cross-examination.

c. Bad Series of Questions Alamo

Q. In summary, have all of your doctors told you that your current pain and discomfort is causally related to the accident on February 2nd?

Counsel: Objection. Hearsay.

Court: Sustained.

Q. In your opinion, is all of your current pain and discomfort causally related to the accident on February 2nd?

Counsel: Objection. Calls for an expert opinion.

Court: Sustained.

Q. Then . . . umm . . . no further questions. I tender the witness for cross-examination.

d. Good Series of Questions Alamo

Q. Prior to this accident, had you ever had a cervical fusion?

A. No.

Q. Prior to this accident, had you ever had an epidural steroid injection in your neck?

A. No.

Q. Prior to this accident, had you ever gone to a chiropractor for neck pain?

A. No.

Q. Prior to this accident, had you ever sought any treatment for neck pain?

A. No.

Q. Prior to this accident, had you ever experienced the type of neck pain you experienced immediately after this accident?

A. No.

Q. No further questions. I tender the witness for cross-examination.

The best Alamos often require trial counsel to organize the direct examination to save that single question or that series of questions for the Alamo. Never count on the court allowing you to ask summary questions. Never start an Alamo question with "in summary" or "again" or "to repeat" or "are you sure . . . ." By starting your Alamo question that way, you are inviting an "asked and answered" objection. Plan ahead. Design and build an Alamo that can withstand any objection.

14. Solicit Denials, Explanations, and Additional Facts during Re-Direct

Actions speak louder than words. When opposing counsel's cross-examination did not hurt your case or the lay witness's credibility, there is no need for re-direct examination. In the Age of Jurors, it is important to know how to handle that (wonderful) situation. When the court asks if you have any re-direct, stand up and say, "No re-direct, Your Honor." Resist the need to be glib. Do not say, "No need, Your Honor," which will draw an objection. Do not chuckle and say, "No, Your Honor." Try not to yawn. The calmness and confidence in your voice is as important as the words you are speaking: "No re-direct, Your Honor."

There are times when opposing counsel's cross-examination creates the need for you to solicit an additional fact, explanation, or denial from a lay witness. When that happens, go to work. Like a waiter methodically setting the table, solicit the additional facts. Like a waiter methodically clearing the table, solicit the additional denials. But re-direct examination should never be synonymous with "repeat examination."

Do not assume that the jury will recognize why you are asking the question. When permitted by the court, refer the witness to the specific question or answer for which you are soliciting the additional fact, explanation, or denial. That way, the jury will recognize the importance of your next question and the witness's next answer.

a. Soliciting a Fact

Q. During cross-examination, were you asked whether you wear prescription glasses?

A. Yes, I was.

Q. During cross-examination, were you asked what *type* of prescription glasses?

A. No, sir.

Q. What type of prescription glasses do you wear?

A. Reading glasses.

Q. Do you normally wear your reading glasses when you are driving?

A. No, I do not.

Q. No further questions. Thank you, Your Honor.

b. Soliciting an Explanation

Q. During cross-examination, were you asked whether you reported neck pain to your primary care physician two days after the accident?

A. Yes, I was.

Q. Were you asked *why* you didn't report neck pain to your primary care physician two days after the accident?

A. No, I was not.

Q. Why didn't you?

A. Because I only see Dr. David for my diabetes, and I already had an appointment scheduled to see an orthopedic surgeon a few days later.

Q. No further questions. Thank you, Your Honor.

c. Soliciting a Denial

Q. During cross-examination, were you asked about your friendship with the plaintiff?

A. Yes, sir.

Q. Before this accident, did you ever lie for the plaintiff at work?

A. No, sir.

Q. Before this accident, did my client ever ask you to lie for him?

A. No, Billy never asked me to do lie for him or anything like that.

Q. Since this accident, has Billy ever asked you to lie for him?

A. No, sir. He just asked me to tell everyone what I saw.

Q. Would you lie for Billy?

A. No, sir. I would not do that for Billy or for anyone else.

Q. No further questions. Thank you, Your Honor.

It is important that your entire trial team be on the same page when it comes to the "re-direct decision." Discuss with your co-counsel and your client who will make that decision. When the court asks if you have any re-direct, will the examining attorney make an executive decision or will your trial team huddle? Whatever you decide, be consistent. If you only huddle once, that huddle may suggest that it is a close call. If your huddle lasts too long, it may suggest that your trial team does not agree.

Have your trial team agree on a signal. When the examining attorney shrugs her or his shoulders and looks at co-counsel as if they can't think of a single question, the entire trial team should recognize the signal and immediately respond by shaking their heads "no" as well. Let the jury see that *nobody* on your trial team can think of a single thing that needs to be fixed or question that needs to be asked on re-direct.

15. Consider or Prepare for the *Jaws* Gambit

Plaintiff attorneys are not legally required to call the plaintiff to the stand during the plaintiff's case-in-chief, especially when liability is not disputed and/or the plaintiff does not recall the accident. Consequently, every civil attorney needs to be aware of what we call the "*Jaws* gambit." Instead of calling the plaintiff to the stand to testify, plaintiff's counsel calls the plaintiff's family, friends, and treating physicians to tell the jury about plaintiff's injuries, recovery, pain, limitations, and challenges. In effect, plaintiff's counsel chooses to play them the *Jaws* music, but not show them the shark.

Properly executed, the *Jaws* gambit can be very effective, especially in a case involving a traumatic brain injury. Jurors are often suspicious or judgmental when a plaintiff describes their own injuries. A single exaggeration can cause jurors to dislike the plaintiff, disregard plaintiff's testimony, or downplay the plaintiff's injuries. In contrast, jurors can be more trusting of the plaintiff's spouse. When the spouse describes the plaintiff's cognitive and behavioral impairment, the jury listens, especially when it is paired with a plaintiff who is in denial (i.e., "he says his memory is fine, but he constantly forgets to . . .").

The *Jaws* gambit can be a difficult decision for a plaintiff attorney, but that decision is becoming easier as success stories spread. After all, why should a plaintiff attorney put the shark on the stand? Why give jurors time to become desensitized to the shark? Why give jurors time to inspect the shark for any seams or signs that the shark is fake? Why not just play the music and let the jury's imagination do the rest?

Every defense attorney has to be prepared for the difficult decision they will face when plaintiff rests their case-in-chief. That is when the defense will have to decide whether to call the plaintiff to the stand. Consider the risk/reward. If the plaintiff attorney has established that the plaintiff *thinks* he can do more than he actually can, what will your cross-examination prove? If even one juror thinks that it is "cruel" to put the plaintiff on the stand (after all, plaintiff's own attorney did not), will that juror hate the defense for dragging the plaintiff into the courtroom? Before every trial involving non-orthopedic injuries, plaintiff attorneys should consider the *Jaws* gambit, and every defense attorney should discuss what their countermove will be.

During the 2003 *Menard* trial, which involved a plaintiff who sustained a severe traumatic brain injury requiring emergency burr hole surgery, our savvy opposing counsel chose not to call his brain-injured plaintiff to the stand. Instead, opposing counsel called (a) his treating neurologist to discuss the location and severity of his brain injury; (b) the neuropsychologist to explain the battery of testing administered to the plaintiff and the objective evidence of cognitive and behavioral impairment; and (c) plaintiff's wife to tell anecdotal stories (i.e., leaves water running, leaves the stove on) and describe how he was not the same person he was before the accident. It was very effective, and we really struggled when deciding whether to call Mr. Menard to the stand during the defense case.

Chapter 12

Flying Blind Cross-Examination

During the Golden Age of Lawyers, it was decided that civil trials should not be "trials by ambush" and civil discovery should be broader than criminal discovery. That decision made no sense whatsoever to criminal defense attorneys, who believed that due process and equal protection required broader discovery in criminal proceedings, where their client's life and liberty were in jeopardy (as opposed to "just their money"). But the decision made perfect sense to prosecutors, who knew the criminal justice system would collapse if criminal defendants—who enjoy a Fifth Amendment right to remain silent—were suddenly given the right to depose every victim, witness, police officer, detective, and expert (for seven hours each).

Right or wrong, challenges to the constitutionality of limited criminal discovery did not fare well. The United States Supreme Court held that there is no general constitutional right to discovery in criminal cases and that *Brady v. Maryland*, 373 U.S. 83, 83 S.Ct. 1194, 10 L.Ed.2d 215 (1963) did not create one.[1] State legislatures continued to enact statutes providing for limited criminal discovery, and state courts continued to rule that the profound differences between civil and criminal discovery were rationally based and constitutional. When the dust settled, civil attorneys had the absolute right to depose every potential witness before trial, and criminal law practitioners (in most jurisdictions) had absolutely no right to depose an available witness.

1. "There is no general constitutional right to discovery in a criminal case, and *Brady* did not create one; as the Court wrote recently, 'the Due Process Clause has little to say regarding the amount of discovery which the parties must be afforded. . . .'" Weatherford v. Bursey, 429 U.S. 545, 559 (1977) (quoting Wardius v. Oregon, 412 U.S. 470, 474 (1973)).

Like Darwin's finches, who adapted to limited food sources by developing different beaks, criminal law practitioners adapted to limited criminal discovery by developing different cross-examination strategies and instincts. Deprived of deposition transcripts, they were forced to cross-examine lay witnesses for the first time (and in front of the jury) without knowing what those witnesses would say. What they developed over time, through trial and error, was the ability to conduct "flying blind" cross-examination.

There is a specific reason why every lay witness takes the stand. Most are called to tell the jury a fact, recite a story, share an observation, or make a denial. During criminal trials, the accused may take the stand to deny or explain the commission of the crime. During civil trials, family and friends may take the stand to share how the plaintiff has changed since the accident. Whatever their purpose may be, a lay witness fulfills that purpose during direct examination.

The goal of flying blind cross-examination is not to un-ring that bell. Without prior statements by the witness or a deposition transcript, there is no reliable cross-examination technique to persuade jurors that the testimony was deceitful, inconsistent, embellished, or a recent fabrication. No cross-examination strategy will consistently persuade a lay witness to remember events differently or to recant their testimony. No combination of words will consistently persuade criminal defendants to admit what they just denied on direct examination. By necessity, flying blind cross-examination must be a means to a different end.

The more realistic goal of flying blind cross-examination is to methodically (a) confirm every favorable admission made by the witness; (b) emphasize the importance of each admission; (c) remind jurors why certain admissions were made; (d) use those admissions to support the credibility of your own witnesses; and (e) highlight when the witness is accusing another witness of lying or being mistaken. Naturally, that is easier said than done, especially when the testimony includes a dozen important admissions and a dozen critical denials.

Trial attorneys need to know *exactly* what to do when forced to conduct a flying blind cross-examination. They don't need war stories. They don't need general advice. They need a proven methodology for preparing questions while listening and objecting to opposing counsel's direct examination of the witness. They need that methodology to produce lines of questioning that convey a simple message to the jurors: "That testimony was neither surprising, nor reliable." At its finest, flying blind cross-examination breaks the spell of direct examination and tells the jury, "We see this all the time. What did you expect the witness to say?"

Every trial attorney can learn something from the exercise of preparing and performing a flying blind cross-examination. So, imagine you are a prosecutor. You rest the State's case, and you sit down. As you lean back in your chair, you hear opposing counsel call to the stand a witness who has never been interviewed or deposed. You have no idea what that witness is going to say, but you can tell by opposing counsel's confident manner that the testimony will be persuasive and clean, leaving you with nothing substantial for impeachment. When opposing counsel's direct examination ends, you will be forced to cross-examine a witness whose answers could take you in any direction. You have no vision of the horizon. You hold no compass. You are about to conduct your first flying blind cross-examination.

1. Show Jurors How the Truth Looks and Sounds

Jurors can sometimes struggle to know whether their own spouse or child is telling the truth, which begs the question, how can trial lawyers expect jurors to know whether the stranger on the stand is testifying truthfully? More than anything, what jurors need is the chance to see how the witness looks and sounds when telling the truth. Like good waiters, let's bring them that glimpse of honesty, and let's do it at the start of our cross-examination.

Lay witnesses want jurors to like them, and they are often more agreeable at the start of cross-examination. That is why the start of cross-examination is the perfect time to ask a series of questions that the witness will be able to answer immediately and with absolute certainty. That series of undisputed factual questions will show jurors how quickly and directly the witness answers questions when telling the truth.

Start that series of undisputed factual questions with a preamble that jurors will remember and that separates the line of questioning. By "tagging" the series of questioning, you create the opportunity to reference that line of questioning during your closing argument.

- "Before we get started, a few **housekeeping** questions . . ."
- "Let me ask you a few **background** questions . . ."
- "Let me start by asking you a few **family** questions . . ."
- "Before we talk about the incident, let me ask a few **work-related** questions . . ."
- "I have a few **earlier-in-the-day** questions . . ."

Resist the temptation to ask leading questions for (only) this part of cross-examination. Yes, jurors can learn from observing truthful responses to leading questions, but they can often learn more from seeing and hearing truthful responses to open-ended questions. Let the jury have both by alternating leading and non-leading questions. The open-ended questions will give the witness the chance to volunteer information and details. The leading questions will give you the chance to establish, restore, and quicken the pace.

Avoid asking factual questions that could solicit "relevance" objections. In most cases, the incident, accident, or crime will provide you with a handful of relevant and undisputed factual questions. If not, consider asking a series of "earlier-in-the-day" factual questions about the day of the incident, accident, or crime:

- Where did you work?
- Were you scheduled to work that night?
- Did you drive your car to work?
- What type of car did you drive?
- Did you have a reserved parking spot?
- Where did you park your car?

Do not get carried away by the ability to harvest information from social media. Remember that people struggle with dates (i.e., "When did you get married"?) more than with locations (i.e., "Where did you get married?"). Avoid questions that, depending on the answer, could solicit sympathy (i.e., "Where did you graduate from high school?," when the answer could be, "I didn't graduate from high school"). And never assume anything about the life of the witness (i.e., "What are the names of your parents?," when the answer could be "I never knew my parents"). You do *not* know their life.

Only as a last resort, and only when you are truly unable to think of any incident-related (undisputed) factual questions, should you ask a series of basic background questions, like the following:

- What is your full name?
- Where were you born?
- What is your date of birth?
- How old are you?
- What color are your eyes?
- What is your approximate height?

Even personal questions like these can give the jury an opportunity to see how quickly and directly the witness answers when telling the truth. No witness asks the attorney to "repeat the question" when asked to state their middle name. No witness pauses for three Mississippi's when asked to state their date of birth. No witness says "umm" before saying their eyes are blue. No witness reassures jurors before stating their age (i.e., "To be honest, I am 45 years old") or sharing their birthplace ("I'm not going to lie, I was born in New Orleans"). And few witnesses will become defensive or difficult when asked their approximate height.

Always ask the series of factual questions routinely and indifferently, like a receptionist at the doctor's office asking required medical questions (i.e., "Has your insurance changed? Have you travelled abroad in the past seven days?"). Be mindful not to ask rapid-fire questions, which could solicit an objection or call attention to what you are trying to do. When necessary, slightly increase the pace of your questions to quicken the response. The faster the response, the better.

Done properly, the way in which a witness answers your series of factual questions can become a (visual and auditory) lie detector test. Pay close attention to the way the witness answers those undisputed factual questions. Notice everything. Did the witness answer quickly and directly? Did the witness lean back in the chair? Did the witness maintain eye contact with you? Did the witness end any answers with "sir" or "ma'am"? That is how the truth looks and sounds.

Later, when asking more important questions, call attention to any aberrations in how the witness responds or behaves. When the witness hesitates, consider calling it to the jury's attention by confronting the witness (i.e., "Why did you hesitate when I asked you . . . ?"). By putting the skunk on the table, you can help jurors remember the question that caused the witness to hesitate. When the witness breaks eye contact, point it out to the jury (i.e., "Why did that question cause you to look up and to the right?"). By pointing it out, you make jurors wonder why the witness's response was different to that question. When the witness begins their answer with an assurance or promise for the *first* time, repeat that assurance or promise:

Q. Were you at the victim's house on the night of the murder?

A. I'm going to be honest with you. I was there that morning, and I did drink out of that glass they found my prints on, but I did not go there that night.

Q. [Pause] That's the first time you started an answer with "I'm going to be honest with you," isn't it?

Welcome objections when calling attention to the way in which the witness hesitated, prefaced an answer, changed their tone, said "umm," shifted in their seat, cursed, or looked at the ceiling. Let opposing counsel make an "argumentative" or "relevance" objection in response to your comment or question. The objection itself will wake the jury up and call their attention to your comment. Days later, jurors will be more likely to remember the aberration if it drew an objection. Picture a friendly Lion reminding undecided Lambs during jury deliberation that the first time the accused said "I'm going to be honest with you" was when asked if he argued with the victim on the night of the murder. "Remember," the Lion will say. "The attorney pointed it out, and the other attorney objected."

During closing argument, you will have the option of telling jurors that the most important series of questions were the housekeeping questions you asked at the start of your cross-examination. You can assure jurors that there was a very good reason why you started with those seemingly unimportant questions. You can explain that your sole reason for asking those questions was to show them how the truth looks and sounds. You can argue that the answers were quick and direct because they were truthful. Then, you can contrast those truthful answers with any subsequently evasive, defensive, reluctant, hesitant, or unusual answers. "Those (later) answers were not quick and direct," you will tell jurors, "because those answers were *not* truthful. You saw how the witness looked and sounded when answering truthfully. Well, that is not the way the witness looked or sounded when I asked . . . ." Like a good waiter, you will have pointed out something about the soup they would otherwise have missed.

2. Prepare a Flying Blind Cross-Examination Chart

Civil practitioners are spoiled. When preparing for a civil jury trial, I can wake up on a Saturday morning, throw on a pair of jeans, drive to the firm, sit down at a clean desk, dissect a 200-page deposition transcript for each witness, carefully select every question, and type a beautiful outline for my cross-examinations. I can take my time. I can anticipate and type potential objections (after each question). I can research responses to those potential objections and type the perfect reply (after each objection). Based on deposition testimony, I can even create "true/false" charts that force the witness to commit, allow the jury to follow along, and provide a visual reminder for closing argument of every admission and denial. Sigh, how I love civil trials.

But as a state prosecutor, I rarely had the benefit of a recorded statement, and I never had the opportunity to depose a criminal defendant. It was a helpless feeling. Sitting at my desk, knowing that my cross-examination of the defendant could be the turning point of a murder trial.

Wanting to prepare for that confrontation, but not knowing how to start. Fearing that I would be unable to take good notes, conjure the perfect cross-examination strategy, and scribble perfectly worded questions on a legal pad *while* listening to and objecting to opposing counsel's direct examination. Desperately wanting to invent a cross-examination kit that I could easily assemble during opposing counsel's direct examination.

The solution was my Flying Blind Cross-Examination Chart. The chart forced me to identify every critical fact. It helped me organize every admission and denial during direct examination. The chart even reminded me of the questions I should be asking *myself* about each fact, including: (a) If admitted, what would be the importance of that admission? (b) What physical evidence will have been (or will be) introduced regarding that fact? (c) If admitted, would that admission support the testimony of my witnesses? and (d) If denied, would that denial be tantamount to accusing another witness of lying, making a mistake, or being wrong? The chart gave me the flexibility to decide during direct examination which columns to pursue during my cross-examination. Table 12.1 shows how a completed Flying Blind Cross-Examination Chart might look *after* the direct examination of a criminal defendant.

Preparing a Flying Blind Cross-Examination Chart should always start with grabbing a legal pad and identifying every fact the witness will have to admit or deny during their direct examination. Before a criminal case, ask yourself what the criminal defendant will have to admit or deny if he takes the stand. Before a civil case, ask yourself what liability and damages issues the plaintiff's spouse will likely address during direct examination. When you have completed your list of facts, consider the best order for listing those facts (column #2) on your chart. Organize and group the facts logically (i.e., chronologically, by legal issue, by factual topic, etc.). Skip every other row. That way, if the witness admits or denies a fact you did not anticipate, you can add that fact to your chart at (or near) the correct spot.

After completing the "Fact" column, determine the "Importance" (column #3) for each fact (if admitted) and identify the physical "Evidence" (column #4) proving each fact. Consider whether an admission would "Confirm" (column #5) the testimony of one of your witnesses. And consider the logical consequences of every denial. By denying a fact, would the witness be "Accusing" (column #6) another witness of lying or a test result of being inaccurate? Because the "Confirms" column assumes an admission and the "Accuses" column assumes a denial, only pencil in what would be true. In theory, every column can be completed prior to direct examination, except whether the witness "Admitted/ Denied" (column #1) each fact.

Table 12.1 How a Completed Flying Blind Chart Might Look After the Direct Examination of a Criminal Defendant

A/D	Fact	Importance	Evidence	Confirms	Accuses
Admits	Dated the victim.	No forced entry	Social media	Neighbor said	
Admits	Dated for 2 years.	No forced entry	Social media	Neighbor said	
Admits	Victim cheated on you.	Motive	Social media	Neighbor said	
Admits	Broke up 1 month before murder.	Motive	Social media	Neighbor said	
Admits	Entered victim's house at 5:00 p.m.	At scene of the Crime	Front door video	Neighbor saw	
Admits	Alone with victim.	Opportunity	Front door video	Neighbor saw	
Admits	Argued with victim.	State of mind		Neighbor heard	
Admits	Left victim's house at 5:30 p.m.	At scene of the crime	Front door video	Neighbor saw	
Denies	Stabbing victim.	The crime (itself)			
Denies	Ignoring neighbor's question when leaving.	State of mind			Neighbor is mistaken.
Denies	Leaving victim's blood on steering wheel.	Guilt	Crime lab testing		Crime lab expert is wrong.
Denies	Telling cellmate he killed victim.				Cellmate is lying.

A completed Flying Blind Cross-Examination Chart can provide you with the compass you need to cross-examine a witness who has never been questioned or deposed. With a glance, you will be able to see: (a) which admissions can be confirmed; (b) the importance of each admission; (c) the evidentiary necessity for certain admissions; (d) whether any admissions support the credibility of your witnesses; and (e) how many people would have to be lying, mistaken, or wrong based on each denial. Of course, there is more than one way to design a Flying Blind Cross-Examination Chart, and every attorney should tailor their chart to their needs and preferences.

Completing a Flying Blind Cross-Examination Chart is an important part of the process, but every trial attorney needs to know how *exactly* how to use that completed chart during cross-examination. What follows is one methodology for conducting a flying blind cross-examination, including the techniques and strategies associated with each column of a completed chart.

3. Confirm and Stack Admissions

An effective flying blind cross-examination can include nothing more than calmly confirming every admission (columns #1 and #2) made during direct examination. Actions speak louder than words and spending your entire cross-examination collecting admissions (a) reminds jurors of each admission; (b) emphasizes the admissions are what *really* matter; and (c) suggests the admissions are all you needed to collect on cross-examination.

Whenever possible, "stack" admissions by including previously confirmed admissions in subsequent questions. Beware conjunctions when stacking admissions. There is a difference between stacking admissions and asking compound questions. Compound questions involve repeating the prior admission and adding a new admission (i.e., "You admit you dated the victim, *and* you admit you dated the victim for two years?"). In contrast, stacking admissions is the technique of adding a single fact to a prior admission. Here is an example of properly stacking admissions by adding a single fact (italicized below) without asking a compound question:

Q. You admit you *dated the victim.*

Q. You admit you dated the victim *for two years.*

Q. You admit that, after two years of dating, you *discovered the victim had been cheating on you.*

Q. You admit that, after two years of dating, you discovered the victim had been cheating on you *with your best friend.*

Q. You admit *your relationship ended* when you discovered the victim had been cheating on you with your best friend.

Many criminal defendants admit everything, except the commission of the crime. During direct examination, opposing counsel will often rush through the events leading up to the commission of the crime because they are so eager to get to their client's denial. Listen carefully to the "admit, admit, admit, deny" testimony. Then, force the witness to confirm every admission:

Q. You admit you entered the victim's house at 5:00 p.m. the night she was murdered.

Q. You admit you were alone in the house with the victim the night she was murdered.

Q. You admit you were alone in the house for at least 30 minutes the night she was murdered.

By collecting admissions, you can also inspire a lay witness to "become who they are." All lay witnesses can be divided into those witnesses who do and those witnesses who do not have an interest in the outcome of the case. Disinterested lay witnesses will listen carefully and confirm every admission without hesitation. In stark contrast, defendants and other lay witnesses who "have a dog in the hunt" will often resist your attempts to confirm and compile admissions. They will avoid the question. They will volunteer nonresponsive information. They will lose their cool. They will object to questions. They will even throw questions back at you (i.e., "Have you never pushed anyone out your way?").

Criminal defendants are at a natural disadvantage. Their taking the stand is almost always an act of desperation. They are so scared of remaining silent and being convicted that they will put themselves in a no-win situation. If they lose their cool on the stand, jurors may fear them and discuss their behavior ("You can tell he has anger issues"). If they keep their cool, jurors may be suspicious of them and discuss their behavior ("If I was wrongfully accused, I would be furious"). If they try to be funny, jurors may dislike them and discuss their behavior ("I wouldn't be joking if I was charged with . . ."). Rarely does a criminal defendant's behavior on the stand perfectly match every juror's idea of appropriate behavior.

Criminal defendants are rarely prepared for cross-examination. For months before the trial, they will myopically focus on what *they* want to tell the jury during direct examination. Whether in jail or on bond, they only practice telling their story. Consequently, about three admissions into your flying blind cross-examination, criminal defendants can sometimes panic. When they do, they can experience a physiological reaction to your line of questioning. The rush of adrenaline in their body can trigger a fight-or-flight response. Their heart rate increases. Their pupils dilate. Their breathing change, and their muscles tighten. That is when they stop cooperating and start fighting back. That is when the jury catches a glimpse of their real personality. That is when some criminal defendants become who they are.

Q. You admit you knew where the victim lived.

A. Yes.

Q. You admit you were in the house with the victim the night she was murdered.

A. Yes. But I didn't kill her.

Q. You admit you were *alone* in the house with the victim the night she was murdered.

A. You're not listening to me. I said, "I did not kill her."

Q. Were you *alone* in the house with the victim the night she was murdered?

A. Yes, I was in the house. Lots of people were in the house that day. But I didn't kill her. End of story.

Q. Were you *alone* in the house with the victim the night she was murdered?

A. I don't know. I didn't search every room of her house, okay? I mean . . . do you do that? Do you search every room when you walk into a house?

Q. Were you *alone* in the house with the victim the night she was murdered?

When collecting admissions, keep the jury focused on the admissions. Never lose your patience. Never lose your temper. Never shine the spotlight on yourself. Never let the defendant distract or detour you with a single comment or answer. Calmly repeat the question as often as necessary. Let the jurors become impatient with the witness.

4. Identify the Importance of Each Admission

After confirming an admission (columns #1 and #2), consider the importance of that admission (column #3). Decide quickly whether to articulate the importance of the admission for the jury or wait until closing argument. Do not hesitate. Do not wait. If the admission is important, immediately ask a question that forces the witness to acknowledge the importance of that admission. Do not try to stack "Importance" admissions the way you stacked "Factual" admissions. When asking the witness to admit the importance of an admission, ask a simple and direct question that is narrowly tailored to the specific admission:

Q. You admit you entered the victim's house at 5:00 p.m. on the night she was murdered (columns #1 and #2).

Q. You admit that, on the night of the murder, there was a point when you were standing where the crime occurred (column #3).

Q. You admit you were alone in the house with the victim the night she was murdered (columns #1 and #2).

Q. So, you admit that, when you were alone in the house with the victim, you had the opportunity to kill the victim (column #3).

Do not fear "argumentative" objections when you are asking the witness to acknowledge the importance of an admission. If opposing counsel objects to your asking a criminal defendant to admit he had the "opportunity" to kill the victim, the jury will remember that the defendant had that opportunity, even if the court sustains the objection.

5. Reveal the Evidentiary Necessity for Any Admissions

Some witnesses only admit what they cannot deny. Always make that clear to the jury by asking a question to establish the evidentiary necessity for each admission. When a criminal defendant admits what the State already proved, remind the jurors of the evidence (column #4) undeniably proving each fact. When the plaintiff's best friend admits only what they can't deny, establish that the witness was aware of the evidence (column #4) undeniably proving each fact. Picture a Lion telling a Lamb who was somehow impressed by the witness's candor, "Look, that guy wasn't being candid. He *had* to admit everything he admitted!"

Never blurt out the reason for an admission (i.e., "You're only admitting that because the video showed it!") or ask the witness to admit the reason for the admission (i.e., "Isn't it true you're only admitting it because the video showed it?"). Both will draw an "argumentative" objection from opposing counsel, and that objection will be sustained. And, even if your comment or question draws no objection, it gives the witness an opportunity to address your accusation (i.e., "I admitted it because it is true") or volunteer information that you might not want to verify (i.e., "When I heard she was murdered, I called my mom and told her that I couldn't believe she was dead because I was at her house the same night!"). There are better ways to make your point.

Trial attorneys do not have to follow (left to right) the columns of the Flying Blind Cross-Examination Chart during their cross-examination. As a prosecutor, if you recognize that a criminal defendant only admitted those facts that had already been proved with evidence, you may want to start by focusing on the evidence that *forced* the criminal defendant to admit each fact. Table 12.2 highlights the two columns to focus on when establishing the reason (column #4) why each admission (column #1) was made. For example, a prosecutor could remind the jury that the defendant was "present in the courtroom" when certain evidence (column #4) was introduced, thereby suggesting the evidence was the only reason for the defendant's subsequent admission:

Q. You were present in the courtroom when we played the front door video, correct?

A. Yes.

Q. You saw yourself on that video entering the victim's house at 5:00 p.m. on the night of her murder, didn't you? (Column #4)

A. Yes.

Q. After seeing yourself captured on that front door video, you admitted to the jury during direct examination that you entered the victim's house at 5:00 p.m. on the night of her murder, correct? (Columns #1 and #2)

A. Yes. But that's not why I admitted it.

Q. But you *are* admitting that, on the night of the murder, there was a point when you were standing where the crime occurred? (Column #3)

Table 12.2 Using a Flying Blind Cross-Examination Chart to Reveal the Reason for Each Admission

A/D	Fact	Importance	Evidence	Confirms	Accuses
Admits	Dated the victim.	No forced entry	Social media	Neighbor said	
Admits	Dated for 2 years.	No forced entry	Social media	Neighbor said	
Admits	Victim cheated on you.	Motive	Social media	Neighbor said	
Admits	Broke up 1 month before murder.	Motive	Social media	Neighbor said	
Admits	Entered victim's house at 5:00 p.m.	At scene of the Crime	Front door video	Neighbor saw	
Admits	Alone with victim.	Opportunity	Front door video	Neighbor saw	
Admits	Argued with victim.	State of mind		Neighbor heard	
Admits	Left victim's house at 5:30 p.m.	At scene of the crime	Front door video	Neighbor saw	
Denies	Stabbing victim.	The crime (itself)			
Denies	Ignoring neighbor's question when leaving.	State of mind			Neighbor is mistaken.
Denies	Leaving victim's blood on steering wheel.	Guilt	Crime lab testing		Crime lab expert is wrong.
Denies	Telling cellmate he killed victim.				Cellmate is lying.

Alternatively, if you want to follow the columns (left to right) and the evidence has not yet been introduced, you can ask the witness to confirm their "knowledge" or "awareness" of the evidence (column #4) after establishing the importance (column #3) of the admission. For example, in a civil case, a defense attorney may have to conduct a flying blind cross-examination of the plaintiff's spouse *before* introducing any evidence:

Q. During direct examination, you admitted that your wife was speeding when she passed my client's truck (columns #1 and #2).

A. Yes.

Q. So, you admit that your wife was violating the posted speed limit of 70 mph when she passed my client's truck (column #3).

A. Yes, she was.

Q. When you made that admission, you were aware that our expert downloaded the Event Data Recorder information from your wife's car, weren't you? (Column #4)

A. Yes, I did know that.

Q. And it was your understanding that the EDR showed your wife was driving at 75 mph, wasn't it? (Column #4)

A. That was my understanding.

Q. During direct examination, you also admitted . . .

Resist the temptation to connect the dots for the jurors. The time for that is closing argument where (if you so choose and the court allows) you can show the jury a version of your Flying Blind Cross-Examination Chart. You can let the jurors see for themselves that the witness only admitted that which could not be denied.

6. Use Admissions to Support the Credibility of Your Witnesses

Jurors are asked to judge the credibility of every witness. After collecting admissions from a lay witness, consider whether those admissions "Confirm" (column #5) the testimony of your own witnesses (Table 12.3). That can be especially important when admissions prove that your witness testified truthfully about numerous facts, and the jury must decide whether your witness was lying or mistaken about the *one* fact the criminal defendant denied.

Table 12.3 Using a Flying Blind Cross-Examination Chart to Support the Testimony of Your Star Witness

A/D	Fact	Importance	Evidence	Confirms	Accuses
Admits	Dated the victim.	No forced entry	Social media	Neighbor said	
Admits	Dated for 2 years.	No forced entry	Social media	Neighbor said	
Admits	Victim cheated on you.	Motive	Social media	Neighbor said	
Admits	Broke up 1 month before murder.	Motive	Social media	Neighbor said	
Admits	Entered victim's house at 5:00 p.m.	At scene of the crime	Front door video	Neighbor saw	
Admits	Alone with victim.	Opportunity	Front door video	Neighbor saw	
Admits	Argued with victim.	State of mind		Neighbor heard	
Admits	Left victim's house at 5:30 p.m.	At scene of the crime	Front door video	Neighbor saw	
Denies	Stabbing victim.	The crime (itself)			
Denies	Ignoring neighbor's question when leaving.	State of mind			Neighbor is mistaken.
Denies	Leaving victim's blood on steering wheel.	Guilt	Crime lab testing		Crime lab expert is wrong.
Denies	Telling cellmate he killed victim.				Cellmate is lying.

This step can be performed at any time. You can establish that the admission supports the testimony of your witness immediately after you solicit the admission (columns #1 and #2), or after you establish the importance of the admission (column #3), or after you establish the evidentiary necessity for the admission (column #4).

There are different ways to perform this step. If your witness has already testified, you can confirm that your witness's testimony was truthful with a single question ("So, Ms. Jones was telling the truth when she testified that she saw you enter the victim's house?"), or you can first confirm that the defendant was in the courtroom ("You were in the courtroom when Ms. Jones testified . . ."). If your witness has not testified yet, it could even be a hypothetical (i.e., "So, if Dr. Davison, our accident reconstruction expert, takes the stand and testifies that your wife was speeding, he would be *absolutely* correct?"). Yes, asking a hypothetical to a lay witness normally draws an objection, but few attorneys will object immediately after the witness admitted the truthfulness of the underlying fact.

Here is an example of how the Flying Blind Cross-Examination Chart can give you the flexibility to address the columns in whatever order you want for each admission (each row):

Q. You were in the courtroom when we played the front door video showing you enter the victim's house at 5:00 p.m. on the night of the murder? (Column #4)

A. Yes.

Q. And, during your direct examination, you admitted that you entered the victim's house at 5:00 p.m., on the night of the murder? (Columns #1 and #2)

A. Yes.

Q. So, when Ms. Jones testified that she saw you enter the victim's house on the night of the murder, she was telling the truth? (Column #5)

A. Yes.

Q. You admit that, at 5:00 p.m. on the night of the murder, you were at the scene of the crime? (Column #3)

A. Yes, but I didn't kill her. She was alive when I left.

When a criminal defendant's admissions prove that your witness testified truthfully about numerous facts, consider creating a separate demonstrative exhibit for your cross-examination. Label a flip-chart page "Neighbor Testified Truthfully" and write down each truthful fact during cross-examination. Or, to save time and spare jurors from seeing your penmanship, prepare a "True/False" chart that allows you to emphasize that the defendant admits that almost everything your witness said was "True."

Do not be afraid to acknowledge the denials made during direct examination. The best way to remind the jury that criminal defendants *always* deny the crime, and the testimony of the plaintiff's family *always* supports the plaintiff's claims, is to let the jury see and hear how unsurprised you are by that testimony. Call attention to what the criminal defendant denied. Show the jury the fork in the road. Create a demonstrative exhibit like the "True/False" chart regarding Ms. Jones' testimony shown in Table 12.4.

Table 12.4 Testimony of Ms. Jones (Neighbor)

	TRUE	FALSE
Dated the victim.	√	
Dated for 2 years.	√	
Victim cheated on you.	√	
Broke up 1 month before murder.	√	
Entered victim's house at 5:00 p.m.	√	
Alone with the victim.	√	
Argued with the victim.	√	
Left victim's house at 5:30 p.m.	√	
Ignored neighbor's question when leaving.		X

There is more than one right way to assemble your cross-examination after you have completed your Flying Blind Cross-Examination Chart. That is the beauty of this methodology. You can take the Flying Blind-Cross-Examination Chart with you to the podium and decide as you go which rows and columns to address. Instead of addressing one admission (one row) at a time, you can choose to address one column at a time. For example, if you find the above "True/False" chart persuasive, you may wait until the end of cross-examination to force the defendant to admit the truthfulness of what Ms. Jones said and repeat his lone denial of Ms. Jones' testimony that the defendant ignored her question when leaving the victim's house.

7. Establish the Logical Consequences of Each Denial

The Flying Blind Cross-Examination Chart saves the best for last. Criminal defendants will often deny facts that incriminate them (or make them look bad), despite the logical consequences of those denials. That is why trial attorneys must take every denial made by a witness during direct examination and force the witness to admit the logical consequences of those denials. More specifically, a trial attorney must force the witness to admit *when* they are claiming that testing is inaccurate and *whether* other people are lying, wrong, or mistaken. The most important part of flying blind cross-examination can be establishing the "Accusations" (column #6), as shown in Table 12.5.

An effective technique for establishing the logical consequences of a denial is (a) to start by confirming what the witness said during direct examination (columns #1 and #2); (b) to solicit the specific denial you want, worded *precisely* the way you want; (c) to confirm the witness is aware of the contradictory physical or testimonial evidence (column #4); and (d) to force the witness to clarify their accusations (column #6).

When trying to nail down those accusations, trust your instincts on whether to ask an open-ended question (i.e., "What are you saying about the neighbor's testimony?"), a multiple-choice question (i.e., "Are you saying the neighbor is lying, mistaken, or wrong?"), or a leading question (i.e., "You are accusing the neighbor of lying, aren't you?"). Whatever question you choose, do not let the witness wiggle out of an answer. The jury has a right to know what the witness is suggesting. Here are some examples of how to clarify a criminal defendant's accusations regarding physical and testimonial evidence.

Q. During direct examination, you denied committing the crime, correct? (Columns #1 and #2)

A. Yes, I didn't kill her.

Q. Do you deny having the victim's blood on you when you left her house and got in your car? (Extrapolation based on denial of crime.)

A. Absolutely.

Q. You were present in the court when the crime lab expert testified that they found the victim's blood on your steering wheel, weren't you? (Column #4)

A. Yes.

Table 12.5 Flying Blind Chart Establishing the Accusations

A/D	Fact	Importance	Evidence	Confirms	Accuses
Admits	Dated the victim.	No forced entry	Social media	Neighbor said	
Admits	Dated for 2 years.	No forced entry	Social media	Neighbor said	
Admits	Victim cheated on you.	Motive	Social media	Neighbor said	
Admits	Broke up 1 month before murder.	Motive	Social media	Neighbor said	
Admits	Entered victim's house at 5:00 p.m.	At scene of the crime	Front door video	Neighbor saw	
Admits	Alone with victim.	Opportunity	Front door video	Neighbor saw	
Admits	Argued with victim.	State of mind		Neighbor heard	
Admits	Left victim's house at 5:30 p.m.	At scene of the crime	Front door video	Neighbor saw	
Denies	Stabbing victim.	The crime (itself)			
Denies	Ignoring neighbor's question when leaving.	State of mind			Neighbor is mistaken.
Denies	Leaving victim's blood on steering wheel.	Guilt	Crime lab testing		Crime lab expert is wrong.
Denies	Telling cellmate he killed victim.				Cellmate is lying.

Q. Are you telling the jury that the crime lab expert lied about finding the victim's blood on your steering wheel? (Column #6)

A. I'm saying that I didn't kill her.

Q. Was the crime lab expert wrong when he testified that they found the victim's blood on your steering wheel? (Column #6)

A. I'm saying that I didn't kill her.

Q. During direct examination, you denied hearing Ms. Jones when you left the victim's house around 5:30 p.m., correct? (Columns #1 and #2)

A. That's right.

Q. You didn't hear Ms. Jones yell, "Is everything okay"? (Columns #1 and #2).

A. No, I didn't.

Q. When Ms. Jones took the stand, she testified that you heard and ignored her when she yelled "Is everything okay?"

A. Yep.

Q. Are you saying Ms. Jones was lying?

When a defendant claims that multiple people are lying, wrong, or mistaken, consider additionally asking that defendant whether they believe that there is a "conspiracy." The conspiracy question itself can be important because it can plant that seed in the mind of jurors. And the answer doesn't really matter. If the defendant claims that there is a conspiracy, you will have earned the right (a) to refer to defendant's "conspiracy theory" for the rest of the trial; (b) to ask the jury whether any of them personally believe defendant's "conspiracy theory" during closing argument; and (c) to argue that any doubt based on defendant's "conspiracy theory" would not be "reasonable." If the defendant admits there is no conspiracy, you can argue that even the defendant admits that there is no conspiracy.

By establishing the logical consequences of every denial, you can help jurors understand what they are really being asked to decide. During a criminal trial, jurors can confuse having a reasonable doubt about a single piece of evidence with having a reasonable doubt about the defendant's guilt. By confirming the logical consequences of the defendant's denials, a trial attorney can articulate *everything* the defendant is asking jurors to find reasonable. For example, based on the admissions and denials in the above Flying Blind Cross-Examination Charts, the criminal defendant would be asking the jury to "buy" that *everything* in the below happened.

a. Facts Based on Defendant's Admissions

- Defendant discovered the victim was cheating on him with his best friend.
- Defendant drove to the victim's house.
- Defendant entered the victim's house at 5:00 p.m.
- Defendant could be heard screaming at the victim.
- Defendant left the victim's house at 5:30 p.m. without touching the victim.

b. Consequences of Defendant's Denials

- Neighbor would *have* to be mistaken about his ignoring her when she yelled "Is everything okay?"
- Crime lab would *have* to be wrong about finding victim's blood on defendant's steering wheel.
- After defendant left, a "mystery killer" would *have* to arrive at the victim's house.
- "Mystery killer" would *have* to enter the victim's house without being seen on the front door video.
- "Mystery killer" would *have* to kill the victim without neighbor's hearing anything.
- "Mystery killer" would *have* to exit the victim's house without being seen on the front door video.
- Defendant's cellmate would *have* to be lying about defendant's admission that he killed the victim.

Not surprisingly, flying blind cross-examinations are most likely to "fly off course" when an attorney is exploring the logical consequences of the denials (column #6). Whereas attorneys are rarely offended by admissions (columns #1 and #2), they are often be offended by false accusations (column #6), especially when a prosecutor "knows" the defendant is guilty or the defense attorney "knows" the witness is lying. The longer the list of accusations (i.e., lying neighbors, lying police officers, and fake test results), the more incredulous and aggressive a prosecutor may become. The more prominent and respected the object of those accusations (i.e., the revered crime lab expert, the decorated police officer, and the beloved pastor who lived next door), the more difficult it will be to hide your indignation and restrain your aggression. But remaining calm and making a list of the defendant's wild accusations or elaborate conspiracy theories can be more effective than laughing or openly attacking the witness.

8. Abandon the Flying-Blind Methodology as Needed

This method of performing a flying blind cross-examination is intended to serve as a reliable compass, but *only* for as long as the attorney needs that compass. So, keep your eyes open and your head on a swivel. If something the witness says or does causes the clouds to break, and you suddenly know *exactly* where you want to steer your cross-examination, trust your trial instincts. Go with your gut. Thank the Flying Blind Cross-Examination Chart for taking you as far as it did, drop the compass, grab hold of the yoke, and fly the plane.

Come on, Maverick. Do some of that pilot stuff.

9. Avoid Asking Questions to Which You Don't Know the Answer

When you do abandon the Flying Blind Cross-Examination Chart, avoid asking cross-examination questions to which you don't know the answer. That is the beauty of the chart. The completed chart allows you to solicit admissions without fear of accidentally soliciting prejudicial testimony. But when you abandon the chart and pursue another line of questioning, you may have no compass or vision of the horizon. Flying blind cross-examination is thrilling, until you fly into the side of a mountain—which is exactly what can happen.

In the 1997 *Derek Williams* trial, our opposing counsel (the public defender) had to perform a flying blind cross-examination of the victim. During direct examination, the victim testified that the defendant walked up to his car, pointed the gun at him, and hit him with the gun. On cross-examination, the public defender aggressively questioned the victim regarding the incident until the victim volunteered, "What really bothers me is my ceiling fan." The courtroom fell silent. You could hear a pin drop. The comment had come completely out of the blue. The public defender smiled, confident he was about to expose that the elderly victim had some form of dementia. "Why does your ceiling fan bother you?" the public defender asked.

The victim did not hesitate. "Because my ceiling fan clicks every time it goes completely around," the victim explained. "And it is exactly the same clicking sound that the empty gun made when he kept pulling the trigger. Click. Click. Click." Instantly, everyone in the courtroom realized that the defendant had tried to kill the victim and should have been charged with attempted murder, instead of aggravated battery. It took the jury less than 15 minutes to find Mr. Williams guilty as charged.

Chapter 13

Mid-Trial Settlements: Strategies for the Courthouse Steps

During the Golden Age of Lawyers, trial attorneys grew fond of bragging to clients that they were "not the type of lawyers who settle on the courthouse steps." That pitch always appealed to clients, and it always appealed to me as a young lawyer. It simplified everything. All trial lawyers could seemingly be divided into two groups: the fearless minority who never settled at trial and the frightened majority who never belonged in a courtroom. Suffice it to say, I knew which club I wanted to join. There was no way that I was *ever* going to "vomit money on the courthouse steps" or discuss settlement after the jury was picked. No, sir. Not me. If opposing counsel rejected my best offer at the end of mediation, we were going to try the case to verdict. "Sorry we couldn't resolve this amicably. I will see you at trial!"

Now, with the benefit of hindsight, I know that I was wrong to disregard settlement opportunities during a jury trial. Few trials go *exactly* as planned. Witnesses answer questions differently, reveal their bias, or lose their cool on the stand. Experts make unexpected admissions and forget how to defend their opinions. Judges make unforeseeable rulings, and attorneys make unfortunate mistakes. When that happens, attorneys on both sides of the aisle should re-evaluate the claims and revisit settlement. The bottom line is that the value of a claim on Day 4 of a jury trial is rarely the same as its value on Day 1.

Jury trials have always involved a degree of uncertainty and risk. That has not changed. Nobody really knows what 12 strangers will do when locked in a room until they agree. But recently, jury verdicts have been particularly unpredictable and alarming. Even the most experienced litigator will admit that their crystal ball is not what it used to be. Trial attorneys are winning trials they should have lost and losing trials they should have won.

Of course, a handful of horror stories about jury verdicts in *other* cases that were tried by *other* attorneys and in *other* states won't scare experienced litigators. Every few years, a string of outrageous verdicts nationwide causes panic in the ranks and seems to herald the end of the civil justice system as we know it. That stopped raising eyebrows a long time ago. But the recent wave of nuclear verdicts does feel different. It is too soon to tell, but the escalation in nuclear verdicts may be more than just perception or publicity. This time, it could be a legitimate trend. In the Age of Jurors, it could be a sign of the times.

Regardless, trial attorneys should prepare for settlement opportunities that manifest during jury trials. Timing is everything. At trial, the window for settlement can slam shut just as quickly as it burst open. So, before you "destroy" the plaintiff's expert on cross-examination, make sure you know (a) *who* will handle any settlement inquiries inspired by your epic cross-examination; (b) *what* types of settlement your client is interested in considering; (c) *whether* unfavorable testimony by the next witness could abruptly end settlement discussions; and (d) *what* you will need to "put on the record" if the parties reach a contingent settlement.

1. Designate a Negotiator for Your Team

Settlement negotiations can poison trial preparation and performance. Instead of preparing for the *next* witness, trial attorneys can waste countless hours calling, texting, and emailing opposing counsel and their clients. Word that the parties are getting closer to settlement can spread through a trial team like a virus. Suddenly, trial attorneys are talking themselves out of filing certain motions, spending less time preparing your witnesses, taking longer dinner breaks, and wondering whether they should cancel their expert's flight.

Settlement negotiations can also cause dissent in the ranks. If opposing counsel has played the game before, they may try to divide and conquer. One moment, opposing counsel is talking with you. The next moment, opposing counsel is speaking with your co-counsel. Suddenly, opposing counsel is asking to speak directly with your client, or worse, the clients decide to grab a coffee without the lawyers. Instead of discussing trial issues and agreeing on trial strategy, your team is discussing risk and disagreeing on the settlement value.

Before the trial starts, designate one individual to handle potential settlement negotiations. Whenever possible, do not pick lead trial counsel to handle settlement negotiations. Make sure that everyone on the defense team knows who has been designated to handle settlement negotiations. When opposing counsel asks if your client has "room to move," point to the designated individual. If opposing counsel asks you if your client has any interest in a high-low agreement, point to the designated individual. Ask that designated individual to tell your trial team when the case settles. Emphasize that the trial team does not need to be told *anything* until the agreement has been confirmed in writing or on the record.

During the 2007 *Lay* trial, our client volunteered to handle in-trial negotiations, and I was grateful for her sacrifice. Every trial recess seemed to involve some form of settlement negotiation, and those negotiations were incredibly frustrating for her. Rather than get dragged into those hallway battles, I stayed in the courtroom and stayed focus, preparing for the next witness. Even when settlement negotiations broke down, and our client flew back to New York on Thursday, I did not engage with opposing counsel. Instead, I worked on my cross-examination of the plaintiff. That cross-examination went extremely well on Friday, and the case settled on Monday. Thanks to our designated negotiator, I was able to stay on target.

2. Identify Windows for Settlement before the Trial Starts

Trial attorneys have always considered the order in which they call their witnesses. Traditionally, that order is designed to have the maximum effect on jurors. Some plaintiff attorneys start with their doctors to give credibility to their clients before their clients take the stand. Some save their best expert for last to clean up any messes. Some always end with their economist, wanting the numbers to be fresh in the jury's mind. Some start with their second-best witness and save their best (most emotional) witness for last. And some plaintiff attorneys will start the trial by calling a despicable defendant to "start with a bang!"

The order of witnesses should still be designed to have the maximum effect on jurors. That should not change. Every decision a trial attorney makes should be based on the premise that the trial will be tried to verdict. That said, trial attorneys would do well to start thinking of opposing counsel's camp as the *other* jury. No, you are never going to convince the *other* jury that you are right, and that they are wrong. That's not going to happen.

But the *other* jury has more skin in the game than the actual jury. The plaintiff may need the money, and a plaintiff attorney working for a contingency fee may have invested too much time and money in the case. The defendant may be facing bankruptcy, the insurance adjuster may be worried that the verdict will exceed their reserve, and the defense attorney may be afraid that losing the trial will mean losing the client. In some ways, it may be easier to persuade the *other* jury to settle the case than to persuade the actual jurors to return a favorable verdict.

Before trial, attorneys should stop, identify potential windows of opportunity for settlement, discuss *when* to first raise the issue of settlement, evaluate the pros and cons of different types of trial settlements, and recognize when those windows for settlement may close.

On one occasion, we parachuted into a case only one month before the jury trial. The plaintiff attorney was threatening to ask for $25 million at trial, and the defendant company did not have anywhere near that amount in insurance. Because the trial could result in a verdict far in excess of the available insurance, the case had everyone's attention. An "eleventh hour" mediation failed. Trial started, and our trial team was living under a microscope.

Prior to that trial, we identified a very small window for settlement. We found evidence that (a) plaintiff's treating doctor had hopped on his computer and allegedly altered an earlier report to support his later diagnosis; (b) one of plaintiff's expert had revisited his interpretation of the diagnostic imaging at counsel's request and (coincidentally) allegedly found evidence of a brain abnormality; and (c) another of plaintiff's experts, when summarizing the medical records, had omitted a sentence that reflected *very* poorly on the plaintiff and established an alternative cause for emotional anguish. But we did not know what order in which opposing counsel would call those three witnesses, who will hereafter be referred to as the "Three Stooges."

Prior to that trial, we also recognized that plaintiff's talented trial counsel was likely going to destroy our weakest defense experts during cross-examination. And so, there was a very small window for settlement. After my cross-examination of the First Stooge, we had our designated negotiator ask them for the *first* time whether they had any interest in a high-low agreement. After my cross-examination of the Second Stooge, our designated negotiator started floating numbers. After my cross-examination of the Third Stooge, and *before* we had to call our Weakest Link, we reached a high-low agreement where the high was less than the $11 million policy limits (eliminating the possibility of an excess judgment against the insured). The window was tight, but that settlement happened because we did not ignore the *other* jury.

3. Amount-Specific Contingent Settlements Based on an Appellate Ruling

Trial attorneys tend to think in absolute terms and to negotiate absolute settlements, which require the defendant to pay a specific amount within a specific period of time. Attorneys rarely negotiate settlement agreements that make the defendant's obligation to pay contingent upon a subsequent verdict, event, or ruling. But there are circumstances when neither party is interested in an absolute settlement, but both parties would benefit from a contingent settlement.

Whenever a single appellate court ruling will ultimately determine the defendant's liability (i.e., a winner-take-all ruling), there will be risk for both parties. Where there is risk to both parties, a contingent settlement can be advantageous for both parties, and that contingent settlement can take different forms.

One option is an amount-specific contingent settlement, where the parties make specific settlement amounts contingent on the outcome of an appellate court ruling by (a) agreeing to the specific amount that defendant will pay if the appellate court ultimately rules in the plaintiff's favor on the issue; and (b) agreeing to the specific amount that defendant will pay if the appellate court ultimately rules in the defendant's favor on the issue. In so doing, an amount-specific contingent settlement shifts the question from "What *is* each party willing to pay/accept in settlement before the appellate court rules?" to "What *would* each party be willing to pay/accept in their worst-case scenario?"

For example, consider the situation created when a trial court denies a defendant's motion for summary judgment on the issue of whether the driver was acting in the course and scope of his employment at the time of the accident. Defendant has a $1 million insurance policy, and both parties recognize the possibility that the jury could award up to $2 million in damages. Mediation fails because neither party is motivated to settle. Defendant is convinced the appellate court will reverse on appeal. Plaintiff is convinced the appellate court will affirm.

In that situation, the parties could make an amount-specific contingent settlement agreement that would make both parties happy in the event of their worst-case scenarios. More specifically, the parties could agree (a) if the defendant is wrong, and the appellate court affirms the trial court's ruling (the defendant's worst-case scenario), the defendant will pay $1 million to the plaintiff; and (b) if the plaintiff is wrong, and the appellate court reverses the trial court's ruling (the plaintiff's worst-case scenario), defendant will pay $250,000. By reaching that agreement, the attorneys would succeed in capping the defendant's exposure and guaranteeing a minimum recovery for the plaintiff.

These amount-specific contingent settlements shift the plaintiff's focus from what plaintiff *could* recover ($2 million) on their best day to what plaintiff *would* want to recover ($250,000) on their worst day. Whereas plaintiff may not be thrilled with the thought of settling for $1 million after the appellate court affirms, plaintiff will absolutely love the idea of being guaranteed $250,000 in the event the appellate court reverses and finds that the defendant is not liable. That is a deal the plaintiff may be willing to make because it would eliminate the possibility of the client's receiving *nothing*.

Similarly, these amount-specific contingent settlements also shift the defendant's focus from what defendant *would* owe ($0) if the appellate court reverses to what defendant *could* owe ($2 million) if the appellate court affirmed. Whereas defendant may not be thrilled with paying $250,000 after the appellate court reverses and finds defendant is not liable, defendant may be absolutely thrilled to pay only $1 million if the appellate court affirms. That is a deal that the defendant may be willing to make because it would eliminate the possibility of a judgment in excess of defendant's $1 million policy limits.

In theory, these amount-specific contingent settlements would moot the need for the jury to determine damages. Once the agreement is made, the specific amount that the defendant will pay solely depends on the appellate court ruling. The jury's award for damages would no longer be relevant or necessary. Thus, the amount-specific contingent settlement agreement would allow the parties to streamline and shorten the trial, asking the jury to determine *only* whether the driver was acting in the course and scope of employment.

4. High-Low Contingent Settlements Based on an Appellate Ruling

Plaintiff attorneys love to talk about a plaintiff's injuries and damages. They want the jurors to know how badly the plaintiff was hurt *before* they determine liability issues like whether the defendant was acting in the course and scope of his employment at the time of the accident. Because amount-specific contingent settlements based on an appellate court ruling (like a ruling on the course and scope issue) moot the need for the jury to award damages, the court would likely exclude all evidence of damages from the trial. For that reason, plaintiff's counsel may demand much higher specific amounts or outright reject an amount-specific settlement agreement.

In the alternative, the parties could make a high-low settlement agreement contingent on the outcome of the appellate court ruling by (a) agreeing to the "high" amount that defendant would pay if the appellate court ultimately affirmed the trial court's ruling on course and scope; (b) agreeing to the "low" amount that defendant would pay if the appellate court reversed the trial court's ruling on course and scope; and (c) agreeing that the defendant would pay the exact amount affirmed on appeal if that amount is greater than the agreed-to "low" and less than the agreed-to "high."

That alternative high-low contingent settlement would not streamline or shorten the trial because the jury's award for damages would still determine the amount owed by the defendant as long as (a) the appellate court affirmed the trial court's ruling on course and scope; (b) the jury's award was for more than the "low" and less than the "high"; and (c) the appellate court affirmed that award on appeal.

This option may be preferred by plaintiff's counsel, especially when plaintiff's counsel believes that introducing evidence of the plaintiff's injuries and damages will increase the probability that the jury will resolve the sole remaining liability issues in the plaintiff's favor.

5. High-Low Contingent Agreements Based on the Jury's Verdict

High-low agreements based on the jury's verdict are what most attorneys think of when they think of high-low agreements. In general, when the high-low agreement is based on the jury's verdict, the parties agree that (a) the plaintiff will recover a specific amount (the "low"), regardless of the jury's verdict; (b) the defendant will never have to pay more than a specific amount (the "high"), regardless of the jury's verdict; and (c) should the jury award an amount between the low and the high, the plaintiff will only be entitled to recover that specific amount awarded by the jury. That may sound simple, but high-low agreements are dangerous creatures.

There are a number of variables that must be specifically addressed by a high-low agreement for that agreement to be effective and enforced. When the parties reach a high-low agreement, always ask the court for the opportunity to have the lawyers (and preferably their clients) confirm the specific terms of the high-low agreement on the record.

High-low agreements can be specifically tailored to the preferences of the parties, but every high-low agreement should address certain issues. In addition to identifying the "high" and the "low," every high-low agreement should answer the following questions.

a. What Will Plaintiff Recover If the Verdict Is Equal to or Less Than the Low?

There will always be a chance that the jury will return a verdict that is equal to or less than the "low" amount agreed to by the parties. Always address what would happen in that event, even if you feel that a high-low agreement is self-explanatory.

Remember that the low amount is only relevant if the jury's award is less than it, which means that a defendant will be dealing with a salty plaintiff. Disappointed plaintiffs may try to tack on whatever they can to the low amount, including court costs, witness fees, attorney fees, and judicial interest.

For that reason, the high-low agreement should provide that, if the jury's verdict is an amount equal to or less than the low, the parties agree that the defendant will pay exactly the low amount to the plaintiff. Always make it clear on the record that the defendant will pay nothing more than the low amount. No court costs. No witness fees. No attorney fees. No judicial interest. No additional amount whatsoever.

b. What Will Plaintiff Recover If the Verdict Is Equal to or Greater Than the High?

There is always a chance that the jury will return a verdict that is equal to or greater than the "high" amount agreed to by the parties. Always address what would happen in that event, even if you feel that a high-low agreement is self-explanatory.

Remember that the high amount is only relevant if the jury's award is greater than it, which means that a defense attorney may be dealing with a salty client. Disappointed clients do not want to be told that the high-low agreement failed to specify whether the defendant would additionally be obligated to pay court costs, witness fees, attorney fees, and judicial interest.

For that reason, the high-low agreement should provide that, if the jury's verdict is an amount equal to or greater than the high, the parties agree that the defendant will pay exactly the high amount to the plaintiff. Always make it clear on the record that the defendant will pay nothing more than the high amount. No court costs. No witness fees. No attorney fees. No judicial interest. No additional amount whatsoever.

c. What Will Plaintiff Recover If the Verdict Is between the Low and the High?

The most likely scenario after a high-low agreement is that the jury returns a verdict that falls between the low and the high amounts agreed to by the parties. Always address what would happen in that event, even if you believe that all high-low agreements should be enforced in exactly the same way with regard to such jury awards.

To avoid additional litigation, the parties should agree that the defendant will pay the exact amount of the jury verdict if that verdict is for an amount greater than the low but less than the high. If the parties reach that agreement, always make it clear on the record that the defendant will pay nothing more than the exact amount of the jury verdict. No court costs. No witness fees. No attorney fees. No judicial interest. No additional amount whatsoever.

d. What Happens If the Jury Is Unable to Reach a Verdict?

Every high-low agreement should establish what will happen if the jury becomes deadlocked (i.e., the trial results in a hung verdict). While everyone is shaking hands and patting themselves on the back over having agreed to a "high" and a "low," take a moment to make sure that this possibility is addressed by the high-low agreement.

First, the parties should reach an agreement on whether the court (a) shall have the discretion to declare a mistrial *at any time* because of a hung verdict; (b) shall be required to give an Allen charge or a "dynamite" charge, encouraging deadlocked jurors to reach a verdict, before declaring a mistrial; (c) shall only have the discretion to declare a mistrial after the jury has deliberated for a specific period of time; or (d) shall be required to declare a mistrial after the jury has deliberated for a specific period of time.

In the 2009 *Craige* case, the jury was deadlocked on the first jury interrogatory, which required jurors to decide whether the accident caused *any* injury to the subsequently paralyzed plaintiff. After hours of deliberation, the jury reportedly voted eight (plaintiff) to four (defense). The court then gave a strongly worded "dynamite" charge, emphasizing that the parties were depending on the jurors to reach a verdict and encouraging the jurors to work with each other. Later, the jury reportedly voted seven (plaintiff) and five (defense). Soon thereafter, the court declared a mistrial. Naturally, as defense counsel, I liked the direction in which the numbers were moving, and I wanted the jury to continue deliberating. By my count, five jurors were now convinced the paralyzed plaintiff sustained no injury. That experience emphasized the need for a high-low agreement to address whether the court will retain complete discretion in declaring a hung jury.

Second, the parties should reach an agreement on whether the defendant shall pay a specific amount in the event of hung jury. To avoid having to retry the case, both parties may be particularly motivated to agree to a specific settlement amount in the event of a mistrial declared because of a hung jury, especially if both parties believe the chances of a hung verdict are remote. In that event, the settlement agreement would more properly be called a "high-low-hung agreement," which is an expression I just coined.

Third, if the parties are unable to reach an agreement regarding a specific amount to be paid in the event of a hung jury, the parties can (a) agree to retry the case with the retrial being subject to the same high-low agreement; (b) agree to retry the case *without* the retrial being subject to the same high-low agreement; (c) agree to settle the case for a specific amount; or (d) agree to an alternative mechanism for settling the case.

e. Do the Parties Agree to Waive All Motions for Mistrial?

High-low agreements made *before* the end of closing arguments should address whether or not the parties waive their right to move for a mistrial. In this regard, high-low agreements traditionally require the parties to waive their right to a mistrial.

There are a number of reasons for that requirement. In theory, the purpose of a high-low agreement is to resolve the matter based on the negotiated high, the negotiated low, and the verdict of the jury, as it is *currently* constituted. A granted motion for mistrial would require a *subsequent* jury to resolve the matter, altering one-third of the agreement. Also, the purpose of a high-low agreement is to resolve the case at the end of the trial.

Fair warning. When the parties reach a high-low agreement and waive their right to move for a mistrial *before* closing arguments, the trial can quickly become the wild, wild west. Opposing counsel can start pushing the envelope with their argument, witnesses, and evidence, knowing that you cannot move for a mistrial. Even if you reach a high-low agreement *immediately* before closing arguments, you may find yourself watching opposing counsel violate the "Golden Rule" by asking jurors to put themselves in the shoes of their client. Or worse, you may hear opposing counsel talk about testimony that was not in the record and evidence that was excluded. Sure, you can object, and the court will sustain your objection, but some bells cannot be un-rung.

During the aforementioned trial, we made a "game-time" decision to reach a high-low agreement before we rested the defense case because: (a) we trusted opposing counsel not to introduce inadmissible evidence and argument and (b) we trusted the judge to be vigilant. That trust was rewarded as neither side engaged in mistrial-worthy conduct, but both sides heard questions during subsequent witness examinations and heard argument during closings that they might not have heard in the absence of a high-low agreement. It was not the wild, wild west, but shots were fired.

When reaching a high-low agreement *before* closing argument, consider raising your concern with opposing counsel. Sometimes, a gentleman's agreement will help both sides resist the temptation to take certain liberties with the argument and evidence. When reading the high-low agreement into the record, consider mentioning that "the parties are aware that, sometimes, after a high-low agreement is reached, the trial can become the wild, wild west, but that is not going to happen here. We know we have a good sheriff (nodding at the judge). We trust each other, and we have reached an understanding."

Of course, if the parties are not willing to waive their right to move for a mistrial, the high-low agreement must additionally address what happens in the event that the court declares a mistrial. The parties should answer specific questions, including: (a) Would the parties agree to retry the case with the retrial being subject to the same high-low agreement? or (b) Would the parties agree to retry the case *without* the retrial being subject to the same high-low agreement?

In theory, the parties could even deter mistrial-worthy misconduct by agreeing that (a) if the court granted a mistrial based on defense misconduct, the subsequent retrial would only be subject to the low (guaranteeing the plaintiff a minimum recovery); and (b) if the court granted a mistrial based on plaintiff misconduct, the subsequent retrial would only be subject to the high (limiting plaintiff's maximum recovery).

f. Do the Parties Agree to Waive Rule 50 Motions and Other Dispositive Motions?

High-low agreements made *before* the end of closing arguments should address whether or not the parties waive their right to subsequently make Rule 50 motions and other dispositive motions. No attorney will want to enter into a high-low agreement that permits opposing counsel to subsequently move for a directed verdict or make a dispositive motion that would (arguably) moot the high-low agreement. That is why the parties often agree to waive Rule 50 motions and any other motion that would ultimately deny the jury the opportunity to reach a verdict.

There may be trials in which a party is convinced that the court is going to grant a Rule 50 motion. In theory, the parties could agree to a high-low agreement in which they agree that (a) the party will still be permitted to make the Rule 50 motion and obtain a ruling; (b) the court will not be advised of the high-low agreement until after the ruling on that Rule 50 motion; (c) the court's granting of the Rule 50 motion would vacate, set aside, revoke, and nullify the high-low agreement; and (d) the court's denial of the Rule 50 motion would be followed by the terms of the high-low agreement being read into the record. But that unique agreement would require the party who intends to file the Rule 50 motion to *really* trust opposing counsel and the court.

g. Do the Parties Retain the Right to Request Curative Instructions?

High-low agreements made *before* the end of closing arguments should address whether or not the parties waive their right to request curative instructions. In the absence of a high-low agreement, trial attorneys commonly move for a mistrial and, in the alternative, move for a curative instruction. When parties reach a high-low agreement and waive their right to move for a mistrial, a curative instruction becomes an attorney's only redress after a sustained objection.

This decision is more about trusting the judge than trusting opposing counsel. There is no inherent danger in agreeing that opposing counsel retains the right to request a curative instruction. The real danger is that the court will give an incredibly inappropriate and prejudicial curative instruction, and you will have no recourse whatsoever (i.e., no right to appeal the court's curative instruction and request a new trial). The more inexperienced the judge, or the more (perceived) favoritism the court has shown opposing counsel, the more difficult this decision may be.

Picture opposing counsel's requesting a curative instruction and the court's telling the jury to disregard something you said during closing argument "because it is absolutely false and absolutely reprehensible. I am disappointed by this conduct, and I am instructing you to ignore counsel's statement." If the parties have waived their right to appeal, there is nothing you can do, except sit down and start writing a settlement check for the "high" amount.

The bottom line is that trust is the real litmus test for determining whether to make a high-low agreement before closing argument. Do you trust opposing counsel? Do you trust the court? Do you trust the court staff? Do you trust yourself?

h. Do the Parties Agree That No Claims or Defenses Will Be Struck?

High-low agreements made *before* the end of closing arguments should address whether or not the parties agree that no claims or defenses will be subsequently struck by the court. When the parties agree to waive their right to move for a mistrial *and* their right to request a curative instruction, their only recourse may be to ask the court to sanction misconduct by ordering claims or affirmative defenses be struck.

Striking claims and defenses is an extreme remedy whether the court is sanctioning opposing counsel's misconduct or the opposing party's misconduct. Trial attorneys should always agree to waive the right to request that the court strike claims and defenses. Again, by not waiving this right, the parties give the court the ability to directly affect the jury's verdict without giving the parties any legal recourse.

Picture opposing counsel's jumping out of the chair and passionately objecting that you just "violated the Golden Rule" during your closing argument. Opposing counsel is furious, and the court *incorrectly* concludes that your argument violated the Golden Rule. What happens next? If the parties have waived the right to move for a mistrial and the right to request a curative instruction, your irate opposing counsel may ask the court to strike a claim (if you represent the plaintiff) or strike an affirmative defense (if you represent the defendant). Think before you give the court that kind of power.

i. Do the Parties Agree That There Will Be No Emergency Supervisory Writs?

Every high-low agreement reached *before* the end of closing arguments should address whether or not the parties waive their right to seek emergency supervisory writs. This can be a difficult decision when the high-low agreement is made before the court has ruled on game-changing evidentiary objections.

j. Do the Parties Agree That There Will Be No Post-Trial Motions?

Every high-low agreement should require the parties to waive their right to make post-trial motions. No motions for a judgment notwithstanding the verdict (JNOV). No motions for new trial. No additur and no remittitur.

Otherwise, the parties will be entering into a high-low agreement that permits the trial court (who, by then, would have knowledge of the specific amounts of the high-low agreement) to substitute the court's opinion on damages for the jury's award for damages. That would be contrary to the purpose of a high-low agreement, which allows the parties to select the "high" and "low" amounts, and reserves for the jury the determination of any award between the "high" and "low." By failing to require the parties to waive post-trial motions, and allowing the court to disregard the jury's award, the trial attorneys can unintentionally render the jury's verdict meaningless. After all, if both parties wanted the judge to ultimately determine damages, they could have proceeded with a judge trial instead of a jury trial.

k. Do the Parties Agree to Waive Their Right to Appeal?

High-low contingent agreements that are based on an appellate ruling cannot require the parties to waive their right to appeal (otherwise, the parties would never obtain the appellate ruling that establishes the high and the low). But every high-low agreement based on a jury award should either (a) require the parties to waive their right to appeal or (b) specify the specific issues that each party retains the right to appeal *and* explain how rulings on each issue will affect the enforcement of the high-low agreement.

l. How Long Will the Defendants Have to Pay the Settlement?

Every high-low agreement should specify how long the defendant has to satisfy the high-low agreement by making payment. If your client needs certain settlement information or documents before issuing the check, make it clear when your clock starts.

Table 13.1 is a checklist summarizing the key points you need to determine when making a high-low settlement; it is available for download at ambar.org/TrialAdvocacy.

Table 13.1 High-Low Agreement Checklist

	The parties agree to a high-low agreement, which will be defined as follows:
1.	The Low shall be [Low].
2.	The High shall be [High].
3.	If the jury's verdict is equal to or less than the amount of [Low], the parties agree that the plaintiff(s) shall only be entitled to and shall only be paid the total amount of [Low]. The defendant(s) shall pay nothing more than the total amount of [Low]. No court costs. No witness fees. No attorney fees. No judicial interest. No additional amount whatsoever.
4.	If the jury's verdict is equal to or greater than the amount of [High], the parties agree that the plaintiff(s) shall only be entitled to and shall only be paid the total amount of [High]. The defendant(s) shall pay nothing more than the total amount of [High]. No court costs. No witness fees. No attorney fees. No judicial interest. No additional amount whatsoever.
5.	If the jury's verdict is for an amount greater than the amount of [Low] and less than the amount of [High], the parties agree that the plaintiff(s) shall only be entitled to and shall only be paid the specific amount of the verdict. The defendant(s) shall pay nothing more than the amount of the verdict. No court costs. No witness fees. No attorney fees. No judicial interest. No additional amount whatsoever.
6.	If the jury is unable to reach a verdict, the parties agree [insert agreement]
7.	The parties [do/not] agree to waive their right to file post-trial motions.
8.	The parties [do/not] agree to waive their right to take an appeal.
9.	The parties agree that the amount owed will be paid within [insert] days of [the verdict/receiving certain settlement information or documents/appellate decision]
	[If the high-low agreement is reached *before* the end of closing arguments] **The parties further agree to the following:**
10.	The parties [do/not] agree to waive all motions for mistrial.
11.	The parties [do/not] agree to waive their right to file dispositive motions, including Rule 50 motions for a directed verdict.
12.	The parties [do/not] agree to waive their right to request curative instructions.
13.	The parties [do/not] agree that no claims or defenses will be struck.
14.	The parties [do/not] agree to waive their right to seek (emergency) supervisory writs.

Chapter 14

Closing Advocacy: Training and Taming Lions

During the Golden Age of Lawyers, trial attorneys took different approaches to closing argument. Some felt compelled to comment on all the evidence, cramming days of trial into a one-hour presentation. Some analyzed only favorable evidence, wanting to make certain it was fresh in the minds of jurors at the start of their deliberation. Some focused on responding to opposing counsel's arguments. Some physically filled in the jury interrogatory, believing jurors were so incompetent or so enamored (with them) that they would copy their answers. What these very different approaches had in common was the deep-seated belief that jurors desperately wanted to hear *their* opinion of the evidence. To be fair, this may have been the case at some point in human history. But it is rarely the case now. So, let's stop thinking that way.

Today, by the end of the trial, jurors know *exactly* what the trial attorneys think and want. They are not remotely interested in pleasing the paid advocates. In the deliberation room, they are only obsessed with being (or at least appearing to be) fair to both parties. If one attorney tells them to award a specific number, they will avoid that number like the bubonic plague. And they have absolutely no interest in parroting the opinions or arguments of either counsel. They are not puppets, and they will reach their own verdict.

Try enough jury trials to verdict and watch enough mock jurors deliberate, and you will reach the inescapable conclusion that jurors genuinely want to do the right thing, but they do *not* want to do what they are told. Like teenagers, they can love you to the moon and back, but they would rather suffer a thousand painful deaths than agree with you in front of their friends. This means that the legal profession stands at a crossroads. We can continue to tell jurors *our* opinion of the evidence and *our* verdict, or we can wake up and write a new playbook for closing argument in the Age of Jurors. Let's do the latter. Let's redefine and redesign closing argument.

Let's start by recognizing that our closing argument had better *not* be the last argument made on behalf of our client. Jurors rarely elect a foreperson and immediately reach a verdict. It is far more likely the jury will spend hours deliberating and the verdict will be determined by one persuasive and persistent juror. We may not know who that Lion is, but we know that he or she is out there, waiting in the tall grass. And we know that Lion needs our help. The longer the jury deliberates, the more likely the Lions will need to eat the Lambs.

Let's shift our focus from persuading Lambs to preparing Lions for deliberation. Instead of telling Lions our opinion of the evidence, let's review the evidence in a way that helps Friendly Lions remember, explain, and defend *their* opinions. Instead of ignoring bias and prejudice, let's prepare Lions for the moment bias and prejudice raises its head in the deliberation room. Instead of trying to change minds during closing argument, let's teach Lions how to change minds during deliberation. Instead of telling jurors our verdict, let's identify a range that allows Lions propose a verdict that appears fair to the other jurors. In short, let's *train* and *tame* our Lions without *telling* our Lions what to do in front of their friends.

1. Review Their Choices without Offering Your Opinion

Good waiters do not make unsolicited arguments. On those rare occasions when a guest admits that they are torn between the fish and the chicken, a good waiter may ask a question ("Do you like curry?"). But when it is time to order, a good waiter never walks up to the table, tells guests what to order, and reviews only the merits of the dish they are recommending. Their job is not to choose for you. Their job is to help you make the right choice *after* they have explained the menu and given you some time to decide.

Similarly, during closing argument, resist the temptation to tell jurors your opinion (which they already know) and to review only the evidence supporting your opinion (which is what jurors expect lawyers to do). Instead, identify the choices or decisions that the jury needs to make together during their deliberation. Then, review all the evidence relevant to each of *their* decisions in a way that makes it clear what decisions *they* should make, without openly telling jurors *your* opinion (which, again, they already know).

Resist the temptation to passionately tell jurors the Beatles were absolutely a better band than the Rolling Stones, and stubbornly review only the Beatles' music catalog and accomplishments. Dedicate yourself to the infinitely more difficult task of discussing the strengths and weaknesses of both bands in a way that will help Lions persuade Lambs that the Beatles were superior, possibly days after your closing argument.

Remember that what you say during closing argument is not as important as what Lions remember. Stop searching for the perfect combination of words to rebut an argument and start searching for the most memorable combination of words. Stop trying to cover every point and start trying to cover what Lions need to remember. Nobody cares if you win the trial on your legal pad. This is not a high school debate competition.

Do not get lost in the weeds. Remember there is a difference between Main Points and Mom Points. If you told your mother about your trial, you might tell her your Main Points. If you called your mother the next day, what she still remembered about your conversation would be Mom Points. Find a way to review the evidence so that your Main Points become Mom Points. You may need Lions to remember those points on day eight of deliberation.

Remember that time equals significance. Do not waste time on trivial evidence and frivolous arguments. Your actions will speak louder than your words. The amount of time you dedicate to a fact, exhibit, or issue often determines its significance. The more time you spend talking about it, the more important it becomes.

If something is trivial, address it with a footnote, not a chapter. During the 1999 *Whitton* first-degree murder trial, the criminal defense attorney's closing argument was primarily based on a bloody fingerprint found inside the house because that bloody fingerprint did *not* match the defendant's fingerprint. Opposing counsel told the jury that the bloody fingerprint "had to belong" to the "real murderer" because it was left after the bloody murders. Tellingly, opposing counsel did not explain that the bloody fingerprint was found directly above the body of the youngest victim, or that the victim's fingers were too decomposed for fingerprint comparison.

During the State's rebuttal in *Whitton*, I walked jurors chronologically through the entire sequence of murders. When I got to the part where the defendant stabbed the youngest victim, wrapped him in a Power Rangers sleeping bag, and left him to bleed to death, I stooped down as if I was next to the victim's sleeping bag. I noted that the fingerprint "which defense counsel spent his entire closing argument talking about" was found less than an arm's length above that victim on the side of the washing machine. I reminded jurors that the victim's finger was too decomposed to print by the time the bodies were discovered, and I told the jurors the victim probably left the fingerprint when he reached up for help. Almost as an aside, I noted that the victim's bloody fingerprint did not belong to some "mystery murderer" and continued with the story. The quickness and indifference with which I dismissed their entire defense emphasized that it had no merit. The jury agreed and found the defendant guilty as charged of all four counts of first-degree murder.

2. Pick One Visual to Help Lions Compare the Evidence

Jurors need to compare the evidence on the ultimate issue, and they often remember what they saw during closing argument better than what they heard. Help Lions by picking one visual reminder like a timeline, graph, table, or chart to compare the evidence on the ultimate issue. What you want is for jurors to be *listening* to you while they are *looking* at your demonstrative exhibit. Picture a Lamb on day two of deliberation confessing to a Lion, "I don't remember all of counsel's points on that issue," and the Lion replying, "Don't you remember *seeing* . . .?"

For the past decade, my favorite method of reviewing the evidence on the ultimate issue has been to display an enlarged image of the scales of justice, and visually stack the physical and testimonial evidence on each side of the scale. By stacking the weights, you can visually and clearly convey what the jury should decide *without* actually telling the jury how to vote.

I have used the scales of justice on different sides of the aisle. As criminal defense counsel, I used the scales during closing argument in the 2010 *Nugent* manslaughter criminal trial in Winn Parish. As lead defense counsel for a trucking company, I used the scales during closing argument in the 2015 *Crayton* personal injury trial in Jefferson Parish. And, as lead plaintiff counsel, I used the scales during closing argument in the 2021 *Lindale* trial in Houston.

Instead of telling jurors that you met your burden of proving the ultimate issue by a preponderance of the evidence, show them how you tipped the scales. Place every witness, exhibit, timeline, document, and even individual sentences (like the exclusivity provision in the contract) that supports your argument on your side of the scale. But be fair to opposing counsel. Place the evidence that supports opposing counsel's argument on their side of the scale. Figure 14.1 shows a scales of justice slide comparing (a) the evidence that Lindale presented proving Equinor had a contractual duty to purchase "all the water" for frack jobs from Lindale and (b) the two witnesses that Equinor called (an employee and an expert) who insisted that Equinor was not obligated to buy "a single drop" of water from Lindale. The scales of justice was the last thing that jurors saw before awarding our clients $26 million in the *Lindale* case.

Figure 14.1 Scales of justice in the *Lindale* trial.

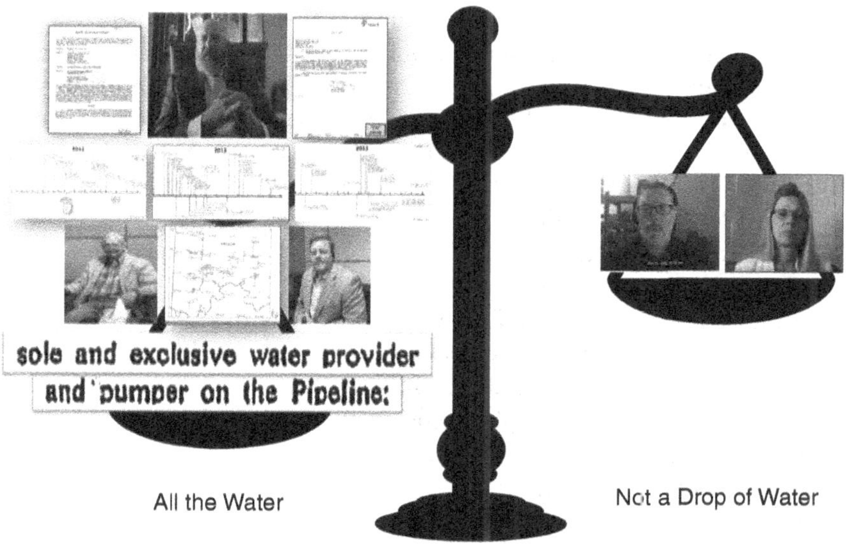

Always resist the temptation to tell jurors what they can plainly see, but feel free to use two different images. Start with the image of a blank scale with perfectly balanced scales. Then switch to a second image showing a tipped scale favoring your client.

During your closing argument, warn jurors up front that the court will not permit the jurors to call for *any* of your demonstrative exhibits, "so this will be the only chance I get to walk through the evidence on both sides of the scale." When jurors realize that the scales of justice won't be in the deliberation room, they will take notes or pay closer attention. Those notes may be exactly what your Lions need during days of deliberation.

Carefully consider the order in which you stack evidence on the scale. Over the years, I have stacked the evidence (a) in chronological order; (b) in the same order in which the evidence was presented at trial; and (c) in the order of importance. Once, I chose to add our key witness to the scale first and then add the additional evidence to visually show the support for his testimony.

Do not feel compelled to use a fancy slide show presentation. During the 2010 *Nugent* trial, the courtroom had no audio/visual and my flip chart was full. With no other options, I took two chairs and placed them in front of the jury. In the "defense chair," I placed all the items in evidence proving that the officer's CEW drive stuns did not cause the suspect's death. By the time I was done, the stack of evidence was so high it was almost falling over. I then pointed out that the State had failed to produce any medical or scientific literature that could be placed in the "State's chair." I asked the jury to imagine how much evidence *should have been* placed in that chair to satisfy the State's burden of proving guilt beyond a reasonable doubt. Visually, it was as effective, if not more effective, than using a fancier slideshow presentation. Similarly, during the 2015 *Crayton* trial, I hand drew the scales on a flip chart, and wrote in the evidence on both sides of the scale.

The scales of justice may not be the most effective visual reminder in personal injury cases involving years of post-accident treatment. In those cases, jurors may struggle to follow your review of the facts, especially if the timeline involves prior accidents, extensive medical treatment, diagnostic images, surveillance dates, independent medical examinations, and different periods of employment. In those cases, it can be effective to use an enlarged and mounted timeline, especially if you checked off each date, event, and finding during your direct and cross-examination of witnesses. Picture yourself standing beside a completely checked-off timeline that you showed them during opening statement, having confirmed every fact.

During opening statement in the 2017 *Stroud* trial, I told jurors that the first seven months could be an "anchor" for them throughout the trial. I showed them a neurological timeline of medical treatment for the first seven months, and I promised them that we would prove that (a) no doctor diagnosed a concussion during the first seven months; (b) all testing (MRI, CT, EEG) was negative; (c) no neurological exam was abnormal; and (d) no cranial nerve exam was abnormal. Throughout the trial, I used different color markers for each expert. I solicited and handwrote every "no" and "negative." Then, during closing argument, I placed the completed neurological timeline (which I called my "board full of no's") on the easel in front of the jury. The visual was a constant reminder that the there was no evidence of a brain injury during the first seven months *and* that the trial had gone exactly as planned.

Sometimes, less is more. Jurors can become desensitized to "fancy" exhibits during a long trial involving many slides and demonstrative exhibits. There is nothing wrong with pulling out a flip chart, drawing a line down the center of the page, and writing down the physical and testimonial evidence on both sides of the ultimate issue. During jury deliberation, Lions may not remember every fact written on your side of the line, but they can remind Lambs that more was written on your side or that your list was longer and better.

3. Replay Video and Show Transcripts of Testimony

Lions prefer for the paid advocates to show the critical testimony rather than repeat, paraphrase, or summarize the critical testimony. Give Lions what they want. Instead of telling jurors what each witness said, replay the critical clip of that juror's testimony (if the juror testified by video) or show the critical quote in the trial transcript. Remember that less is more. Never replay video of more than the specific question and answer, and always highlight the specific question and answer in the trial transcript.

Providing the jury with video clips and transcripts during closing argument does not happen the night before closing argument. Before trial, do all of the following:

- Prepare video clips for any videotaped trial perpetuation deposition that will be played during the trial.
- Request that the court arrange for daily trial transcripts. If the court or the court reporter cannot accommodate your request, find out whether the court will permit you to pay for a certified court reporter to attend the trial and prepare daily transcripts (which you should offer to share with opposing counsel).
- Request and arrange for any testimony presented remotely (i.e., "live by Zoom") to be recorded to permit your team to nightly edit video clips.

During the 2011 *Wiltz* trial, opposing counsel used a document overhead projector to display trial transcripts. It was ridiculously effective. I watched helplessly as the jurors read along with him, and I listened nervously as counsel explained why each quote was important to the outcome of the trial. Instead of telling jurors what each witness said, counsel was showing them the testimony. And, during deliberation, Lions would be able to remind fellow jurors that they saw the transcript instead of arguing "that's not what counsel said."

Always ask the court, perhaps during the pretrial conference, whether you will be allowed to use trial transcripts during closing argument. Unfortunately, some courts will not permit attorneys to replay video or show/read trial transcripts during closing argument. During the 2012 *Fahy* trial, I started reading excerpts from the daily trial transcripts to make certain the jurors correctly recalled what was said by a critical witness. Opposing counsel objected and the court sustained that objection, basically ruling that the jury had to rely on their memory of the testimony. Whether or not the court's ruling was erroneous, I failed to consider the court's reaction to my using the daily transcripts during closing argument.

Think before you object to opposing counsel's use of a trial transcript during closing argument. During the *Fahy* trial, after the court ruled that I could not read directly from the trial transcript, plaintiff's counsel repeatedly objected whenever he thought I was reading from or quoting the trial transcript. Plaintiff's counsel later regretted that decision because he felt it made him look like a lawyering lawyer who wanted to deprive jurors of the benefit of trial transcript. After the jury returned a zero verdict, plaintiff's counsel filed a motion for new trial alleging, in part, that *his objections* prejudiced his client.

> Counsel for Defendant, during closing argument continuously and repeatedly read from the daily transcripts of the trial testimony when the Court had previously ruled that it would not be permitted. Counsel for Plaintiff was forced to object numerous times to the Defendant's violation of the Court's rulings on this issue in front of the jury, creating the prejudicial impression that Plaintiff did not want the jury to hear testimony from witnesses.

That motion was denied as having no merit, but the above-quoted excerpt from that motion is a reminder that transcript issues are best addressed with the court before closing argument.

4. Identify a Turning Point in the Trial

Perception is reality. In hindsight, people perceive most long-term endeavors as having a turning point. Every war has a turning point. Every career has a turning point. Every successful and unsuccessful relationship has a turning point. And every courtroom movie or television drama has a turning point. Consequently, Lions may search for a turning point in your trial, and Lambs may be persuaded by a Lion's ability to identify one.

Whenever possible, identify a specific witness, exhibit, or event as "the turning point in the trial," and calmly explain why it was a turning point. But do not take it too far. Do not tell jurors the turning point requires a certain verdict for your client. Let them decide that for themselves.

Identifying a moment as a turning point can become a self-fulfilling prophecy. History proves that the turning point in a war is often remembered long after the countless skirmishes are forgotten. Similarly, the longer the jury deliberates, the more likely jurors will remember and discuss the turning point you identified during closing argument. Picture a Lion referring to the "turning point" admission for the entire deliberation. Picture a Lion politely asking if they could spend some time discussing the "turning point" exhibit. Imagine how reluctant Lambs would be to admit they don't understand *why* something was a turning point. The sheer repetition of the phrase "turning point" can reinforce the importance of any testimony, exhibit, or event.

A single answer or a single line of questioning can be turning point in the trial. During the *Fahy* trial, plaintiffs asked the jury to award $12 million in compensatory damages plus punitive damages. Plaintiffs claimed our client, the leading manufacturer of conducted electrical weapons (CEWs), was liable for failing to warn officers to "avoid the chest when possible." During closing argument, I told jurors the turning point in the trial was when the police officer testified that she had "no time to aim" because the fists-up plaintiff was only six feet away and coming right at her. I argued that if the officer had no time to aim, then an additional warning to avoid aiming at the chest would not have changed the outcome.

Turning points can evoke a visceral reaction by opposing counsel. During the *Fahy* trial, I reminded jurors that when the officer testified that she had "no time to aim," opposing counsel responded by repeatedly and unsuccessfully trying to get the officer to change her testimony and say she "fired at" center mass or "pointed" at the center of the chest. As the trial transcript reflects:

> Q: And so you fired . . . just like you had been trained to at center body mass, correct?
>
> A. I didn't know where it was going to hit him, I just shot it. That's all I could do. I couldn't aim. I was surprised it shot him in the chest because his fists were up like this.
>
> Q. And you had it pointed at the center of his chest, correct?
>
> A. No, I had it down, and as he's approaching me, I just pulled it up and shot it.

Q. And you followed that muscle memory when you fired . . . at center body mass, correct?

A. Again, I didn't have time to aim, I didn't know where I was hitting him, that's the only recourse I had to keep him from approaching me any further and protect myself and my partner.

After the *Fahy* trial, opposing counsel spoke with jurors before he himself was interviewed. The subsequent article quoted plaintiff's counsel as saying that "some of the jurors felt that we didn't make our case that the state of the science in 2007, when this device was sold, was enough to require TASER to issue a warning on chest shots" and "other jurors felt that the dynamics of the situation did not give the officer time to aim differently and so a warning wouldn't have made any difference."[1] Which suggests that Lions discussed the turning point during deliberation, and the turning point directly affected the outcome of the trial.

Turning points are not limited to physical and testimonial evidence regarding liability. During the 2004 *Molo* trial, we defended an excess insurer against the claim that a falling blowtorch caused severe brain damage, requiring constant supervision and care. During direct examination, plaintiff's wife testified that she was afraid to leave him alone; but, during cross-examination, she admitted to leaving their six-month-old grandchild alone with plaintiff while she worked. That admission was the turning point in the trial. That one act of trust spoke louder than anything the experts said about plaintiff's cognitive or behavioral impairment. Accordingly, my co-counsel Bob discussed that turning point during his closing argument. The jury agreed. Their verdict did not exceed the primary policy, and no judgment was entered against our client.

5. Prepare Lions to Discuss the Burden of Proof

Lions need to be prepared to raise, discuss, and enforce the burden of proof. Do not assume that Lions will listen, understand, or remember the court's jury instructions regarding burden of proof. Always address the burden of proof during your closing argument. In civil cases, always give Lions a visual that will remind Lions of the number of elements and the burden of proof.

---

1. Juan Carlos Rodriguez, *Taser Beats Heart Attack Victim's Failure to Warn Suit*, LAW360 (Dec. 14, 2012), https://www.law360.com/articles/401669/taser-beats-heart-attack-victim-s-failure-to-warn-suit.

As a civil defense attorney, consider comparing disputed legal elements to a series of bridges the prosecutor and plaintiff must build with evidence to get where they want to go. If they fail to meet their burden of producing sufficient physical and testimonial evidence regarding even one bridge, the jury must return a defense verdict. Figure 14.2 shows the three bridges I presented in the 2012 *Fahy* trial, where the jury reportedly found that the plaintiff failed to prove that the addition of a warning would have changed what happened that day.

Figure 14.2 Three bridges presented at trial.

Three Bridges

Eads	Golden Gate	Tower
TASER ***Knew*** **X26 Caused VF**	**Warning** ***Would Have*** ***Changed*** **Probe Location**	**X26** **Actually** ***Caused*** **VF**

Again, the order of the bridges can matter. During the 2010 *Nugent* trial, I started opening statement by drawing three bridges on a flip chart and identifying those three bridges as follows: (1) the CEW *can* cause cardiac arrest (general causation); (2) the CEW *did* cause cardiac arrest (specific causation); and (3) the officer's conduct was unreasonable. During closing argument, the State dedicated most of their time discussing the third bridge (the officer's conduct), and I focused on the State's failure to prove the first two bridges. The bridge visual allowed me to respectfully suggest that the jury should never reach the third bridge, and it gave Lions a visual reminder that they should start deliberation by discussing the first bridge. The jury found our client not guilty, having never reached the third bridge.

As a plaintiff attorney in a civil case, I prefer to use the scales of justice and argue that my burden of proving the case by a preponderance of the evidence only required me "a feather" more evidence to our side of the scale. I have heard other plaintiff attorneys use a sports metaphor to define a preponderance of the evidence as only requiring them to "get the football across the 50-yard line, not into the end zone." But never be content to tell Lions that preponderance of the evidence only requires you "to prove 50.0001 percent," unless your goal is to confuse Lions and Lambs.

Prosecutors and criminal defense attorneys both struggle to define the burden of proof, and there is no classic metaphor or visual to explain "beyond a reasonable doubt." As a prosecutor, you may be able to think of a visual, but I preferred to focus on the definition of "reasonable." More specifically, I chose to explain why the criminal defendant's excuse, defense, or conspiracy theory was "not reasonable." During the 1998 *Duncan* second-degree murder trial, the defendant beat his wife to death with a bat and set their house on fire. At trial, the defendant took the stand and insisted that he left his wife alone in the house with her drug dealer (moments before her murder) and went to his sister's house, where he was seen minutes later washing and bleaching his jeans. Rather than confuse Lions with a visual or definition of "beyond a reasonable doubt," I focused on all the reasons why it was "not reasonable" to conclude the defendant left his wife with a "mystery murderer" to go bleach his jeans. The Lions agreed, and the jury found the defendant guilty as charged.

As a criminal defense attorney, you may also be able to think of a visual, but I prefer to focus on what constitutes "unreasonable" doubt. More specifically, I try to arm Lions with the knowledge that their doubt (as to my client's guilt) constitutes a "reasonable" doubt as long as their doubt does not "violate reason." During the *Nugent* trial, I suggested that any doubt regarding the cause of death did not "violate reason" because it was supported by evidence, and I listed all the evidence supporting that reasonable doubt, including the testimony of the forensic pathologist who performed the autopsy and concluded that the officer's CEW did not cause the subject's cardiac arrest. Personally, I felt it would be easier for Lions to defend their doubt by asking "Why does my doubt violate reason?" than for Lions to prove their doubt was "reasonable." The Lions agreed, and the jury found my client not guilty of manslaughter.

6. Remind Lions to Call for Exhibits

Every jury deliberation starts with Lions and Lambs walking into a room with an empty table. If you could walk into that room with them, and spread out all the exhibits you wanted Lions to discuss during deliberation, which exhibits would you pick? During your closing argument, remind Lions they have the right to call for any exhibit during deliberation. If deliberation lasts more than a day, a Lion may need to call for an exhibit to gobble up a Lamb.

Suggesting that Lions call for a specific exhibit can emphasize the importance of that exhibit, shows confidence in your case, and directly affect jury deliberation. During the 1998 *Allen* first-degree robbery trial, the prosecution had to prove it was reasonable for a cashier to think the accused was armed when he ran into a video store, said he had a gun, demanded money, and started pushing his fist into the cashier's back. During closing argument, I encouraged (practically begged) jurors to call for the ring the accused was wearing and to take turns pushing it into each other's backs. I reminded jurors that it was a cold night, and the flat, circular ring would have felt like the cold steel of a gun. The Lions called for the ring, reportedly took turns pushing it into each other's backs and found the defendant guilty as charged.

Suggesting Lions call for all of your closing argument exhibits can also be effective. Never force Lions to comb through stacks or binders of paper trying to find the specific note you read during closing argument. Make certain you prepare a list of your closing argument exhibits and (if possible) keep those exhibits separate. Consider placing them in a folder marked "closing argument exhibits" before returning them to the clerk, because the court may send all the exhibits to the jury if you can't quickly identify the requested ones.

Remember that attorneys cannot highlight exhibits after they have been admitted into evidence. During the pretrial conference, ask the court if it allows the parties to admit highlighted exhibits into evidence. If the court does, highlight what you want the Lion to read when they call for an exhibit. If there are only a handful of exhibits involved in your trial, consider color-coding your highlights based on the specific legal or factual issue they address. Picture yourself encouraging Lions to call for your closing argument exhibits and telling them that *all* evidence of a cervical herniation is highlighted green.

During closing argument, make certain Lions can see any document you discuss. Whether the courtroom has a single projector screen or monitors for every juror, make certain jurors can read the note and see where that note is located on the document, because Lions may have to find that note later without you. If the courtroom has no screens or monitors, enlarge and mount your documents on an easel.

Avoid putting all your eggs in one slideshow presentation. During the *Craige* trial, my clicker became stuck, and my opening statement slide show started racing through more than 30 slides. I was forced to finish my discussion of the witnesses and evidence from memory. Consider enlarging and mounting a handful of your closing argument exhibits as a back-up plan should your computer or your clicker betray you.

7. Provide Photos, Bios, and Tags for Witnesses

Lions may have trouble remembering the names of your witnesses or connecting names with faces. Do not launch directly into a discussion of what "Miss Nelson" said on the stand. Do not assume the jury remembers her name, what she looked like, or why anyone should believe a word she said.

Always take a photograph of your witnesses while they are on the stand, and immediately after their testimony.[2] Make sure they are wearing the exact same clothes and the photograph shows whatever they placed (i.e., glasses, tissue box, a book, stack of papers, anatomical spine model) on the ledge of the witness stand. During closing argument, when you discuss that witness, show a photograph of the witness to remind jurors who that witness was and what they (the jurors) thought of that witness. Picture Lions thinking "ooh, I liked her" and later describing "Miss Nelson" as the "witness who wore red-rimmed glasses with a matching red sweater." Picture Lions describing one of your seven medical experts as "the doctor with the bow tie who brought the anatomical model of the spine."

Always remind Lions of why they should care about your witness's testimony. Olympic broadcasts always show viewers background stories about the Olympians *before* the event because they want viewers to care about the Olympians' performance *during* the event. During direct examination, you asked the right questions and made certain the jury learned enough about your witnesses to care about their testimony. Your closing argument is your last chance to repeat those biographies, and the jury may not remember the witness until you do.

Start by reminding jurors who called the witness ("We called Jody Nelson"). If you don't have a photograph of Miss Nelson on the stand, remind them what she looked like ("Jody was the very nice lady who wore red-rimmed glasses and a matching red sweater"). Remind them Jody has served as a crossing guard for the past ten years. Remind them that Jody testified she knows that intersection like the back of her hand.

2. Similarly, if you anticipate reading the transcript of a witness deposition to the jury, always list as an exhibit, introduce into evidence, and publish to the jury a photograph of the witness so that the jurors can put a face to the name.

Then, and only then, put the diagram on the easel, point to where Jody was standing, and tell the jury what Jody saw.

Whenever possible, give Lions a catchy "tag" for your opponent's witness before criticizing his or her testimony. The tags should always be based on some critical aspect of the witnesses' testimony and should instantly remind the jury why that testimony is suspect. Clever tags are irresistible to jurors, especially when the trial involves many witnesses and jury deliberation lasts more than one day.

Tagging is a simple process, but it must be done correctly. Start by reminding the jury of the relevant testimony or event, and immediately refer to the witness by the tag instead of his or her real name. It is important to sound professional, not snarky or childish. Remember that tagging a witness can rub some jurors the wrong way.

Factual admissions make good tags. When Dr. Bailey admits she only read the abstract of the seminal article, she becomes "Doctor Cliff Notes." When a witness admits he assumed it was the defendant, he becomes "John 'I Assume So' Robinson" or "Assuming John" or "The Assumer." When the orthopedic surgeon admits her physical examination only lasted five minutes, she becomes "Doctor Five-Minute Exam." When the witness admits he has an awful memory, he becomes "Mr. Forgetful." When Susan Johnson testifies that she saw everything through her rear-view mirror, she becomes "Susan 'Rear-View Mirror' Johnson."

Trial events make good tags. When the court is forced to instruct an expert witness to answer a question, remind the jury of the court's instruction and then discuss the testimony of "Dr. Evasive." When an overcoached witness named Ben Robinson repeatedly and obnoxiously begins his answers to your cross-examination questions by saying "to the best of my knowledge," he becomes "To the Best of My Knowledge Ben."

During the 2021 *Lindale* trial, opposing counsel played the video deposition of Russel Rankin, who participated in the contract negotiations. Rather than focusing on Mr. Rankin's testimony on (what he recalled was) the intent of the parties when the contract was signed, we focused on Mr. Rankin's inability to remember a laundry list of events and details. During closing argument, I told the jury that the defense called "Russell 'I Can't Remember' Rankin," showed the jury a chart listing everything the witness could not remember, and then reviewed each item by saying "Russell 'I Can't Remember' Rankin can't remember . . . ." The jury loved the tag and completely disregarded the testimony of Russell "I Can't Remember" Rankin.

Bias can provide the best tag. When a witness has been friends with a party since high school, he becomes the "Lifelong Friend." When a witness was not promoted or frequently complains, he becomes the "Disgruntled Employee" or the "Guy with a Grudge." When a witness was completing for the same job or business, he becomes "The Competitor." And when a witness has a financial interest in the outcome of the case, he becomes "The Guy Who Stands to Gain."

Clothing only provides a good tag when the lay witness appears in offensive or wildly inappropriate clothing (i.e., racist, sexist, or immature T-shirts) or an expert witness appears unprofessional. During the *Craige* trial, the treating neurosurgeon took the stand wearing blue jeans, and I wrestled all night with whether to call him "Doctor Blue Jeans" during my closing argument. I pictured Lions forcing Lambs to choose between our brilliant neurosurgeon or "Doctor Blue Jeans." Ultimately, I chose not to use that tag because it was too cutesy for a paralysis case, and I did not want to give opposing counsel the chance to criticize me for focusing on what he was wearing instead of what he said.

Be warned. Tagging one witness suggests the tag was obvious and appropriate. Tagging more than one witness, or unfairly tagging a witness, can make you look like a lawyering lawyer (or, worse, make you look desperate). Never incorrectly or unfairly tag a witness. And always try to limit yourself to tagging one witness. Choose wisely.

Never base the tag on the witnesses' physical appearance or anything beyond the witness's personal control. Do not describe a witness as Professor Nose Hair, Mr. Stutter, Miss Screechy-Voice, or Dr. Two Chins. You will be held in contempt, and you will lose the trial. Here is a helpful rule: when in doubt, *don't* use the tag you're thinking about.

8. Give Lions Realistic Ranges and Options, Not *Your* Verdict

During the Golden Age of Lawyers, Gray Hairs handling civil cases adopted the practice of walking jurors through the jury interrogatory and telling jurors what their responses and verdict should be. Over time, and with advances in courtroom technology, that practice evolved into attorneys showing and telling jurors how to fill out the jury interrogatory. And it wasn't just Gray Hairs. As recently as 2015, I recommended telling Lions *your* answer to each jury interrogatory and *your* verdict.[3]

3. I made that recommendation in a chapter I authored entitled "Feeding Lions during Closing Argument" in FROM THE TRENCHES: TRIAL TIPS FROM 21 OF THE NATION'S TOP TRIAL LAWYERS 275–94 (John S. Worden ed., ABA Publishing 2015).

Nothing seems more basic to our profession than telling jurors what their verdict should be. Our clients expect us to tell jurors what to do. Our mentors taught us to tell jurors what the right verdict is. Our opposing counsel is going to tell jurors what to do. How can we let opposing counsel tell Lions a verdict or number without telling Lions ours? How can we take the chance that Lions will be smart enough to agree with us, but not smart enough to correctly answer the jury interrogatory? Plus, if the jury loves and respects us as much as we think they do, how can we abandon them during closing argument, when they need us the most?

Nobody is abandoning anybody. Depending on the type of trial, jurors may need their waiter to walk them through the jury interrogatory, point out important words they may struggle to define, or call their attention to the specific question that requires them to weigh certain evidence. There is nothing wrong with helping Lions negotiate the jury interrogatory and reminding them of the evidence that is relevant to each question. But resist the temptation to burden Friendly Lions with *your* opinions and *your* verdict.

Continue to identify and discuss tricky legal issues. During the 1999 *Whitton* trial, the defendant was accused of killing three victims and waiting hours for the fourth victim to return home. The State of Louisiana charged the defendant with four counts of first-degree murder, which the court instructed the jury was the killing of a human being when the defendant had the specific intent to kill "more than one person." Because I failed to discuss the defendant's intent when he killed the fourth of the four victims, the jurors reportedly struggled for hours to decide whether the defendant had the intent to kill *more* than one person when he killed the final victim. I spent those hours waiting with the families of the victims. To this day, I regret my failure to discuss that legal issue with the jury, who (thankfully) returned a verdict of guilty as charged on all four counts.

Continue to help Lions with tricky calculations. Consider how hard it could be for jurors who find liability but reject plaintiff's numbers to determine what constitutes fair compensation without your help. During the 2006 *Swain* trial, plaintiff asked the jury for a total award of $500,000, claiming plaintiff's minor injuries and (subsequent) heart problems were caused by the accident. During my closing argument, I admitted the accident caused plaintiff's minor injuries, reviewed the evidence that plaintiff's heart problems were unrelated, and asked the jury to fairly compensate the plaintiff for *only* his minor injuries. But I failed to add up the undisputed amount of past medical expenses associated with plaintiff's minor injuries. The jury was forced to call for all the medical invoices and spend hours adding up the expenses related to plaintiff's minor injuries. To this day, I don't know how the jury reached their award of $55,845.28, but I still feel guilty that the Lions didn't get any help from me.

Trial attorneys must stop telling jurors what they want the jurors to do. Instead, provide a realistic verdict range that gives Lions the flexibility and independence they need to reach their own verdict. During the 2017 *Stroud* trial, plaintiff's counsel ended his first closing argument by filling out the jury interrogatory and telling jurors to award his client a total of $18.5 million for her cervical injury and traumatic brain injury. My co-counsel believed the jury was with us and recommended I tell the jury to award only $1.5 million. The client was reluctant to tell them $1.5 million, concerned the jury would "split the baby" between our number ($1.5 million) and theirs ($18.5 million) and award the mid-point ($10 million). The decision was mine, and I decided to provide the jury with a realistic range. During my closing argument, after reviewing the lack of evidence of traumatic brain injury, I identified the "real" verdict range as being $180,000 "for just her cervical injury" to $2.8 million "if we caused everything plaintiff said we caused."

During the *Stroud* trial, the Lions refused to do what plaintiff's counsel told them to do. In fact, they completely ignored the number ($18.5 million) that opposing counsel told them to write down as their verdict. Instead, the Lions used my realistic range ($180,000 to $2.8 million), determined the mid-point of my range ($1.49 million), and awarded $1.5 million. Their award was a verdict that *neither* attorney had recommended, which is why Lions liked it.

By providing Lions with evidence-supported options, you can help Lions make a reasonable verdict appear reasonable. If your client is willing to pay for six months of plaintiff's recovery, discuss with Lions the options of finding that plaintiff reached maximum medical improvement when she completed physical therapy (three months), when she returned to work (six months), or when she was discharged by her treating physician (one year). Given the choice between three hats, some jurors will pick the middle-sized hat whether it fits their head or not, and those jurors may be tempted to pick the middle date whether it fits the facts or not.

When appropriate, consider pursuing "throw away" claims that give Lions the flexibility and independence they need to devour Lambs. During the 2021 *Lindale* trial, the court excluded several claims, but allowed our client to bring two separate claims for two separate breaches of the same contract. By the end of the two-week trial, we had proven our primary claim, but we had concerns about whether an appellate court would affirm *any* award for our secondary claim. With the client's permission, we decided to give Lions a realistic range for the primary claim and only half-heartedly sell the secondary claim. During closing argument, I gave a realistic range of $27,144,404.50 (if diesel cost $4/gallon) to $27,943,268.50 (if diesel cost $2/gallon) for the primary claim. Then, I admitted that we did not know the specific amount owed on the secondary claim and told the jury they could award up to $7,791,033.60. In response, opposing counsel told them to award my client nothing.

In *Lindale*, the Lions refused to do what defense counsel told them to do. Instead, they found the defendant breached the exclusivity provision (our primary claim), accepted my realistic range, and awarded (to the penny) the *bottom* of that range, awarding our client $27,144,404.50. The jury proceeded to find that the defendant breached the other contractual provision (our secondary claim) but awarded *nothing* for that breach. When we visited with jurors afterwards, they were quick to explain that they could not give us anything for our secondary claim because we failed to prove a specific amount. Their verdict was "fair" because they did not give us *everything* we wanted.

9. Prepare Lions for Sympathy, Bias, and Prejudice

It has become customary for trial lawyers to file motions *in limine* asking the court to prohibit opposing counsel from making prejudicial comments during closing argument. Before filing those motions, always consider the possibility that jurors will make the same prejudicial remarks during jury deliberation. How could those comments affect other jurors? How would you want a Lion to respond? If you successfully exclude the remark, and say nothing during closing argument, will a Lion recognize that the comment is not relevant to the jury's deliberation? Will a Lion be able to persuade the Lambs to ignore the prejudicial comment?

Sometimes, you need to "put the skunk on the table."[4] Discuss with your client whether you should openly discuss sympathy, bias, and prejudice during your closing argument. Your decision will always depend on the specific trial, but you should always be prepared to discuss why and how you can "put the skunk on the table."

Consider preparing Lions for expressions of sympathy during jury deliberation. Most civil jurors are not millionaires. Many live paycheck

4. Proper credit should be given to my mentor, Robert E. Kerrigan, Jr., who was the first attorney I heard use the expression "put the skunk on the table."

to paycheck. Many are unemployed. Many receive some form of government assistance. Some are powerless to change their own lives, and they have just been given the power to change the life of an injured or cheated plaintiff.

In a civil trial, a defense attorney should always consider acknowledging that the desire to help another person is natural, strong, and good. Acknowledge that you picked good people and you expect good people to feel sympathy for the plaintiff, but explain that justice requires a fair and objective weighing of the evidence. Remind Lions their verdict should be based solely on the physical and testimonial evidence. If there is a specific jury instruction to that effect, show it to them and read it to them. Warn Lions what they might hear during deliberation and suggest (without telling them what to say) the appropriate response.

- If a juror says, "We have to help that family," that juror has stopped weighing the evidence.
- If a juror asks, "If the defendant doesn't pay, what are they going to do?," that juror has stopped weighing the evidence.
- If a juror thinks, "They won't get any money if we blame the empty chair," that juror has stopped weighing the evidence.

Consider calling the Lion's attention to any overt attempts to bias or prejudice the Lambs. During the *Pyles* case, we defended a French Quarter gentlemen's club against a former entertainer's claim of negligent security. While on the stand, plaintiff volunteered that the club always closed for the Bayou Classic, an annual football game held at the Superdome in New Orleans that brings in fans and alumni of Southern University and Grambling State University, two historically African American universities. The suggestion was that our client, the Caucasian owner of the club, closed the club because he did not like African Americans.

During his closing argument in *Pyles*, my co-counsel Bob directly addressed the allegation of racism by telling the jury (paraphrasing): "When the facts are on your side, argue the facts. When the law is on your side, argue the law. And when the law and the facts are *not* on your side, tell the predominantly African American jury that the club closed for the Bayou Classic." By putting the skunk on the table, Bob forced opposing counsel (who was African American) to spend his rebuttal insisting that the plaintiff did not mention the club's closure to bias or prejudice the jury. The Lions were listening. Plaintiff asked the jury to award more than $1 million against the club, and the jury awarded $90,000.

Consider taming Lions by sharing an appropriate response to potential momentum-shifting comments. Figure out the most likely bias or prejudice, and warn Lions what they might hear during jury deliberation, like the following in a criminal case:

- If a juror says, "I'm afraid of what will happen if we let him back on the streets," that juror has stopped weighing the evidence.
- If a juror says, "I'm not sending anyone to jail," that juror has stopped weighing the evidence.
- If a juror tells a personal story about being wrongfully arrested or detained by other officers, that juror has stopped weighing the evidence.
- If a juror starts talking about the accused's children, that juror has stopped weighing the evidence.

Pay attention to more than just the verdict during mock trials and focus groups. Note every comment that distracts or prejudices the jury against your client. Label a page "Ideas for Voir Dire and Closing Argument," and write down comments like the following in a civil case:

- "That's the price of doing business."
- "That's why they have insurance."
- "Why wouldn't they warn about everything?"
- "If it happened on their property, I don't care if it's their fault."
- "This is a drop in the bucket for them."

After the mock trial or focus group, show the prejudicial comments to your client and co-counsel. Discuss with them the risk that jurors might be saying or thinking this during deliberation. Discuss whether you should "put the skunk on the table" by calling the Lion's attention to the prejudice and sharing or suggesting your response.

10. Prepare Lions for "Split the Baby" Suggestions

At some point during deliberation, Lions may be surrounded by Lambs who want to agree on a compromise verdict and go home. Picture a juror suggesting they "split the baby" by awarding a mid-point between requested awards in a civil trial or by convicting the defendant of a lesser and included offense in a criminal trial. How do you want Lions to respond to that suggestion?

Prepare Lions for that moment. Lions often despise splitting the baby because they hate compromise and truly believe in their position. If not careful, Lions can permanently scare off Lambs (or be exiled and ignored) by emotionally or quickly rejecting the concept of compromise. That is why it is important to tame Lions by sharing your response to splitting the baby.

If your client does *not* want a compromise verdict, tame Lions by sharing with them a more diplomatic response than "No!" During the *Craige* trial, we admitted that our client was 100 percent responsible for causing the car accident, but we denied the allegation that the accident caused plaintiff's paralysis. Based on the testimony, it was an all-or-nothing case, and our client was concerned the jury would decide to split the baby and return a verdict of more than a million dollars. With the client's permission, I shared a story that would decrease the likelihood of a compromise verdict.

During closing argument in the *Craige* trial, I told jurors that "Solomon-like" wisdom was a misnomer because King Solomon did not actually split the baby. Solomon is considered wise because he refused to split the baby. Solomon only threatened to split the baby to discover which woman would object to his harming the child. People forget that Solomon ultimately gave the *whole* baby to the woman who was entitled to the whole baby and gave *nothing*—not even a hair of the baby—to the woman who was not entitled. The Lions were listening, and the jury never got past the first question of the jury interrogatory. After hours of deliberating, the jury notified the court that they were hopelessly deadlocked.

Remember that sharing the King Solomon story is dangerous business. Before you suggest that justice requires Lions to give the "whole baby" or "no baby" to a civil plaintiff, always discuss the risks with your client and get their permission (again, preferably in writing).

If your client *does* want a compromise verdict, and your marching orders are to tell the jury your verdict (instead of offering a realistic range), discuss what you can do during closing argument to improve the likelihood that Lions will respond *favorably* to splitting the baby, including: (1) acknowledging both parties seem to have taken extreme positions; (2) conceding that jurors have the right to reach a compromise verdict; (3) acknowledging any jury instruction that encourages compromise or working together; (4) encouraging jurors to reach an equitable solution; and (5) reminding jurors that good settlements are often defined as "settlements that leave both parties unhappy."

Never openly encourage jurors to split the baby. If you tell jurors to split the baby during your rebuttal argument and encourage them to award the mid-point ($500,000) between your $800,000 request and the defendant's $200,000 response, Lions may consider your mid-point ($500,000) an admission: (a) that your original demand of $800,000 was patently unreasonable; and (2) that you would be happy with a $500,000 verdict. In so doing, you may inspire Lions to start deliberation by saying, "Okay, plaintiffs are at $500,000 and defense is at $200,000."

11. Motivate Lions with Your Alamo

Lions and Lambs will remember the last thing you say during closing argument. You cannot and should not try to memorize your entire closing argument, but you owe it to your client to nail the last 15 to 60 seconds of your closing argument, which we call our "Alamo."[5] Write it down. Make it perfect. Memorize it and practice it.

The Alamo is where you make your last stand. If you get lost or nervous, remember the Alamo! If your closing argument starts to lag, remember the Alamo! When you realize you have only one minute left, remember the Alamo!

A good Alamo is an absolute necessity whenever the court places a time limit on your closing argument. Practice your Alamo. Know exactly how long it takes you to deliver. Give yourself at least two additional minutes to wrap up whatever point you are covering. Ask the court to let you know when you have the time needed for your Alamo plus two more minutes remaining. And, when the court tells you, "Counselor, you have [Alamo plus two minutes] remaining," thank the court, wrap up your point, and head for the Alamo!

There are no hard-and-fast rules for building your Alamo. Basing your Alamo on your opening statement teaser can be effective when your teaser was based on your most important fact, exhibit, or argument. Ending your closing argument with your opening statement teaser can also bookend the trial, create symmetry, and emphasize that the trial went according to plan. Basing your Alamo on your trial theme or the turning point in the trial can also be effective.

An effective Alamo can be the presentation of a single exhibit. During the 1997 *Collor* second-degree murder trial, the detective testified that after receiving an anonymous tip, he confronted the defendant, who gave a taped statement claiming he shot the victim out of fear for his life. During the trial, the defendant took the stand and retracted his statement to the detective. He testified that he saw another man shoot the victim over a drug deal and insisted the detective forced him to make a false statement. My co-counsel ended the State's rebuttal by placing a tape player directly in front of the jury, inserting the audio tape (rewound to the admission), and pressing play. The last thing the jury heard was the

---

5. Proper credit should be given to Greg L. Johnson, Brett D. Wise, and the other attorney-coaches who developed and polished the concept of an effective Alamo during the many years we coached the Jesuit High School mock trial team.

tape of the defendant admitting that he shot the victim. It was an effective Alamo, and the jury found the defendant guilty as charged.

Plaintiffs and prosecutors should save their Alamo for rebuttal. During a 1997 cocaine distribution jury trial, defense counsel called witnesses who testified that the defendant had a job and was an enterprising young man. There was no guarantee the veteran public defender was going to give a closing argument, and I felt we needed to answer the question, "Why would this defendant sell drugs?" During my closing argument, I told the urban legend about the reporter who asked Willie Sutton, a prolific American bank robber, "Why do you rob banks?" Sutton replied, "Because that's where the money is." I produced the cash found on the defendant, and asked the jury, "Why would an enterprising young man sell drugs?" One by one, I started stacking the bills in front of the jury until an elderly juror in the front row muttered, "Because that's where the money is."

That dream trial moment soon became a nightmare as the criminal defense attorney pointed out that I was wrong about the bank robber (I said Jesse James instead of Willie Sutton) and wrong about his client. He aptly focused the jury's attention on my decision to focus on motive in a drug distribution case instead of on evidence of a sale. Learn from my mistake: Always save the perfect Alamo for your rebuttal close!

Remember that it can be risky for plaintiffs and prosecutors to save their Alamo for their rebuttal because opposing counsel is not required to give a closing argument. During the *Whitton* trial, we convicted the defendant of four counts of first-degree murder and proceeded to the penalty phase of the trial, during which evidence of mitigating and aggravating circumstances was presented. At the conclusion of the penalty phase, my co-counsel gave a very good closing argument in support of the death penalty, but we saved many of our best points for my rebuttal (a strategy that had worked well during the guilt phase). This time, opposing counsel looked over at me, stood up, and waived his closing argument. I was not allowed to give a rebuttal, and the jury—who never heard my Alamo—recommended a life sentence.

12. End with a "Father Tompson Pause"

Help your Lions by ending with a bang, not a whimper. There are no scoreboards in a courtroom, and Lambs can get the impression you won or lost based on your body language and demeanor. Never make it harder for your Lions to gobble up Lambs by ending your closing argument sheepishly. Instead, when you finish your Alamo, do the "Tompson Pause."

The late Father Harry Tompson, S.J., was a dynamic and beloved president of Jesuit High School in New Orleans. Before every football game, he would hold a mass for the football players and coaches in the very small chapel inside the school. His homily doubled as a pep talk, and it always ended on a feverish pitch. Father Tompson would then stand there, in dead silence, staring fiercely into the eyes of the players. The bigger the game, the longer the pause. The better the homily, the longer the pause. The pause conveyed absolute pride and confidence in his message.

One Easter Sunday, Father Tompson reportedly walked up the stairs of the pulpit in front of a packed church to deliver what is traditionally a very long homily. He waited a few moments and then loudly declared: "He is Risen!" Then Father Tompson stood there in total silence, staring at the congregation for several seconds, possibly years, before slowly turning around and walking down the stairs.

Similarly, when you finish your closing argument, stand before the jury in silence and have the confidence to look into their eyes. Thank them and walk slowly back to your chair. When performed correctly, the Tompson Pause can make a good Alamo great.

Remember to say thank you. I had the misfortune of using the Tompson Pause while the judge, who was later removed from the bench by the Louisiana Supreme Court for being a threat to the judicial system (yes, seriously), was playing computer solitaire. When the judge heard the silence, she looked up from her computer, saw me walking back to the State's table, and asked, "Are ya done?" I had to stop, turn around, and say, "Yes, your honor."

Make certain you say "thank you" slowly and sincerely. Do not smile when you say it, and try not to sound like you just finished a comedy performance (i.e., "Thank you very much, you've been a great jury!"). Do not quickly mutter it, because this may be interpreted as disingenuous or perfunctory. If the Tompson Pause is a beautiful balloon, then smiling, stuttering, or squeaking "thank you" can be the pin that pops that balloon.

13. Stop Confusing Argument with Advocacy

During the Golden Age of Lawyers, it became fashionable for Gray Hairs at cocktail parties to boldly declare that trials are over by the end of *voir dire* or opening statement. That nothing you say or do during your closing argument will change the outcome of the trial. Today, some lawyers still feel that way. Do not listen to them. They are not your friends.

Approach every closing argument as if only one juror is on your side—a juror who will never know the facts as well as you will and who will only remember a fraction of what you say during closing argument. For your own sanity, convince yourself that juror is a Lion.

Stop confusing advocacy with argument. There is a reason why every parent predicts that their kid would make a great lawyer because they "argue so much!" That is the distinct impression of jurors as they enter the courtroom. That is exactly what they expect to hear from the paid advocates during their last chance to address them. Surprise them by cleverly advocating, instead of passionately arguing your case. Surprise them by helping them review the evidence on both sides, without constantly offering your opinion. Surprise them by helping them identify *their* choices and decisions, without telling them *your* opinion or *your* verdict. The legal profession may be married to the term "closing argument," but let's start thinking of it as "closing advocacy."

Embrace the new playbook. Resolve that, by the end of your closing advocacy, your Lions on the jury will: (a) know what exhibits to call for and what to do with those exhibits; (b) be able to identify a turning point in the trial; (c) remember the bios of your key witnesses and the tags of your opponents'; (d) be able to picture how the evidence stacks up on both sides of the scale; (e) be prepared for prejudicial and emotional comments; and (f) know how you would respond to compromise. Then wait and listen . . . for the silence of the Lambs.

Conclusion

For generations, lawyers have referred to the "art" of trial advocacy. The declaration that there exists a "new science of trial advocacy" challenges that fundamental assumption. It suggests we have learned something new about jurors, their perceptions, and their preferences. It implies that old strategies and techniques are proving less reliable. It promises that a different approach can be effective. It openly invites lawyers to consider the possibility that their advocacy can be more scientific. It offers hope, and it heralds change.

That change is already happening. Other attorneys have already changed their approach to trial advocacy. They are out there, resisting the urge to treat exhibit books like dumpsters. Maximizing their limited time for voir dire. Disclosing the good, the bad, and the ugly during opening statement. Winning their first two objections. Pulling their punches during cross-examination. Creating opportunities for their experts to establish their independence and superiority. Showing the jury how the evidence stacks up on both sides, but never telling the jury what their verdict should be. Engaging in closing advocacy instead of closing argument.

Many of these strategies have been percolating for years. Most attorneys will be reminded of a trial where they observed or personally tried *at least* one of the specific techniques discussed in this book. And as radical as certain trial strategies may seem to Gray Hairs, some readers will already consider those strategies old news. That's the thing about change. When change is real, it happens everywhere and is (eventually) felt by everyone.

To be clear, there is more than one way to try and win a case. Yes, there may be times when justice depends on a prosecutor's unleashing his fierce anger and calling down the Wrath of God. Yes, an innocent man's life may someday depend on defense counsel's ability to malign law enforcement officers, inspire outrage, and sell injustice. Yes, the outcome of some civil trials may turn on whether the jury can be manipulated into sending a message to the plaintiff, or to the defendant, or to an entire industry. And, yes, trials involving beloved and hated celebrities may prove to be the exception to every trial advocacy rule. But for all those untelevised civil and criminal trials, involving ordinary people in ordinary courtrooms, we need a new playbook.

I am not a psycho-historian like Vico, Hegel, or Seldon. But I see the pendulum of public perception swinging in the wrong direction. In a handful of generations, jurors have gone from admiring lawyers, to distrusting lawyers, to resenting our advocacy. We can't stop that pendulum with legislation or marketing. We need to make our stand in the courtroom.

Gray Hairs will always prefer more direct advocacy and more traditional trial techniques. But times have changed, and trial lawyers must change with the times. Jurors have grown tired of "mad dog" litigators. They find them annoying, not entertaining. They want lawyers to stop fighting with each other, roll up their sleeves, and start helping them with the dishes.

The idea of being wonderful waiters, instead of lawyering lawyers, already appeals to our common sense. There is a reason why "kill all the lawyers" is such a popular misinterpretation of Shakespeare, and a reason why fancy restaurants don't need "tip your waiter" signs. People are tired of being told what to do by lawyers, car salesmen, and other paid advocates. What they appreciate is a waiter who quietly and professionally makes their life a little easier. Who brings them everything they could possibly want and helps them make their *own* decision. That waiter has their respect. That waiter has their attention. That waiter has their ear.

The waiter pivot offers an alternative approach to trial advocacy. It can surprise, disarm, and influence the jury. It can build trust with the jurors and conceal flaws in our case. Consider the cover of this book. At first glance, did you recognize that the table setting was imperfect? Did you notice that the spoon should have been placed to the right of the fork? Or was your attention naturally drawn to the waiter's tuxedo sleeve and white glove? The more professional the waiter, the more likely the guest will trust that waiter instead of scrutinizing the service.

Trial lawyers will always be paid advocates. Fortunately, we don't have to become professional waiters. We just have to play them in the courtroom. And the better we become at helping jurors, the more patient, forgiving, and appreciative those jurors will be.

The Golden Age of Lawyers has ended. The Age of Jurors has begun. We should welcome this new era as an opportunity to change the way we practice law and the way our legal profession is perceived. Let's redefine trial advocacy and reinvent ourselves. Let's remind jurors how helpful lawyers can be during a trial. Let's impress jurors with our courtesy and professionalism. Let's send them home with a new appreciation for what we do and a better understanding of why we are needed in the courtroom. Let's find a way to win our trials and win back our jurors. One trial at a time. One juror at a time.

Index

Page numbers followed by f indicate figure and by t indicate table

C

D

E

H

I

J

Q

R

S

T

V